A Prince of Sinners

E. Phillips Oppenheim

Alpha Editions

This edition published in 2024

ISBN 9789362099211

Design and Setting By

Alpha Editions
www.alphaedis.com

Email - info@alphaedis.com

As per information held with us this book is in Public Domain.
This book is a reproduction of an important historical work.
Alpha Editions uses the best technology to reproduce historical work
in the same manner it was first published to preserve its original nature.
Any marks or number seen are left intentionally to preserve.

Contents

CHAPTER I MR. KINGSTON BROOKS, POLITICAL AGENT	- 2 -
CHAPTER II THE BULLSOM FAMILY AT HOME	- 5 -
CHAPTER III KINGSTON BROOKS HAS A VISITOR	- 12 -
CHAPTER IV A QUESTION FOR THE COUNTRY	- 18 -
CHAPTER V THE MARQUIS OF ARRANMORE	- 25 -
CHAPTER VI THE MAN WHO WENT TO HELL	- 31 -
CHAPTER VII A THOUSAND POUNDS	- 37 -
CHAPTER VIII KINGSTON BROOKS MAKES INQUIRIES	- 42 -
CHAPTER IX HENSLOW SPEAKS OUT	- 49 -
CHAPTER X A TEMPTING OFFER	- 54 -
CHAPTER XI WHO THE DEVIL IS BROOKS?	- 62 -
CHAPTER XII MR. BULLSOM GIVES A DINNER-PARTY	- 68 -
CHAPTER XIII CHARITY THE "CRIME"	- 75 -
CHAPTER XIV AN AWKWARD QUESTION	- 83 -
CHAPTER XV A SUPPER-PARTY AT THE "QUEEN'S"	- 92 -
CHAPTER XVI UNCLE AND NIECE	- 98 -
CHAPTER XVII FIFTEEN YEARS IN HELL	- 106 -
CHAPTER XVIII MARY SCOTT PAYS AN UNEXPECTED CALL	- 113 -
CHAPTER XIX THE MARQUIS MEPHISTOPHELES	- 119 -
CHAPTER XX THE CONFIDENCE OF LORD ARRANMORE	- 125 -
CHAPTER I LORD ARRANMORE'S AMUSEMENTS	- 133 -
CHAPTER II THE HECKLING OF HENSLOW	- 141 -

CHAPTER III MARY SCOTT'S TWO VISITORS	- 147 -
CHAPTER IV A MARQUIS ON MATRIMONY	- 154 -
CHAPTER V BROOKS ENLISTS A RECRUIT	- 161 -
CHAPTER VI KINGSTON BROOKS, PHILANTHROPIST	- 168 -
CHAPTER VII BROOKS AND HIS MISSIONS	- 176 -
CHAPTER VIII MR. BULLSOM IS STAGGERED	- 182 -
CHAPTER IX GHOSTS	- 188 -
CHAPTER X A NEW DON QUIXOTE	- 193 -
CHAPTER I AN ARISTOCRATIC RECRUIT	- 202 -
CHAPTER II MR. LAVILETTE INTERFERES	- 207 -
CHAPTER III THE SINGULAR BEHAVIOUR OF MARY SCOTT	- 213 -
CHAPTER IV LORD ARRANMORE IN A NEW ROLE	- 218 -
CHAPTER V LADY SYBIL LENDS A HAND	- 225 -
CHAPTER VI THE RESERVATION OF MARY SCOTT	- 231 -
CHAPTER VII FATHER AND SON	- 237 -
CHAPTER VIII THE ADVICE OF MR. BULLSOM	- 243 -
CHAPTER IX A QUESTION AND AN ANSWER	- 249 -
CHAPTER X LADY SYBIL SAYS "YES"	- 254 -
CHAPTER XI BROOKS HEARS THE NEWS	- 259 -
CHAPTER XII THE PRINCE OF SINNERS SPEAKS OUT	- 271 -

PART I

CHAPTER I
MR. KINGSTON BROOKS, POLITICAL AGENT

Already the sweepers were busy in the deserted hall, and the lights burned low. Of the great audience who had filled the place only half-an-hour ago not one remained. The echoes of their tumultuous cheering seemed still to linger amongst the rafters, the dust which their feet had raised hung about in a little cloud. But the long rows of benches were empty, the sweepers moved ghostlike amongst the shadows, and an old woman was throwing tealeaves here and there about the platform. In the committee-room behind a little group of men were busy with their leave-takings. The candidate, a tall, somewhat burly man, with hard, shrewd face and loosely knit figure, was shaking hands with every one. His tone and manner savoured still of the rostrum.

"Good-night, sir! Good-night, Mr. Bullsom! A most excellent introduction, yours, sir! You made my task positively easy. Good-night, Mr. Brooks. A capital meeting, and everything very well arranged. Personally I feel very much obliged to you, sir. If you carry everything through as smoothly as this affair to-night, I can see that we shall lose nothing by poor Morrison's breakdown. Good-night, gentlemen, to all of you. We will meet at the club at eleven o'clock to-morrow morning. Eleven o'clock precisely, if you please."

The candidate went out to his carriage, and the others followed in twos and threes. A young man, pale, with nervous mouth, strongly-marked features and clear dark eyes, looked up from a sheaf of letters which he was busy sorting.

"Don't wait for me, Mr. Bullsom," he said. "Reynolds will let me out, and I had better run through these letters before I leave."

Mr. Bullsom was emphatic to the verge of gruffness.

"You'll do nothing of the sort," he declared. "I tell you what it is, Brooks. We're not going to let you knock yourself up. You're tackling this job in rare style. I can tell you that Henslow is delighted."

"I'm much obliged to you for saying so, Mr. Bullsom," the young man answered. "Of course the work is strange to me, but it is very interesting, and I don't mean to make a mess of it."

"There is only one chance of your doing that," Mr. Bullsom rejoined, "and that is if you overwork yourself. You need a bit of looking after. You've got a rare head on your shoulders, and I'm proud to think that I was the one to bring your name before the committee. But I'm jolly well certain of one thing. You've done all the work a man ought to do in one day. Now listen to me. Here's my carriage waiting, and you're going straight home with me to have a bite and a glass of wine. We can't afford to lose our second agent, and I can see what's the matter with you. You're as pale as a ghost, and no wonder. You've been at it all day and never a break."

The young man called Brooks had not the energy to frame a refusal, which he knew would be resented. He took down his overcoat, and stuffed the letters into his pocket.

"You're very good," he said. "I'll come up for an hour with pleasure."

They passed out together into the street, and Mr. Bullsom opened the door of his carriage.

"In with you, young man," he exclaimed. "Home, George!"

Kingston Brooks leaned back amongst the cushions with a little sigh of relief.

"This is very restful," he remarked. "We have certainly had a very busy day. The inside of electioneering may be disenchanting, but it's jolly hard work."

Mr. Bullsom sat with clasped hands in front of him resting upon that slight protuberance which denoted the advent of a stomach. He had thrown away the cigar which he had lit in the committee-room. Mrs. Bullsom did not approve of smoking in the covered wagonette, which she frequently honoured with her presence.

"There's nothing in the world worth having that hasn't to be worked for, my boy," he declared, good-humoredly.

"By other people!" Brooks remarked, smiling.

"That's as it may be," Mr. Bullsom admitted. "To my mind that's where the art of the thing comes in. Any fool can work, but it takes a shrewd man to keep a lot of others working hard for him while he pockets the oof himself."

"I suppose," the younger man remarked, thoughtfully, "that you would consider Mr. Henslow a shrewd man?"

"Shrewd! Oh, Henslow's shrewd enough. There's no question about that!"

"And honest?"

Mr. Bullsom hesitated. He drew his hand down his stubbly grey beard.

"Honest! Oh, yes, he's honest! You've no fault to find with him, eh?"

"None whatever," Brooks hastened to say. "You see," he continued more slowly, "I have never been really behind the scenes in this sort of thing before, and Henslow has such a very earnest manner in speaking. He talked to the working men last night as though his one desire in life was to further the different radical schemes which we have on the programme. Why, the tears were actually in his eyes when he spoke of the Old Age Pension Bill. He told them over and over again that the passing of that Bill was the one object of his political career. Then, you know, there was the luncheon to-day—and I fancied that he was a little flippant about the labour vote. It was perhaps only his way of speaking."

Mr. Bullsom smiled and rubbed the carriage window with the cuff of his coat. He was very hungry.

"Oh, well, a politician has to trim a little, you know," he remarked. "Votes he must have, and Henslow has a very good idea how to get them. Here we are, thank goodness." The carriage had turned up a short drive, and deposited them before the door of a highly ornate villa. Mr. Bullsom led the way indoors, and himself took charge of his guest's coat and hat. Then he opened the door of the drawing-room.

"Mrs. Bullsom and the girls," he remarked, urbanely, "will be delighted to see you. Come in!"

CHAPTER II
THE BULLSOM FAMILY AT HOME

There were fans upon the wall, and much bric-a-brac of Oriental shape but Brummagem finish, a complete suite of drawing-room furniture, incandescent lights of fierce brilliancy, and a pianola. Mrs. Peter Bullsom, stout and shiny in black silk and a chatelaine, was dozing peacefully in a chair, with the latest novel from the circulating library in her lap; whilst her two daughters, in evening blouses, which were somehow suggestive of the odd elevenpence, were engrossed in more serious occupation. Louise, the elder, whose budding resemblance to her mother was already a protection against the over-amorous youths of the town, was reading a political speech in the Times. Selina, who had sandy hair, a slight figure, and was considered by her family the essence of refinement, was struggling with a volume of Cowper, who had been recommended to her by a librarian with a sense of humour, as a poet unlikely to bring a blush into her virginal cheeks. Mr. Bullsom looked in upon his domestic circle with pardonable pride, and with a little flourish introduced his guest.

"Mrs. Bullsom," he said, "this is my young friend, Kingston Brooks. My two daughters, sir, Louise and Selina." The ladies were gracious, but had the air of being taken by surprise, which, considering Mr. Bullsom's parting words a few hours ago, seemed strange.

"We've had a great meeting," Mr. Bullsom remarked, sidling towards the hearthrug, and with his thumbs already stealing towards the armholes of his waistcoat, "a great meeting, my dears. Not that I am surprised! Oh, no! As I said to Padgett, when he insisted that I should take the chair, 'Padgett,' I said, 'mark my words, we're going to surprise the town. Mr. Henslow may not be the most popular candidate we've ever had, but he's on the right side, and those who think Radicalism has had its day in Medchester will be amazed.' And so they have been. I've dropped a few hints during my speeches at the ward meetings lately, and Mr. Brooks, though he's new at the work, did his best, and I can tell you the result was a marvel. The hall was packed—simply packed. When I rose to speak there wasn't an empty place or chair to be seen."

"Dear me!" Mrs. Bullsom remarked, affably. "Supper is quite ready, my love."

Mr. Bullsom abandoned his position precipitately, and his face expressed his lively satisfaction.

"Ah!" he exclaimed. "I was hoping that you would have a bite for me. As I said to Mr. Brooks when I asked him to drop in with me, there's sure to be something to eat. And I can tell you I'm about ready for it."

Brooks found an opportunity to speak almost for the first time. He was standing between the two Misses Bullsom, and already they had approved of him. He was distinctly of a different class from the casual visitors whom their father was in the habit of introducing into the family circle.

"Mr. Bullsom was kind enough to take pity on an unfortunate bachelor," he said, with a pleasant smile. "My landlady has few faults, but an over-love of punctuality is one of them. By this time she and her household are probably in bed. Our meeting lasted a long time."

"If you will touch the bell, Peter," Mrs. Bullsom remarked, "Ann shall dish up the supper."

The young ladies exchanged shocked glances. "Dish up." What an abominable phrase! They looked covertly at their guest, but his face was imperturbable.

"We think that we have been very considerate, Mr. Brooks," Selina remarked, with an engaging smile. "We gave up our usual dinner this evening as papa had to leave so early."

Mr. Brooks smiled as he offered his arm to Mrs. Bullsom—a courtesy which much embarrassed her.

"I think," he said, "that we shall be able to show you some practical appreciation of your thoughtfulness. I know nothing so stimulating to the appetite as politics, and to-day we have been so busy that I missed even my afternoon tea."

"I'm sure that we are quite repaid for giving up our dinner," Selina remarked, with a backward glance at the young man. "Oh, here you are at last, Mary. I didn't hear you come in."

"My niece, Miss Scott," Mr. Bullsom announced. "Now you know all the family."

A plainly-dressed girl with dark eyes and unusually pale cheeks returned his greeting quietly, and followed them into the dining-room. Mrs. Bullsom spread herself over her seat with a little sigh of relief. Brooks gazed in silent wonder at the gilt-framed oleographs which hung thick upon the walls, and Mr. Bullsom stood up to carve a joint of beef.

"Plain fare, Mr. Brooks, for plain people," he remarked, gently elevating the sirloin on his fork, and determining upon a point of attack. "We don't understand frills here, but we've a welcome for our friends, and a hearty one."

"If there is anything in the world better than roast beef," Brooks remarked, unfolding his serviette, "I haven't found it."

"There's one thing," Mr. Bullsom remarked, pausing for a moment in his labours, "I can give you a good glass of wine. Ann, I think that if you look in the right-hand drawer of the sideboard you will find a bottle of champagne. If not I'll have to go down into the cellar."

Ann, however, produced it—which, considering that Mr. Bullsom had carefully placed it there a few hours ago, was not extraordinary—and Brooks sipped the wine with inward tremors, justified by the result.

"I suppose, Mr. Brooks," Selina remarked, turning towards him in an engaging fashion, "that you are a great politician. I see your name so much in the papers."

Brooks smiled.

"My political career," he answered, "dates from yesterday morning. I am taking Mr. Morrison's place, you know, as agent for Mr. Henslow. I have never done anything of the sort before, and I have scarcely any claims to be considered a politician at all."

"A very lucky change for us, Brooks," Mr. Bullsom declared, with the burly familiarity which he considered justified by his position as chairman of the Radical committee. "Poor Morrison was past the job. It was partly through his muddling that we lost the seat at the last election. I'd made up my mind to have a change this time, and so I told 'em."

Brooks was tired of politics, and he looked across the table. This pale girl with the tired eyes and self-contained manner interested him. The difference, too, between her and the rest of the family was puzzling.

"I believe, Miss Scott," he said, "that I met you at the Stuarts' dance."

"I was there," she admitted. "I don't think I danced with you, but we had supper at the same table."

"I remember it perfectly," he said. "Wasn't it supposed to be a very good dance?"

She shrugged her shoulders.

"I believe so," she answered. "There was the usual fault—too many girls. But it was very pretty to watch."

"You do not care for dancing, yourself, perhaps?" he hazarded.

"Indeed I do," she declared. "But I knew scarcely any one there. I see a good deal of Kate sometimes, but the others I scarcely know at all."

"You were in the same position as I was, then," he answered, smiling.

"Oh, you—you are different," she remarked. "I mean that you are a man, and at a dance that means everything. That is why I rather dislike dances. We are too dependent upon you. If you would only let us dance alone."

Selina smiled in a superior manner. She would have given a good deal to have been invited to the dance in question, but that was a matter which she did not think it worth while to mention.

"My dear Mary!" she said, "what an idea. I am quite sure that when you go out with us you need never have any difficulty about partners."

"Our programmes for the Liberal Club Dance and the County Cricket Ball were full before we had been in the room five minutes," Louise interposed.

Mary smiled inwardly, but said nothing, and Brooks was quite sure then that she was different. He realized too that her teeth were perfect, and her complexion, notwithstanding its pallor, was faultless. She would have been strikingly good-looking but for her mouth, and that—was it a discontented or a supercilious curl? At any rate it disappeared when she smiled.

"May I ask whether you have been attending a political meeting this evening, Miss Scott?" he asked. "You came in after us, I think."

She shook her head.

"No, I have a class on Wednesday evening."

"A class!" he repeated, doubtfully.

Mr. Bullsom, who thought he had been out of the conversation long enough, interposed.

"Mary calls herself a bit of a philanthropist, you see, Mr. Brooks," he explained. "Goes down into Medchester and teaches factory girls to play the piano on Wednesday evenings. Much good may it do them."

There was a curious gleam in the girl's eyes for a moment which checked the words on Brooks' lips, and led him to precipitately abandon the conversation. But afterwards, while Selina was pedalling at the pianola and playing havoc with the expression-stops, he crossed the room and stood for a moment by her chair.

"I should like you to tell me about your class," he said. "I have several myself—of different sorts."

She closed her magazine, but left her finger in the place.

"Oh, mine is a very unambitious undertaking," she said. "Kate Stuart and I started it for the girls in her father's factory, and we aim at nothing higher than an attempt to direct their taste in fiction. They bring their Free Library lists to us, and we mark them together. Then we all read one more serious book at the same time—history or biography—and talk about it when we meet."

"It is an excellent idea," he said, earnestly. "By the bye, something occurs to me. You know, or rather you don't know, that I give free lectures on certain books or any simple literary subject on Wednesday evenings at the Secular Hall when this electioneering isn't on. Couldn't you bring your girls one evening? I would be guided in my choice of a subject by you."

"Yes, I should like that," she answered, "and I think the girls would. It is very good of you to suggest it."

Louise, with a great book under her arm, deposited her dumpy person in a seat by his side, and looked up at him with a smile of engaging candour.

"Mr. Brooks," she said, "I am going to do a terrible thing. I am going to show you some of my sketches and ask your opinion."

Brooks turned towards her without undue enthusiasm.

"It is very good of you, Miss Bullsom," he said, doubtfully; "but I never drew a straight line in my life, and I know nothing whatever about perspective. My opinion would be worse than worthless."

Louise giggled artlessly, and turned over the first few pages.

"You men all say that at first," she declared, "and then you turn out such terrible critics. I declare I'm afraid to show them to you, after all."

Brooks scarcely showed that desire to overcome her new resolution which politeness demanded. But Selina came tripping across the room, and took up her position on the other side of him.

"You must show them now you've brought them out, Louise," she declared. "I am sure that Mr. Brooks' advice will be most valuable. But mind, if you dare to show mine, I'll tear them into pieces."

"I wasn't going to, dear," Louise declared, a little tartly. "Shall I begin at the beginning, Mr. Brooks, or—"

"Oh, don't show those first few, dear," Selina exclaimed. "You know they're not nearly so good as some of the others. That mill is all out of drawing."

Mary, who had been elbowed into the background, rose quietly and crossed to the other end of the room. Brooks followed her for a moment with regretful eyes. Her simple gown, with the little piece of ribbon around her graceful neck, seemed almost distinguished by comparison with the loud-patterned and dressier blouses of the two girls who had now hemmed him in. For a moment he ignored the waiting pages.

"Your cousin," he remarked, "is quite unlike any of you. Has she been with you long?"

Louise looked up a little tartly.

"Oh, about three years. You are quite right when you say that she is unlike any of us. It doesn't seem nice to complain about her exactly, but she really is terribly trying, isn't she, Selina?"

Selina nodded, and dropped her voice.

"She is getting worse," she declared. "She is becoming a positive trouble to us."

Brooks endeavoured to look properly sympathetic, and considered himself justified in pursuing the conversation. "Indeed! May I ask in what way?"

"Oh, she has such old-fashioned ideas," Louise said, confidentially. "I've quite lost patience with her, and so has Selina; haven't you, dear? She never goes to parties if she can help it, she is positively rude to all our friends, and the sarcastic things she says sometimes are most unpleasant. You know, papa is very, very good to her."

"Yes, indeed," Selina interrupted. "You know, Mr. Brooks, she has no father and mother, and she was living quite alone in London when papa found her out and brought her here—and in the most abject poverty. I believe he found her in a garret. Fancy that!"

"And now," Louise continued, "he allows her for her clothes exactly the same as he does us—and look at her. Would you believe it, now? She is like that nearly every evening, although we have friends dropping in continually. Of course I don't believe in extravagance, but if a girl has relations who are generous enough to give her the means, I do think that, for their sake, she ought to dress properly. I think that she owes it to them, as well as to herself."

"And out of doors it is positively worse," Selina whispered, impressively. "I declare," she added, with a simper, "that although nobody can say that I am proud, there are times when I am positively ashamed to be seen out with her. What she does with her money I can't imagine."

Brooks, who was something of a critic in such matters, and had recognized the art of her severely simple gown, smiled to himself. He was wise enough, however, not to commit himself.

"Perhaps," he suggested, "she thinks that absolute simplicity suits her best. She has a nice figure."

Selina tossed her much-beaded slipper impatiently.

"Heaven only knows what Mary does think," she exclaimed, impatiently.

"And Heaven only knows what I am to say about these," Brooks groaned inwardly, as the sketch-book fell open before him at last, and its contents were revealed to his astonished eyes.

CHAPTER III
KINGSTON BROOKS HAS A VISITOR

Kingston Brooks was twenty-five years old, strong, nervous, and with a strenuous desire to make his way so far as was humanly possible into the heart of life. He was a young solicitor recently established in Medchester, without friends save those he was now making, and absolutely without interest of any sort. He had a small capital, and already the beginnings of a practice. He had some sort of a reputation as a speaker, and was well spoken of by those who had entrusted business to him. Yet he was still fighting for a living when this piece of luck had befallen him. Mr. Bullsom had entrusted a small case to him, and found him capable and cheap. Amongst that worthy gentleman's chief characteristics was a decided weakness for patronizing younger and less successful men, and he went everywhere with Kingston Brooks' name on his lips. Then came the election, and the sudden illness of Mr. Morrison, who had always acted as agent for the Radical candidates for the borough. Another agent had to be found. Several who would have been suitable were unavailable. An urgent committee meeting was held, and Mr. Bullsom at once called attention to an excellent little speech of Kingston Brooks' at a ward meeting on the previous night. In an hour he was closeted with the young lawyer, and the affair was settled. Brooks knew that henceforth the material side of his career would be comparatively easy sailing.

He had accepted his good fortune with something of the same cheerful philosophy with which he had seen difficulty loom up in his path a few months ago. But to-night, on his way home from Mr. Bullsom's suburban residence, a different mood possessed him. Usually a self-contained and somewhat gravely minded person, to-night the blood went tingling through his veins with a new and unaccustomed warmth. He carried himself blithely, the cool night air was so grateful and sweet to him that he had no mind even to smoke. There seemed to be no tangible reason for the change. The political excitement, which a few weeks ago he had begun to feel exhilarating, had for him decreased now that his share in it lay behind the scenes, and he found himself wholly occupied with the purely routine work of the election. Nor was there any sufficient explanation to be found in the entertainment which he had felt himself bound to accept at Mr. Bullsom's hands. Of the wine, which had been only tolerable, he had drunk, as was his custom, sparingly, and of Mary Scott, who had certainly interested him in a manner which the rest of the family had not, he had after all seen but very little. He found himself thinking with fervor of the desirable things in life, never had the various tasks which he had set himself seemed so easy an accomplishment, his own powers more real and alive. And beneath it all he was conscious of a vague sense of excitement, a nervous dancing of the blood, as though even now the time were at hand when he might find himself in touch with some of the greater forces of life, all of which he intended some day to realize. It was delightful after all to be young and strong, to be stripped for the race in the morning of life, when every indrawn breath seems sweet with the perfume of beautiful things, and the heart is tuned to music.

The fatigue of the day was wholly forgotten. He was surprised indeed when he found himself in the little street where his rooms were. A small brougham was standing at the corner, the liveries and horse of which, though quiet enough, caused him a moment's surprise as being superior to the ordinary equipages of the neighborhood. He passed on to the sober-fronted house where he lived, and entering with his latch-key made his way to his study. Immediately he entered he was conscious of a man comfortably seated in his easy-chair, and apparently engrossed in a magazine.

He advanced towards him inquiringly, and his visitor, carefully setting down the magazine, rose slowly to his feet. The young man's surprise at finding his rooms occupied was increased by the appearance of his visitor. He was apparently of more than middle age, with deeply-lined face, tall, and with an expression the coldness of which was only slightly mitigated by a sensitive mouth that seemed at once cynical and humorous. He was of more than ordinary height, and dressed in the plainest dinner garb of the day, but his dinner jacket, his black tie and the set of his shirt were revelations to Brooks, who dealt only with the Medchester tradespeople. He did not hold out his hand, but he eyed Brooks with a sort of critical survey, which the latter found a little disconcerting.

"You wished to see me, sir?" Brooks asked. "My name is Kingston Brooks, and these are my rooms."

"So I understood," the new-comer replied imperturbably. "I called about an hour ago, and took the liberty of awaiting your return."

Brooks sat down. His vis-a-vis was calmly selecting a cigarette from a capacious case. Brooks found himself offering a light and accepting a cigarette himself, the flavour of which he at once appreciated.

"Can I offer you a whisky-and-soda?" he inquired.

"I thank you, no," was the quiet reply.

There was a short pause.

"You wished to see me on some business connected with the election, no doubt?" Brooks suggested.

His visitor shook his head slowly. He knocked the ash from his cigarette and smiled whimsically.

"My dear fellow," he said, "I haven't the least idea why I came to see you this evening."

Brooks felt that he had a right to be puzzled, and he looked it. But his visitor was so evidently a gentleman and a person of account, that the obvious rejoinder did not occur to him. He merely waited with uplifted eyebrows.

"Not the least idea," his visitor repeated, still smiling. "But at the same time I fancy that before I leave you I shall find myself explaining, or endeavouring to explain, not why I am here, but why I have not visited you before. What do you think of that?"

"I find it," Brooks answered, "enigmatic but interesting."

"Exactly. Well, I hate talking, so my explanation will not be a tedious one. Your name is Kingston Brooks."

"Yes."

"Your mother's name was Dorothy Kenneir. She was, before her marriage, the matron of a home in the East End of London, and a lady devoted to philanthropic work. Your father was a police-court missionary."

Brooks was leaning a little forward in his chair. These things were true enough. Who was his visitor?

"Your father, through over-devotion to the philanthropic works in which he was engaged, lost his reason temporarily, and on his partial recovery I understand that the doctors considered him still to be mentally in a very weak state. They ordered him a sea voyage. He left England on the Corinthia fifteen years ago, and I believe that you heard nothing more of him until you received the news of his death—probably ten years back."

"Yes! Ten years ago.

"Your mother, I think, lived for only a few months after your father left England. You found a guardian in Mr. Ascough of Lincoln's Inn Fields. There my knowledge of your history ceases.

"How do you know these things?" Brooks asked.

"I was with your father when he died. It was I who wrote to you and sent his effects to England."

"You were there—in Canada?"

"Yes. I had a dwelling within a dozen miles of where your father had built his hut by the side of the great lake. He was the only other Englishman within a hundred miles. So I was with him often."

"It is wonderful—after all these years," Brooks exclaimed. "You were there for sport, of course?"

"For sport!" his visitor repeated in a colourless tone.

"But my father—what led him there? Why did he cut himself off from every one, send no word home, creep away into that lone country to die by himself? It is horrible to think of."

"Your father was not a communicative man. He spoke of his illness. I always considered him as a person mentally shattered. He spent his days alone, looking out across the lake or wandering in the woods. He had no companions, of course, but there were always animals around him. He had the look of a man who had suffered."

"He was to have gone to Australia," Brooks said. "It was from there that we expected news from him. I cannot see what possible reason he had for changing his plans. There was no mystery about his life in London. It was one splendid record of self-denial and devotion to what he thought his duty."

"From what he told me," his vis-a-vis continued, handing again his cigarette-case, and looking steadily into the fire, "he seems to have left England with the secret determination never to return. But why I do not know. One thing is certain. His mental state was not altogether healthy. His desire for solitude was almost a passion. Towards the end, however, his mind was clear enough. He told me about your mother and you, and he handed me all the papers, which I subsequently sent to London. He spoke of no trouble, and his transition was quite peaceful."

"It was a cruel ending," Brooks said, quietly. "There were people in London whom he had befriended who would have worked their passage out and faced any hardships to be with him. And my mother, notwithstanding his desertion, believed in him to the last."

There was a moment's intense silence. This visitor who had come so strangely was to all appearance a man not easily to be moved. Yet Brooks fancied that the long white fingers were trembling, and that the strange quiet of his features was one of intense self-repression. His tone when he spoke again, however, was clear, and almost indifferent.

"I feel," he said, "that it would have been only decently courteous of me to have sought you out before, although I have, as you see, nothing whatever to add to the communications I sent you. But I have not been a very long time in England, and I have a very evil habit of putting off things concerning which there is no urgency. I called at Ascough's, and learned that you were in practice in Medchester. I am now living for a short time not far from here, and reading of the election, I drove in to-night to attend one of the meetings—I scarcely cared which. I heard your name, saw you on the platform, and called here, hoping to find you."

"It was very kind," Brooks said.

He felt curiously tongue-tied. This sudden upheaval of a past which he had never properly understood affected him strangely.

"I gathered from Mr. Ascough that you were left sufficient means to pay for your education, and also to start you in life," his visitor continued. "Yours is considered to be an overcrowded profession, but I am glad to understand that you seem likely to make your way."

Brooks thanked him absently.

"From your position on the platform to-night I gather that you are a politician?"

"Scarcely that," Brooks answered. "I was fortunate enough to be appointed agent to Mr. Henslow owing to the illness of another man. It will help me in my profession."

The visitor rose to his feet. He stood with his hands behind him, looking at the younger man. And Brooks suddenly remembered that he did not even know his name.

"You will forgive me," he said, also rising, "if I have seemed a little dazed. I am very grateful to you for coming. I have always wanted more than anything in the world to meet some one who saw my father after he left England. There is so much which even now seems mysterious with regard to his disappearance from the world."

"I fear that you will never discover more than you have done from me," was the quiet reply. "Your father had been living for years in profound solitude when I found him. Frankly, I considered from the first that his mind was unhinged. Therein I fancy lies the whole explanation of his silence and his voluntary disappearance. I am assuming, of course, that there was nothing in England to make his absence desirable."

"There was nothing," Brooks declared with conviction. "That I can personally vouch for. His life as a police-court missionary was the life of a militant martyr's, the life of a saint. The urgent advice of his physicians alone led him to embark upon that voyage; I see now that it was a mistake. He left before he had sufficiently recovered to be safely trusted alone. By the bye," Brooks continued, after a moment's hesitation, "you have not told me your name, whom I have to thank for this kindness. Your letters from Canada were not signed."

There was a short silence. From outside came the sound of the pawing of horses' feet and the jingling of harness.

"I was a fellow-traveller in that great unpeopled world," the visitor said, "and there was nothing but common humanity in anything I did. I lived out there as Philip Ferringshaw, here I have to add my title, the Marquis of Arranmore. I was a younger son in those days. If there is anything which I have forgotten, I am at Enton for a month or so. It is an easy walk from Medchester, if your clients can spare you for an afternoon. Good-night, Mr. Brooks."

He held out his hand. He was sleepy apparently, for his voice had become almost a drawl, and he stifled a yawn as he passed along the little passage. Kingston Brooks returned to his little room, and threw himself back into his easy-chair. Truly this had been a wonderful day.

CHAPTER IV
A QUESTION FOR THE COUNTRY

For the first time in many years it seemed certain that the Conservatives had lost their hold upon the country. The times were ripe for a change of any sort. An ill-conducted and ruinous war had drained the empire of its surplus wealth, and every known industry was suffering from an almost paralyzing depression—Medchester, perhaps, as severely as any town in the United Kingdom. Its staple manufactures were being imported from the States and elsewhere at prices which the local manufacturers declared to be ruinous. Many of the largest factories were standing idle, a great majority of the remainder were being worked at half or three-quarters time. Thoughtful men, looking ten years ahead, saw the cloud, which even now was threatening enough, grow blacker and blacker, and shuddered at the thought of the tempest which before long must break over the land. Meanwhile, the streets were filled with unemployed, whose demeanour day by day grew less and less pacific. People asked one another helplessly what was being done to avert the threatened crisis. The manufacturers, openly threatened by their discharged employees, and cajoled by others higher in authority and by public opinion, still pronounced themselves helpless to move without the aid of legislation. For the first time for years Protection was openly spoken of from a political platform.

Henslow, a shrewd man and a politician of some years' standing, was one of the first to read the signs of the times, and rightly to appreciate them. He had just returned from a lengthened visit to the United States, and what he had seen there he kept at first very much to himself. But at a small committee meeting held when his election was still a matter of doubt, he unbosomed himself at last to some effect.

"The vote we want," he said, "is the vote of those people who are losing their bread, and who see ruin and starvation coming in upon them. I mean the middle-class manufacturers and the operatives who are dependent upon them. I tell you where I think that as a nation we are going wrong. We fixed once upon a great principle, and we nailed it to our mast—for all time. That is a mistake. Absolute Free Trade, such as is at present our national policy, was a magnificent principle in the days of Cobden—but the times have changed. We must change with them. That is where the typical Englishman fails. It is a matter of temperament. He is too slow to adapt himself to changing circumstances."

There was a moment's silence. These were ominous words. Every one felt that they were not lightly spoken. Henslow had more behind. A prominent manufacturer, Harrison by name, interposed from his place.

"You are aware, Mr. Henslow," he said, "that many a man has lost an assured seat for a more guarded speech than that. For generations even a whisper of the sort has been counted heresy—especially from our party."

"Maybe," Henslow answered, "but I am reminded of this, Mr. Harrison. The pioneers of every great social change have suffered throughout the whole of history, but the man who has selected the proper moment and struck hard, has never failed to win his reward. Now I am no novice in politics, and I am going to make a prophecy. Years ago the two political parties were readjusted on the Irish question. Every election which was fought was simply on these lines—it was upon the principle of Home Rule for Ireland, and the severance of that country from the United Kingdom, or the maintenance of the Union. Good! Now, in more recent times, the South African war and the realization of what our Colonies could do for us has introduced a new factor. Those who have believed in a doctrine of expansion have called themselves 'Imperialists,' and those who have favoured less wide-reaching ideals, and perhaps more attention to home matters, have been christened 'Little Englanders.' Many elections have been fought out on these lines, if not between two men absolutely at variance with one another on this question, still on the matter of degree. Now, I am going to prophesy. I say that the next readjustment of Parties, and the time is not far ahead, will be on the tariff question, and I believe that the controversy on this matter, when once the country has laid hold of it, will be the greatest political event of this century. Listen, gentlemen. I do not speak without having given this question careful and anxious thought, and I tell you that I can see it coming."

The committee meeting broke up at a late hour in the afternoon amidst some excitement, and Mr. Bullsom walked back to his office with Brooks. A fine rain was falling, and the two men were close together under one umbrella.

"What do you think of it, Brooks?" Bullsom asked anxiously.

"To tell you the truth, I scarcely know," the younger answered. "Ten years ago there could have been but one answer—to-day—well, look there."

The two men stood still for a moment. They were in the centre of the town, at a spot from which the main thoroughfares radiated into the suburbs and manufacturing centres. Everywhere the pavements and the open space where a memorial tower stood were crowded with loiterers. Men in long lines stood upon the kerbstones, their hands in their pockets, watching, waiting—God knows for what. There were all sorts, of course, the professional idlers and the drunkard were there, but the others—there was no lack of them. There was no lack of men, white-faced, dull-eyed, dejected, some of them actually with the brand of starvation to be seen in their sunken cheeks and wasted limbs. No wonder that the swing-doors of the public-houses, where there was light and warmth inside, opened and shut continually.

"Look," Brooks repeated, with a tremor in his tone. "There are thousands and thousands of them—and all of them must have some sort of a home to go to. Fancy it—one's womankind, perhaps children—and nothing to take home to them. It's such an old story, that it sounds hackneyed and commonplace. But God knows there's no other tragedy on His earth like it."

Mr. Bullsom was uncomfortable.

"I've given a hundred pounds to the Unemployed Fund," he said.

"It's money well spent if it had been a thousand," Brooks answered. "Some day they may learn their strength, and they will not suffer then, like brute animals, in silence. Look here. I'm going to speak to one of them."

He touched a tall youth on the shoulder. "Out of work, my lad?" he asked. The youth turned surlily round. "Yes. Looks like it, don't it?"

"What are you?" Brooks asked.

"Clicker."

"Why did you leave your last place?"

"Gaffer said he's no more orders—couldn't keep us on. The shop's shut up. Know of a job, guv'nor?" he asked, with a momentary eagerness. "I've two characters in my pocket—good 'uns."

"You've tried to get a place elsewhere?" Brooks asked.

"Tried? D'ye suppose I'm standing here for fun? I've tramped the blessed town. I went to thirty factories yesterday, and forty to-day. Know of a job, guv'nor? I'm not particular."

"I wish I did," Brooks answered, simply. "Here's half-a-crown. Go to that coffee-palace over there and get a meal. It's all I can do for you."

"Good for you, guv'nor," was the prompt answer. "I can treat my brother on that. Here, Ned," he caught hold of a younger boy by the shoulder, "hot coffee and eggs, you sinner. Come on."

The two scurried off together. Brooks and his companion passed on.

"It is just this," Brooks said, in a low tone, "just the thought of these people makes me afraid, positively afraid to argue with Henslow. You see—he may be right. I tell you that in a healthily-governed country there should be work for every man who is able and willing to work. And in England there isn't. Free Trade works out all right logically, but it's one thing to see it all on paper, and it's another to see this—here around us—and Medchester isn't the worst off by any means."

Bullsom was silent for several moments.

"I tell you what it is, Brooks," he said. "I'll send another hundred to the Unemployed Fund to-night."

"It's generous of you, Mr. Bullsom," the young lawyer answered. "You'll never regret it. But look here. There's a greater responsibility even than feeding these poor fellows resting upon us to-day. They don't want our charity. They've an equal right to live with us. What they want, and what they have a right to, is just legislation. That's where we come in. Politics isn't a huge joke, or the vehicle for any one man's personal ambition. We who interest ourselves, however remotely, in them, impose upon ourselves a great obligation. We've got to find the truth. That's why I hesitate to say anything against Henslow's new departure. We're off the track now. I want to hear all that Henslow has to say. We must not neglect a single chance whilst that terrible cry is ever in our ears."

They parted at the tram terminus, Mr. Bullsom taking a car for his suburban paradise. As usual, he was the centre of a little group of acquaintances.

"And how goes the election, Bullsom?" some one asked him.

Mr. Bullsom was in no hurry to answer the question. He glanced round the car, collecting the attention of those who might be supposed interested.

"I will answer that question better," he said, "after the mass meeting on Saturday night. I think that Henslow's success or failure will depend on that."

"Got something up your sleeve, eh?" his first questioner remarked.

"Maybe," Mr. Bullsom answered. "Maybe not. But apart from the immediate matter of this election, I can tell you one thing, gentlemen, which may interest you."

He paused. One thumb stole towards the armhole of his waistcoat. He liked to see these nightly companions of his hang upon his words. It was a proper and gratifying tribute to his success as a man of affairs.

"I have just left," he said, "our future Member."

The significance of his speech was not immediately apparent.

"Henslow! Oh, yes. Committee meeting this afternoon, wasn't it?" some one remarked.

"I do not mean Henslow," Mr. Bullsom replied. "I mean Kingston Brooks."

The desired sensation was apparent.

"Why, he's your new agent, isn't he?"

"Young fellow who plays cricket rather well."

"Great golfer, they say!"

"Makes a good speech, some one was saying."

"Gives free lectures at the Secular Hall." "Rather a smart young solicitor, they say!"

Mr. Bullsom looked around him.

"He is all these things, and he does all these things. He is one of these youngsters who has the knack of doing everything well. Mark my words, all of you. I gave him his first case of any importance, and I got him this job as agent for Henslow. He's bound to rise. He's ambitious, and he's got the brains. He'll be M.P. for this borough before we know where we are."

Half-a-dozen men of more or less importance made a mental note to nod to Kingston Brooks next time they saw him, and Mr. Bullsom trudged up his avenue with fresh schemes maturing in his mind. In the domestic circle he further unburdened himself.

"Mrs. Bullsom," he said, "I am thinking of giving a dinner-party. How many people do we know better than ourselves?"

Mrs. Bullsom was aghast, and the young ladies, Selina and Louise, who were in the room, were indignant.

"Really, papa," Selina exclaimed, "what do you mean?"

"What I say," he answered, gruffly. "We're plain people, your mother and I, at any rate, and when you come to reckon things up, I suppose you'll admit that we're not much in the social way. There's plenty of people living round us in a sight smaller houses who don't know us, and wouldn't if they could—and I'm not so sure that it's altogether the fault of your father and mother either, Selina," he added, breaking ruthlessly in upon a sotto-voce remark of that young lady's.

"Well, I never!" Selina exclaimed, tossing her head.

"Come, come, I don't want no sauce from you girls," he added, drifting towards the fireplace, and adopting a more assured tone as he reached his favourite position. "I've reasons for wishing to have Mr. Kingston Brooks here, and I'd like him to meet gentlefolk. Now, there's the Vicar and his wife. Do you suppose they'd come?"

"Well, I should like to know why not," Mrs. Bullsom remarked, laying down her knitting, "when it's only three weeks ago you sent him ten guineas for the curates' fund. Come indeed! They'd better."

"Then there's Dr. Seventon," Mr. Bullsom continued, "and his wife. Better drop him a line and tell him to look in and see me at the office. I can invent something the matter with me, and I'd best drop him a hint. They say Mrs. Seventon is exclusive. But I'll just let him know she's got to come. Now, who else, girls?"

"The Huntingdons might come—if they knew that it was this sort of an affair," Selina remarked, thoughtfully.

"And Mr. Seaton," Louise added. "I'm sure he's most gentlemanly."

"I don't want gentlemanly people this time," Mr. Bullsom declared, "I want gentle-people. That's all there is about it. I let you ask who you like to the house, and give you what you want for subscriptions and clothes and such-like. You've had a free 'and. Now let's see something for it. Half-a-dozen couples'll be enough if you can't get more, but I Won't have the Nortons, or the Marvises, or any of that podgy set. You understand that? And, first of all, you, Selina, had better write to Mr. Brooks and ask him to dine with us in a friendly way one night the week after next, when the election is over and done with."

"In a friendly way, pa?" Selina repeated, doubtfully. "But we can't ask these other people whom we know so slightly like that—and, besides, Mr. Brooks might not dress if we put it like that."

"A nice lot you know about gentle-people and their ways," Mr. Bullsom remarked, with scorn. "A young fellow like Brooks would tog himself out for dinner all right even if we were alone, as long as there were ladies there. And as for the dinner, you don't suppose I'm such a mug as to leave that to Ann. I shall go to the Queen's Hotel, and have 'em send a cook and waiters, and run the whole show. Don't know that I shan't send to London. You get the people! I'll feed 'em!"

"Do as your father says, Selina," Mrs. Bullsom said, mildly. "I'm sure he's very considerate."

"Where's Mary?" Mr. Bullsom inquired. "This is a bit in her line."

Selina tossed her head.

"I'm sure I don't know why you should say that, papa," she declared. "Mary knows nothing about society, and she has no friends who would be the least use to us."

"Where is she, anyway?" Mr. Bullsom demanded. No one knew. As a matter of fact she was having tea with Kingston Brooks.

CHAPTER V
THE MARQUIS OF ARRANMORE

They had met almost on the steps of his office, and only a few minutes after he had left Mr. Bullsom. Brooks was attracted first by a certain sense of familiarity with the trim, well-balanced figure, and immediately afterwards she raised her eyes to his in passing. He wheeled sharply round, and held out his hand.

"Miss Scott, isn't it? Do you know I have just left your uncle?"

She smiled a little absently. She looked tired, and her boots and skirt were splashed as though with much walking.

"Indeed! I suppose you see a good deal of him just now while the election is on?"

"I must make myself a perfect nuisance to him," Brooks admitted. "You see the work is all new to me, and he has been through it many times before. Are you just going home?"

She nodded.

"I have been out since two o'clock," she said.

"And you are almost wet through, and quite tired out," he said. "Look here. Come across to Mellor's and have some tea with me, and I will put you in a car afterwards."

She hesitated—and he led the way across the Street, giving her no opportunity to frame a refusal. The little tea-place was warm and cosy. He found a comfortable corner, and took her wet umbrella and cape away.

"I believe," he said, sitting down opposite her, "that I have saved your life."

"Then I am not sure," she answered, "that I feel grateful to you. I ought to have warned you that I am not in the least likely to be a cheerful companion. I have had a most depressing afternoon."

"You have been to your tailor's," he suggested, "and your new gown is a failure—or is it even worse than that?"

She laughed dubiously. Then the tea was brought, and for a moment their conversation was interrupted. He thought her very graceful as she bent forward and busied herself attending to his wants. Her affinity to Selina and Louise was undistinguishable. It was true that she was pale, but it was the pallor of refinement, the student's absence of colour rather than the pallor of ill-health.

"Mr. Brooks," she said, presently, "you are busy with this election, and you are brought constantly into touch with all classes of people. Can you tell me why it is that it is so hard just now for poor people to get work? Is it true, what they tell me, that many of the factories in Medchester are closed, and many of those that are open are only working half and three-quarter time?"

"I am afraid that it is quite true, Miss Scott," he answered. "As for the first part of your question, it is very hard to answer. There seem to be so many causes at work just now.

"But it is the work of the politician surely to analyze these causes.

"It should be," he answered. "Tell me what has brought this into your mind."

"Some of the girls in our class," she said, "are out of work, and those who have anything to do seem to be working themselves almost to death to keep their parents or somebody dependent upon them. Two of them I am anxious about. I have been trying to find them this afternoon. I have heard things, Mr. Brooks, which have made me ashamed—sick at heart—ashamed to go home and think how we live, while they die. And these girls—they have known so much misery. I am afraid of what may happen to them."

"These girls are mostly boot and shoe machinists, are they not?"

"Yes. But even Mr. Stuart says that he cannot find them work."

"It is only this afternoon that we have all been discussing this matter," he said, gravely. "It is serious enough, God knows. The manufacturer tells us that he is suffering from American competition—here and in the Colonies. He tells us that the workpeople themselves are largely to blame, that their trades unions restrict them to such an extent that he is hopelessly handicapped from the start. But there are other causes. There is a terrible wave of depression all through the country. The working classes have no money to spend. Every industry is flagging, and every industry seems threatened with competition from abroad. Do you understand the principles of Free Trade at all?"

"Not in the least. I wish I did."

"Some day we must have a talk about it. Henslow has made a very daring suggestion to-day. He has given us all plenty to think about. We are all agreed upon one thing. The crisis is fast approaching, and it must be faced.

These people have the right to live, and they have the right to demand that legislation should interfere on their behalf."

She sighed.

"It is a comfort to hear you talk like this," she said. "To me it seems almost maddening to see so much suffering, so many people suffering, not only physically, but being dragged down into a lower moral state by sheer force of circumstances and their surroundings, and all the time we educated people go on our way and live our lives, as though nothing were happening—as though we had no responsibility whatever for the holocaust of misery at our doors. So few people stop to think. They won't understand. It is so easy to put things behind one."

"Come," he said, cheerfully, "you and I, at least, are not amongst those. And there is a certain duty which we owe to ourselves, too, as well as to others—to look upon the brighter side of things. Let us talk about something less depressing."

"You shall tell me," she suggested, "who is going to win the election."

"Henslow!" he answered, promptly.

"Owing, I suppose—"

"To his agent, of course. You may laugh, Miss Scott, but I can assure you that my duties are no sinecure. I never knew what work was before."

"Too much work," she said, "is better than too little. After all, more people die of the latter than the former."

"Nature meant me," he said, "for a hazy man. I have all the qualifications for a first-class idler. And circumstances and the misfortune of my opinions are going to keep me going at express speed all my life. I can see it coming. Sometimes it makes me shudder."

"You are too young," she remarked, "to shrink from work. I have no sympathy to offer you."

"I begin to fear, Miss Scott," he said, "that you are not what is called sympathetic."

She smiled—and the smile broke into a laugh, as though some transient idea rather than his words had pleased her.

"You should apply to my cousin Selina for that," she said. "Every one calls her most delightfully sympathetic."

"Sympathy," he remarked, "is either a heaven-sent joy—or a bore. It depends upon the individual."

"That is either enigmatical or rude," she answered. "But, after all, you don't know Selina."

"Why not?" he asked. "I have talked with her as long as with you—and I feel that I know you quite well."

"I can't be responsible for your feelings," she said, a little brusquely, "but I'm quite sure that I don't know you well enough to be sitting here at tea with you even."

"I won't admit that," he answered, "but it was very nice of you to come.

"The fact of it was," she admitted, "my headache and appetite were stronger than my sense of the conventions. Now that the former are dissipated the latter are beginning to assert themselves. And so—"

She began to draw on her gloves. Just then a carriage with postilions and ladies with luggage came clattering up the street. She watched it with darkening face.

"That is the sort of man I detest," she said, motioning her head towards the window. "You know whose carriage it is, don't you?"

He shook his head.

"No, I did not know that any one round here drove with positions."

"It is the Marquis of Arranmore. He has a place at Enton, I believe, but he is only here for a few months in the year."

Brooks started and leaned eagerly forward.

"Why do you hate him?" he asked. "What has he done?"

"Didn't you hear how he treated the Mayor when he went out for a subscription to the Unemployed Fund?"

Brooks shook his head.

"No! I have heard nothing."

"Poor old Mr. Wensome went out all that way purposely to see him. He was kept waiting an hour, and then when he explained his errand the Marquis laughed at him. 'My dear fellow,' he said, 'the poor people of Medchester do not interest me in the least. I do not go to the people who are better off than I am and ask them to help support me, nor do I see the least reason why those who are worse off than I am should expect me to support them.' Mr. Wensome tried to appeal to his humanity, and the brute only continued to laugh in a cynical way. He declared that poor people did not interest him. His tenants he was prepared to look after—outside his own property he didn't care a snap of the fingers whether people lived or died. Mr. Wensome said it was perfectly awful to hear him talk, and he came away without a penny. Yet his property in this country alone is worth fifty thousand a year.

"It is very surprising," Brooks said, thoughtfully. "The more surprising because I know of a kind action which he once did."

"Sh! they're coming here!" she exclaimed. "That is the Marquis."

The omnibus had pulled up outside. A tall footman threw open the door, and held an umbrella over the two ladies who had descended. The Marquis and two other men followed. They trooped into the little place, bringing with them a strange flavour of another world. The women wore wonderful furs, and one who had ermine around her neck wore a great bunch of Neapolitan violets, whose perfume seemed to fill the room.

"This is a delightful idea," the taller one said, turning towards her host. "An eight-mile drive before tea sounded appalling. Where shall we sit, and may we have muffins?"

"There is nothing about your youth, Lady Sybil, which I envy more than your digestion," he answered, motioning them towards a table. "To be able to eat muffins with plenty of butter would be unalloyed bliss. Nevertheless, you shall have them. No one has ever called me selfish. Let us have tea, and toast, and bread-and-butter and cakes, and a great many muffins, please, young lady," he ordered. "And will you send out some tea to my servants, please? It will save them from trying to obtain drinks from the hotel next door, and ensure us a safe drive home."

"And don't forget to send out for that pack of cards, Arranmore," the elder lady said. "We are going to play bridge driving home with that wonderful little electric lamp of yours.

"I will not forget," he promised. "We are to be partners, you know."

He was on the point of sitting down when he saw Brooks at the next table. He held out his hand.

"How do you do, Mr. Brooks?" he said. "I am glad to see that you are going to get your man in.

"Thank you," Brooks answered, rising and waiting for his companion, who was buttoning her gloves. "I was afraid that your sympathies would be on the other side."

"Dear me, no," the Marquis answered. "My enemies would tell you that I have neither sympathy nor politics, but I assure you that at heart I am a most devout Radical. I have a vote, too, and you may count upon me.

"I am very glad to hear it," Brooks answered. "Shall I put you down on the list 'to be fetched'?"

The Marquis laughed.

"I'll come without," he declared. "I promise. Just remind me of the day."

He glanced towards Mary Scott, and for a moment seemed about to include her in some forthcoming remark. But whatever it might have been—it was never made. She kept her eyes averted, and though her self-possession was absolutely unruffled she hastened her departure. "I am not hurrying you, Mr. Brooks?" she asked. "Not in the least," he assured her.

He raised his hat to the Marquis and his party, and the former nodded good-humouredly. There was silence until the two were in the street. Then one of the men who had been looking after them dropped his eye-glass.

"I tell you what," he said to his vis-a-vis. "There's some chance for us in Medchester after all. I don't believe Arranmore is popular amongst the ladies of his own neighbourhood."

The Marquis laughed softly.

"She has a nice face," he remarked, "and I should imagine excellent perceptions. Curiously enough, too, she reminded me of some one who has every reason to hate me. But to the best of my belief I never saw her before in my life. Lady Caroom, that weird-looking object in front of you is a teapot—and those are teacups. May I suggest a use for them?"

CHAPTER VI
THE MAN WHO WENT TO HELL

The Hon. Sydney Chester Molyneux stood with his cue in one hand, and an open telegram in the other, in the billiard-room at Enton. He was visibly annoyed.

"Beastly hard luck," he declared. "Parliament is a shocking grind anyway. It isn't that one ever does anything, you know, but one wastes such a lot of time when one might have been doing something worth while."

"Do repeat that, Sydney," Lady Caroom begged, laying down her novel for a moment. "It really sounds as though it ought to mean something."

"I couldn't!" he admitted. "I wish to cultivate a reputation for originality, and my first object is to forget everything I have said directly I have said it, in case I should repeat myself."

"A short memory," Arranmore remarked, "is a politician's most valuable possession, isn't it?"

"No memory at all is better," Molyneux answered.

"And your telegram?" Lady Caroom asked.

"Is from my indefatigable uncle," Molyneux groaned. "He insists upon it that I interest myself in the election here, which means that I must go in to-morrow and call upon Rochester."

The younger girl looked up from her chair, and laughed softly.

"You will have to speak for him," she said. "How interesting! We will all come in and hear you."

Molyneux missed an easy cannon, and laid down his cue with an aggrieved air.

"It is all very well for you," he remarked, dismally, "but it is a horrible grind for me. I have just succeeded in forgetting all that we did last session, and our programme for next. Now I've got to wade through it all. I wonder why on earth Providence selected for me an uncle who thinks it worth while to be a Cabinet Minister?"

Sybil Caroom shrugged her shoulders.

"I wonder why on earth," she remarked, "any constituency thinks it worth while to be represented by such a politician as you. How did you get in, Sydney?"

"Don't know," he answered. "I was on the right side, and I talked the usual rot."

"For myself," she said, "I like a politician who is in earnest. They are more amusing, and more impressive in every way. Who was the young man you spoke to in that little place where we had tea?" she asked her host.

"His name is Kingston Brooks," Arranmore answered. "He is the agent for Henslow, the Radical candidate."

"Well, I liked him," she said. "If I had a vote I would let him convert me to Radicalism. I am sure that he could do it."

"He shall try—if you like," Arranmore remarked.

I am going to ask him to shoot one day."

"I am delighted to hear it," the girl answered. "I think he would be a wholesome change. You are all too flippant here."

The door opened. Mr. Hennibul, K.C., inserted his head and shoulders.

"I have been to look at Arranmore's golf-links," he remarked. "They are quite decent. Will some one come and play a round?"

"I will come," Sybil declared, putting down her book.

"And I," Molyneux joined in. "Hennibul can play our best ball."

Lady Caroom and her host were left alone. He came over to her side.

"What can I do to entertain your ladyship?" he asked, lightly. "Will you play billiards, walk or drive? There is an hour before lunch which must be charmed away."

"I am not energetic," she declared. "I ought to walk for the sake of my figure. I'm getting shockingly stout. Marie made me promise to walk a mile to-day. But I'm feeling deliciously lazy."

"/Embonpoint/ is the fashion," he remarked, "and you are inches short of even that yet. Come and sit in the study while I write some letters." She held out her hands.

"Pull me up, then! I am much too comfortable to move unaided."

She sprang to her feet lightly enough, and for a moment he kept her hands, which rested willingly enough in his. They looked at one another in silence. Then she laughed.

"My dear Arranmore," she protested, "I am not made up half carefully enough to stand such a critical survey by daylight. Your north windows are too terrible."

"Not to you, dear lady," he answered, smiling. "I was wondering whether it was possible that you could be forty-one."

"You brute," she exclaimed, with uplifted eyebrows. "How dare you? Forty if you like—for as long as you like. Forty is the fashionable age, but one year over that is fatal. Don't you know that now-a-days a woman goes straight from forty to sixty? It is such a delicious long rest. And besides, it gives a woman an object in life which she has probably been groping about for all her days. One is never bored after forty."

"And the object?"

"To keep young, of course. There's scope for any amount of ingenuity. Since that dear man in Paris has hit upon the real secret of enamelling, we are thinking of extending the limit to sixty-five. Lily Cestigan is seventy-one, you know, and she told me only last week that Mat Harlowe—you know Harlowe, he's rather a nice boy, in the Guards had asked her to run away with him. She's known him three months, and he's seen her at least three times by daylight. She's delighted about it."

"And is she going?" Arranmore asked.

"Well, I'm not sure that she'd care to risk that," Lady Caroom answered, thoughtfully. "She told him she'd think about it, and, meanwhile, he's just as devoted as ever."

They crossed the great stone hall together—the hall which, with its wonderful pillars and carved dome, made Enton the show-house of the county. Arranmore's study was a small octagonal room leading out from the library. A fire of cedar logs was burning in an open grate, and he wheeled up an easy-chair for her close to his writing-table.

"I wonder," she remarked, thoughtfully, "what you think of Syd Molyneux?"

"Is there anything—to be thought about him?" he answered, lighting a cigarette.

"He's rather that way, isn't he?" she assented. "I mean for Sybil, you know."

"I should let Sybil decide," he answered.

"She probably will," Lady Caroom said. "Still, she's horribly bored at having to be dragged about to places, you know, and that sort of thing, just because she isn't married, and she likes Syd all right. He's no fool!"

"I suppose not," Arranmore answered. "He's of a type, you know, which has sprung up during my—absence from civilization. You want to grow up with it to appreciate it properly. I don't think he's good enough for Sybil."

Lady Caroom sighed.

"Sybil's a dear girl," she said, "although she's a terrible nuisance to me. I shouldn't be at all surprised either if she developed views. I wish you were a marrying man, Arranmore. I used to think of you myself once, but you would be too old for me now. You're exactly the right age for Sybil."

Arranmore smiled. He had quite forgotten his letters. Lady Caroom always amused him so well.

"She is very like what you were at her age," he remarked. "What a pity it was that I was such a poverty-stricken beggar in those days. I am sure that I should have married you."

"Now I am beginning to like you," she declared, settling down more comfortably in her chair. "If you can keep up like that we shall be getting positively sentimental presently, and if there's anything I adore in this world—especially before luncheon—it is sentiment. Do you remember we used to waltz together, Arranmore?"

"You gave me a glove one night," he said. "I have it still."

"And you pressed my hand—and—it was in the Setons' conservatory—how bold you were."

"And the next day," he declared, in an aggrieved tone, "I heard that you were engaged to Caroom. You treated me shamefully."

"These reminiscences," she declared, "are really sweet, but you are most ungrateful. I was really almost too kind to you. They were all fearfully anxious to get me married, because Dumesnil always used to say that my complexion would give out in a year or two, and I wasted no end of time upon you, who were perfectly hopeless as a husband. After all, though, I believe it paid. It used to annoy Caroom so much, and I believe he proposed to me long before he meant to so as to get rid of you."

"I," Arranmore remarked, "was the victim."

She sat up with eyes suddenly bright.

"Upon my word," she declared, "I have an idea. It is the most charming and flattering thing, and it never occurred to me before. After all, it was not eccentricity which caused you to throw up your work at the Bar—and disappear. It was your hopeless devotion to me. Don't disappoint me now by denying it. Please don't! It was the announcement of my engagement, wasn't it?"

"And it has taken you all these years to find it out?

"I was shockingly obtuse," she murmured. "The thing came to me just now as a revelation. Poor, dear man, how you must have suffered. This puts us on a different footing altogether, doesn't it?" "Altogether," he admitted.

"And," she continued, eyeing him now with a sudden nervousness, "emboldens me to ask you a question which I have been dying to ask you for the last few years. I wonder whether you will answer it."

"I wonder!" he repeated.

A change in him, too, was noticeable. That wonderful impassivity of feature which never even in his lighter moments passed altogether away, seemed to deepen every line in his hard, clear-cut face. His mouth was close drawn, his eyes were suddenly colder and expressionless. There was about him at such times as—these an almost repellent hardness. His emotions, and the man himself, seemed frozen. Lady Caroom had seen him look like it once before, and she sighed. Nevertheless, she persevered.

"For nearly twenty years," she said, "you disappeared. You were reported at different times to be in every quarter of the earth, from Zambesia to Pekin. But no one knew, and, of course, in a season or two you were forgotten. I always wondered, I am wondering now, where were you? What did you do with yourself?

"I went down into Hell," he answered. "Can't you see the marks of it in my face? For many years I lived in Hell—for many years."

"You puzzle me," she said, in a low tone. "You had no taste for dissipation. You look as though life had scorched you up at some time or other. But how? where? You were found in Canada, I know, when your brother died. But you had only been there for a few years. Before then?"

"Ay! Before then?"

There was a short silence. Then Arranmore, who had been gazing steadily into the fire, looked up. She fancied that his eyes were softer.

"Dear friend," he said, "of those days I have nothing to tell—even you. But there are more awful things even than moral degeneration. You do me justice when you impute that I never ate from the trough. But what I did, and where I lived, I do not think that I shall ever willingly tell any one."

A piece of burning wood fell upon the hearthstone. He stooped and picked it up, placed it carefully in its place, and busied himself for a moment or two with the little brass poker. Then he straightened himself.

"Catherine," he said, "I think if I were you that I would not marry Sybil to Molyneux. It struck me to-day that his eyeglass-chain was of last year's pattern, and I am not sure that he is sound on the subject of collars. You know how important these things are to a young man who has to make his own way in the world. Perhaps, I am not sure, but I think it is very likely I might be able to find a husband for her."

"You dear man," Lady Caroom murmured. "I should rely upon your taste and judgment so thoroughly."

There was a discreet knock at the door. A servant entered with a card.

Arranmore took it up, and retained it in his fingers.

"Tell Mr. Brooks," he said, "that I will be with him in a moment. If he has ridden over, ask him to take some refreshment."

"You have a visitor," Lady Caroom said, rising. "If you will excuse me I will go and lie down until luncheon-time, and let my maid touch me up. These sentimental conversations are so harrowing. I feel a perfect wreck."

She glided from the room, graceful, brisk and charming, the most wonderful woman in England, as the Society papers were never tired of calling her. Arranmore glanced once more at the card between his fingers.

"Mr. Kingston Brooks."

He stood for a few seconds, motionless. Then he rang the bell.

"Show Mr. Brooks in here," he directed.

CHAPTER VII
A THOUSAND POUNDS

Brooks had ridden a bicycle from Medchester, and his trousers and boots were splashed with mud. His presence at Enton was due to an impulse, the inspiration of which he had already begun seriously to doubt. Arranmore's kindly reception of him was more than ordinarily welcome.

"I am very glad to see you, Mr. Brooks," he said, holding out his hand. "How comes it that you are able to take even so short a holiday as this? I pictured you surrounded by canvassers and bill-posters and journalists, all clamouring for your ear."

Brooks laughed, completely at his ease now, thanks to the unspoken cordiality of the other man. He took the easy-chair which the servant had noiselessly wheeled up to him.

"I am afraid that you exaggerate my importance,—Lord Arranmore," he said. "I was very busy early this morning, and I shall be again after four. But I am allowed a little respite now and then."

"You spend it very sensibly out of doors," Arranmore remarked. "How did you get here?"

"I cycled," Brooks answered. "It was very pleasant, but muddy."

"What will you have?" Lord Arranmore asked. "Some wine and biscuits, or something of that sort?"

His hand was upon the bell, but Brooks stopped him.

"Nothing at all, thank you, just now."

"Luncheon will be served in half-an-hour," the Marquis said. "You will prefer to wait until then?"

"I am much obliged to you," Brooks answered, "but I must be getting back to Medchester as soon as possible. Besides," he added, with a smile, "I am afraid when I have spoken of the object of my visit you may feel inclined to kick me out."

"I hope not," Arranmore replied, lightly. "I was hoping that your visit had no object at all, and that you had been good enough just to look me up.

"I should not have intruded without a purpose," Brooks said, quietly, "but you will be almost justified in treating my visit as an impertinence when I have disclosed my errand. Lord Arranmore, I am the secretary for the fund which is being raised in Medchester for the relief of the Unemployed."

Arranmore nodded.

"Oh, yes," he said. "I had a visit a few days ago from a worthy Medchester gentleman connected with it."

"It is concerning that visit, Lord Arranmore, that I have come to see you," Brooks continued, quietly. "I only heard of it yesterday afternoon, but this morning it seems to me that every one whom I have met has alluded to it."

The Marquis was lounging against the broad mantelpiece. Some part of the cordiality of his manner had vanished.

"Well?"

"Lord Arranmore, I wondered whether it was not possible that some mistake had been made," Brooks said. "I wondered whether Mr. Wensome had altogether understood you properly—"

"I did my best to be explicit," the Marquis murmured.

"Or whether you had misunderstood him," Brooks continued, doggedly. "This fund has become absolutely necessary unless we wish to see the people starve in the streets. There are between six and seven thousand operatives and artisans in Medchester to-day who are without work through no fault of their own. It is our duty as citizens to do our best for them. Nearly every one in Medchester has contributed according to their means. You are a large property-owner in the town. Cannot you consider this appeal as an unenforced rate? It comes to that in the long run."

The Marquis shrugged his shoulders.

"I think," he said, "that on the subject of charity Englishmen generally wholly misapprehend the situation. You say that between six and seven thousand men are out of work in Medchester. Very well, I affirm that there must be a cause for that. If you are a philanthropist it is your duty to at once investigate the economic and political reasons for such a state of things, and alter them. By going about and collecting money for these people you commit what is little short of a crime. You must know the demoralizing effect of charity. No man who has ever received a dole is ever again an independent person. Besides that, you are diverting the public mind from the real point of issue, which is not that so many thousand people are hungry, but that a flaw exists in the administration of the laws of the country so grave that a certain number of thousands of people who have a God-sent right to productive labour haven't got it. Do you follow me?"

"Perfectly," Brooks answered. "You did not talk like this to Mr. Wensome."

"I admit it. He was an ignorant man in whom I felt no interest whatever, and I did not take the trouble. Besides, I will frankly admit that I am in no sense of the word a sentimentalist. The distresses of other people do not interest me particularly. I have been poor myself, and I never asked for, nor was offered, any sort of help. Consequently I feel very little responsibility concerning these unfortunate people, whose cause you have espoused."

"May I revert to your first argument?" Brooks said. "If you saw a man drowning then, instead of trying to save him you would subscribe towards a fund to teach people to swim?"

"That is ingenious," Lord Arranmore replied, smiling grimly, "but it doesn't interest me. If I saw a man drowning I shouldn't think of interfering unless the loss of that man brought inconvenience or loss to myself. If it did I should endeavour to save him—not unless. As for the fund you speak of, I should not think of subscribing to it. It would not interest me to know that other people were provided with a safeguard against drowning. I should probably spend the money in perfecting myself in the art of swimming. Don't you see that no man who has ever received help from another is exactly in the same position again? As an individual he is a weaker creature. That is where I disagree with nearly every existing form of charity. They are wrong in principle. They are a debauchment."

"Your views, Lord Arranmore," Brooks said, "are excellent for a model world. For practical purposes I think they are a little pedantic. You are quite right in your idea that charity is a great danger. I can assure you that we are trying to realize that in Medchester. We ask for money, and we dispense it unwillingly, but as a necessary evil. And we are trying to earnestly see where our social system is at fault, and to readjust it. But meanwhile, men and women and children even are starving. We must help them."

"That is where you are wholly wrong, and where you retard all progress," Arranmore remarked. "Can't you see that you are continually plugging up dangerous leaks with putty instead of lead? You muffle the cry which but for you must ring through the land, and make itself heard to every one. Let the people starve who are without means. Legislation would stir itself fast enough then. It is the only way. Charity to individuals is poison to the multitude. You create the criminal classes with your charities, you blindfold statesmen and mislead political economists. I tell you that the more you give away the more distress you create."

Brooks rose from his seat.

"Charity is older than nations or history, Lord Arranmore," he said, "and I am foolish enough to think that the world is a better place for it. Your reasoning is very excellent, but life has not yet become an exact science. The weaknesses of men and women have to be considered. You have probably never seen a starving person."

Lord Arranmore laughed, and Brooks looked across the room at him in amazement. The Marquis was always pale, but his pallor just then was as unnatural as the laugh itself.

"My dear young man," he said, "if I could show you what I have seen your hair would turn grey, and your wits go wandering. Do you think that I know nothing of life save its crust? I tell you that I have been down in the depths, aye, single-handed, there in the devil's own cauldron, where creatures in the shape of men and women, the very sight of whom would turn you sick with horror, creep like spawn through life, brainless and soulless, foul things who would murder one another for the sake of a crust, or—Bah! What horrible memories."

He broke off abruptly. When he spoke again his tone was as usual.

"Come," he said, "I mustn't let you have this journey for nothing. After all, the only luxury in having principles is in the departing from them. I will give you a cheque, Mr. Brooks, only I beg you to think over what I have said. Abandon this doling principle as soon as it is possible. Give your serious attention to the social questions and imperfect laws which are at the back of all this distress."

Brooks felt as though he had been awakened from a nightmare. He never forgot that single moment of revelation on the part of the man who sat now smiling and debonair before his writing-table.

"You are very kind indeed, Lord Arranmore," he said. "I can assure you that the money will be most carefully used, and amongst my party, at any rate, we do really appreciate the necessity for going to the root of the matter."

Arranmore's pen went scratching across the paper. He tore out a cheque, and placing it in an envelope, handed it to Brooks.

"I noticed," he remarked, thoughtfully, "that a good many people coming out of the factories hissed my carriage in Medchester last time I was there. I hope they will not consider my cheque as a sign of weakness. But after all," he added, with a smile, "what does it matter? Let us go in to luncheon, Brooks."

Brooks glanced down at his mud-splashed clothes and boots.

"I must really ask you to excuse me," he began, but Arranmore only rang the bell.

"My valet will smarten you up," he said. "Here, Fritz, take Mr. Brooks into my room and look after him, will you. I shall be in the hall when you come down."

As he passed from the dressing-room a few minutes later, Brooks paused for a moment to look up at the wonderful ceiling above the hall. Below, Lord Arranmore was idly knocking about the billiard balls, and all around him was the murmur of pleasant conversation. Brooks drew the envelope from his pocket and glanced at the cheque. He gave a little gasp of astonishment. It was for a thousand pounds.

CHAPTER VIII
KINGSTON BROOKS MAKES INQUIRIES

At luncheon Brooks found himself between Sybil Caroom and Mr. Hennibul.

She began to talk to him at once.

"I want to know all about your candidate, Mr. Brooks," she declared. "You can't imagine how pleased I am to have you here. I have had the feeling ever since I came of being shut up in a hostile camp. I am a Radical, you know, and these good people, even my mother, are rabid Conservatives."

Brooks smiled as he unfolded his serviette.

"Well, Henslow isn't exactly an ornamental candidate," he said, "but he is particularly sound and a man with any amount of common-sense. You should come and hear him speak."

"I'd love to," she answered, "but no one would bring me from here. They are all hopeless. Mr. Molyneux there is going to support Mr. Rochester. If I wasn't sure that he'd do more harm than good, I wouldn't let him go. But I don't suppose they'll let you speak, Sydney," she added. "They won't if they've ever heard you."

Molyneux smiled an imperturbable smile.

"Personally," he said, "I should prefer to lend my moral support only, but my fame as an orator is too well known. There is not the least chance that they will let me off."

Sybil looked at Brooks.

"Did you ever hear such conceit?" she remarked, in a pitying tone. "And I don't believe he's ever opened his mouth in the House, except to shout 'Hear, hear'! Besides, he's as nervous as a kitten. Tell me, are you going to return Mr. Henslow?"

"I think so," Brooks answered. "It is certain to be a very close contest, but I believe we shall get a small majority. The Jingo element are our greatest trouble. They are all the time trying to make people believe that Conservatives have the monopoly of the Imperial sentiment. As a matter of fact, I think that Henslow is almost rabid on the war question."

"Still, your platform—to use an Americanism," Mr. Hennibul interposed, "must be founded upon domestic questions. Medchester is a manufacturing town, and I am given to understand is suffering severely. Has your man any original views on the present depression in trade?"

Brooks glanced towards the speaker with a smile.

"You have been reading the Medchester Post!" he remarked.

The barrister nodded.

"Yes. It hinted at some rather surprising revelation."

"You must read Henslow's speech at the mass meeting to-morrow night," Brooks said. "At present I mustn't discuss these matters too much, especially before a political opponent," he remarked, smiling at Mr. Molyneux. "You might induce Mr. Rochester to play our trump card."

"If your trump card is what I suspect it to be," Mr. Hennibul said, "I don't think you need fear that. Rochester would be ready enough to try it, but some of his supporters wouldn't listen to it."

The conversation drifted away from politics. Brooks found himself enjoying his luncheon amazingly. Sybil Caroom devoted herself to him, and he found himself somehow drawn with marvellous facility into the little circle of intimate friends. Afterwards they all strolled into the hall together for coffee, and Arranmore laid his hand upon his arm.

"I am sorry that you will not have time to look round the place," he said. "You must come over again before long."

"You are very kind," Brooks said, dropping his voice a little. "There are one or two more things which I should like to ask you about Canada."

"I shall always be at your service," Lord Arranmore answered.

"And I cannot go," Brooks continued, "without thanking you—"

"We will take that for granted," Arranmore interrupted. "You know the spirit in which I gave it. It is not, I fear, one of sympathy, but it may at any rate save me from having my carriage windows broken one dark night. By the bye, I have ordered a brougham for you in half-an-hour. As you see, it is raining. Your bicycle shall be sent in to-morrow."

"It is very kind of you indeed," Brooks declared.

"Molyneux has to go in, so you may just as well drive together," Arranmore remarked. "By the bye, do you shoot?"

"A little," Brooks admitted.

"You must have a day with us. My head keeper is coming up this afternoon, and I will try and arrange something. The election is next week, of course. We must plan a day after then."

"I am afraid that my performance would scarcely be up to your standard," Brooks said, "although it is very kind of you to ask me. I might come and look on."

Arranmore laughed.

"Hennibul is all right," he said, "but Molyneux is a shocking duffer. We'll give you an easy place. We have some early callers, I see."

The butler was moving towards them, followed by two men in hunting-clothes.

"Sir George Marson and Mr. Lacroix, your lordship," he announced.

For a second Arranmore stood motionless. His eyes seemed to pass through the man in pink, who was approaching with outstretched hand, and to be fastened upon the face of his companion. It chanced that Brooks, who had stepped a little on one side, was watching his host, and for the second time in one day he saw things which amazed him. His expression seemed frozen on to his face—something underneath seemed struggling for expression. In a second it had all passed away. Brooks could almost have persuaded himself that it was fancy.

"Come for something to eat, Arranmore," Sir George declared, hungrily. "My second man's gone off with the sandwich-case—hunting on his own, I believe. I'll sack him to-morrow. Here's my friend Lacroix, who says you saved him from starvation once before out in the wilds somewhere. Awfully sorry to take you by storm like this, but we're twelve miles from home, and it's a God-forsaken country for inns."

"Luncheon for two at once, Groves," Lord Arranmore answered. "Delighted to meet you again, Mr. Lacroix. Last time we were both of us in very different trim."

Lady Caroom came gliding up to them, and shook hands with Sir George.

"This sounds so interesting," she murmured. "Did you say that you met Lord Arranmore in his exploring days?" she asked, turning to Mr. Lacroix.

"I found Lord Arranmore in a log hut which he had built himself on the shores of Lake Ono," Lacroix said, smiling. "And when I tell you that I had lost all my stores, and that his was the only dwelling-place for fifty miles around, you can imagine that his hospitality was more welcome to me then even than to-day."

Brooks, who was standing near, could not repress a start. He fancied that Lord Arranmore glanced in his direction.

Lady Caroom shuddered.

"The only dwelling-house for fifty miles," she repeated. "What hideous misanthropy."

"There was no doubt about it," Lacroix declared, smiling. "My Indian guide, who knew every inch of the country, told me so many times. I can assure you that Lord Arranmore, whom I am very pleased to meet again, was a very different person in those days."

The butler glided up from the background.

"Luncheon is served in the small dining-room, Sir George," he announced.

* * * * *

Molyneux and Brooks drove in together to Medchester, and the former was disposed—for him to be talkative.

"Queer thing about Lacroix turning up," he remarked. "I fancy our host looked a bit staggered."

"It was enough to surprise him," Brooks answered. "From Lake Ono to Medchester is a long way."

Molyneux nodded.

"By Jove, it is," he affirmed. "Queer stick our host. Close as wax. I've known him ever since he dropped in for the title and estates, and I've never yet heard him open his mouth on the subject of his travels."

"Was he away from England for very long?" Brooks asked.

"No one knows where he was," Molyneux replied. "Twenty years ago he was reading for the Bar in London, and he suddenly disappeared. Well, I have never met a soul except Lacroix to-day who has seen anything of him in the interval between his disappearance and his coming to claim the estates. That means that for pretty well half a lifetime he passed completely out of the world. Poor beggar! I fancy that he was hard up, for one thing." To Brooks the subject was fascinating, but he had an idea that it was scarcely the best of form to be discussing their late host with a man who was comparatively a stranger to him. So he remained silent, and Molyneux, with a yawn, abandoned the subject.

"Where does Rochester hang out, do you know?" he asked Brooks. "I don't suppose for a moment I shall be able to find him."

"His headquarters are at the Bell Hotel," Brooks replied. "You will easily be able to come across him, for he has a series of ward meetings to-night. I am sorry that we are to be opponents."

"We shan't quarrel about that," Molyneux answered. "Here we are, at Medchester, then. Better let him put you down, and then he can go on with me. You're coming out to shoot at Enton, aren't you?"

"Lord Arranmore was good enough to ask me," Brooks answered, dubiously, "but I scarcely know whether I ought to accept. I am such a wretched shot."

Molyneux laughed.

"Well, I couldn't hit a haystack," he said, "so you needn't mind that. Besides, Arranmore isn't keen about his bag, like some chaps. Are these your offices? See you again, then."

Brooks found a dozen matters waiting for his attention. But before he settled down to work he wrote two letters. One was to the man who was doing his work as Secretary to the Unemployed Fund during the election, and with a brief mention of a large subscription, instructed him to open several relief stations which they had been obliged to chose a few days ago. And the other letter was to Victor Lacroix, whom he addressed at Westbury Park, Sir George Marson's seat.

"DEAR SIR,

"I should be exceedingly obliged if you would accord me a few minutes' interview on a purely personal matter. I will wait upon you anywhere, according to your convenience.

"Yours faithfully,

"KINGSTON BROOKS."

CHAPTER IX
HENSLOW SPEAKS OUT

The bomb was thrown. Some ten thousand people crowded together in the market-place at Medchester, under what seemed to be one huge canopy of dripping umbrellas, heard for the first time for many years a bold and vigorous attack upon the principles which had come to be considered a part of the commercial ritual of the country. Henslow made the best of a great opportunity. He spoke temperately, but without hesitation, and concluded with a biting and powerful onslaught upon that class of Englishmen who wilfully closed their eyes to the prevailing industrial depression, and endeavoured to lure themselves and others into a sense of false security as to the well-being of the country by means of illusive statistics. In his appreciation of dramatic effect, and the small means by which an audience can be touched, Henslow was a past master. Early in his speech he had waved aside the umbrella which a supporter was holding over him, and regardless of the rain, he stood out in the full glare of the reflected gaslight, a ponderous, powerful figure.

"No one can accuse me," he cried, "of being a pessimist. Throughout my life I have striven personally, and politically, to look upon the brightest side of things. But I count it a crime to shut one's eyes to the cloud in the sky, even though it be no larger than a man's hand. Years ago that cloud was there for those who would to see. To-day it looms over us, a black and threatening peril, and those who, ostrich-like, still hide their heads in the sand, are the men upon whose consciences must rest in the future the responsibility for those evil things which are even now upon us. Theories are evil things, but when theory and fact are at variance, give me fact. Theoretically Free Trade should—I admit it—make us the most prosperous nation in the world. As a matter of fact, never since this country commenced to make history has our commercial supremacy been in so rotten and insecure a position. There isn't a flourishing industry in the country, save those which provide the munitions of war, and their prosperity is a spasmodic, and I might almost add, an undesirable thing. Now, I am dealing with facts to-night, not theories, and I am going to quote certain unassailable truths, and I am going to give you the immediate causes for them. The furniture and joinery trade of England is bad. There are thousands of good hands out of employment. They are out of work because the manufacturer has few or no orders. I want the immediate cause for that, and I go to the manufacturer. I ask him why he has no orders. He tells me, because every steamer from America is bringing huge consignments of ready-made office and general furniture, at such prices or such quality that the English shopkeepers prefer to stock them. Consequently trade is bad with him, and he cannot find employment for his men. I find here in Medchester the boot and shoe trade in which you are concerned bad. There are thousands of you who are willing to work who are out of employment. I go to the manufacturer, and I say to him, 'Why don't you find employment for your hands?' 'For two reasons,' he answers. 'First, because I have lost my Colonial and some of my home trade through American competition, and secondly, because of the universally depressed condition of every kindred trade throughout the country, which keeps people poor and prevents their having money to spend.' Just now I am not considering the question of why the American can send salable boots and shoes into this country, although the reasons are fairly obvious. They have nothing to do with my point, however. We are dealing to-night with immediate causes!

"And now as to that depression throughout the country which keeps people poor, as the boot manufacturer puts it, and prevents their having money to spend. I am going to take several trades one by one, and ascertain the immediate cause of their depression—"

He had hold of his audience, and he made good use of his advantage. He quoted statistics, showing the decrease of exports and relative increase of imports. How could we hope to retain our accumulated wealth under such conditions?—and finally he abandoned theorizing and argument, and boldly declared his position.

"I will tell you," he concluded, "what practical means I intend to bring to bear upon the situation. I base my projected action upon this truism, which is indeed the very kernel of my creed. I say that every man willing and able to work should have work, and I say that it is the duty of legislators to see that he has it. To-day there are one hundred thousand men and women hanging about our streets deteriorating morally and physically through the impossibility of following their trade. I say that it is time for legislators to inquire into the cause of this, and to remedy it. So I propose to move in the House of Commons, should your votes enable me to find myself there, that a Royal Commission be immediately appointed to deal with this matter. And I propose, further, to insist that this Commission be composed of manufacturers and business men, and that we dispense with all figure-heads, and I can promise you this, that the first question which shall engage the attention of these men shall be an immediate revision of our tariffs. We won't have men with theories which work out beautifully on paper, and bring a great country into the throes of commercial ruin. We won't have men who think that the laws their fathers made are good enough for them, and that all change is dangerous, because Englishmen are sure to fight their way through in the long run—a form of commercial Jingoism to which I fear we are peculiarly prone. We don't want scholars or statisticians. We want a commission of plain business men, and I promise you that if we get them, there shall be presented to Parliament before I meet you again practical measures which I honestly and firmly believe will start a wave of commercial prosperity throughout the country such as the oldest amongst you cannot remember. We have the craftsmen, the capital, and the brains—all that we need is legislation adapted to the hour and not the last century, and we can hold our own yet in the face of the world."

* * * * *

Afterwards, at the political club and at the committee-room, there was much excited conversation concerning the effect of Henslow's bold declaration. The general impression was, this election was now assured. A shouting multitude followed him to his hotel, popular Sentiment was touched, and even those who had been facing the difficulty of life with a sort of dogged despair for years were raised into enthusiasm. His words begat hope.

In the committee-room there was much excitement and a good deal of speculation. Every one realized that the full effect of this daring plunge could not be properly gauged until after it had stood the test of print. But on the whole comment was strikingly optimistic. Brooks for some time was absent. In the corridor he had come face to face with Mary Scott. Her eyes flashed with pleasure at the sight of him, and she held out her hand frankly.

"You heard it all?" he asked, eagerly.

"Yes—every word. Tell me, you understand these things so much better than I do. Is this an election dodge, or—is he in earnest? Was he speaking the truth?

"The honest truth, I believe," he answered, leading her a little away from the crowd of people. "He is of course pressing this matter home for votes, but he is very much in earnest himself about it."

"And you think that he is on the right track?"

"I really believe so," he answered. "In fact I am strongly in favour of making experiments in the direction he spoke of. By the bye, Miss Scott, I have something to tell you. You remember telling me about Lord Arranmore and his refusal to subscribe to the Unemployed Fund?"

"Yes!"

"He has been approached again—the facts have been more fully made known to him, and he has sent a cheque for one thousand pounds."

She received the news with a coldness which he found surprising.

"I think I can guess," she said, quietly, "who the second applicant was."

"I went to see him myself," he admitted.

"You must be very eloquent," she remarked, with a smile which he could not quite understand. "A thousand pounds is a great deal of money."

"It is nothing to Lord Arranmore," he answered.

"Less than nothing," she admitted, readily. "I would rather that he had stopped in the street and given half-a-crown to a hungry child."

"Still—it is a magnificent gift," he declared. "We can open all our relief stations again. I believe that you are a little prejudiced against Lord Arranmore."

"I?" She shrugged her shoulders. "How should I be? I have never spoken a word to him in my life. But I think that he has a hard, cynical face, and a hateful expression."

Brooks disagreed with her frankly.

"He seems to me," he declared, "like a man who has had a pretty rough time, and I believe he had in his younger days, but I do not believe that he is really either hard or cynical. He has some odd views as regards charity, but upon my word they are logical enough."

She smiled.

"Well, we'll not disagree about him," she declared. "I wonder how long my uncle means to be."

"Shall I find out?" he asked.

"Would it be troubling you? He is so excited that I dare say he has forgotten all about me."

Which was precisely what he had done. Brooks found him the centre of an animated little group, with a freshly-lit cigar in his mouth, and every appearance of having settled down to spend the night. He was almost annoyed when Brooks reminded him of his niece.

"God bless my soul, I forgot all about Mary," he exclaimed with vexation. "She must go and sit somewhere. I shan't be ready yet. Henslow wants us to go down to the Bell, and have a bit of supper."

"In that case," Brooks said, "you had better allow me to take Miss Scott home, and I will come then to you."

"Capital, if you really don't mind," Mr. Bullsom declared. "Put her in a cab. Don't let her be a bother to you."

Brooks found her reluctant to take him away, but he pleaded a headache, and assured her that his work for the night was over. Outside he led her away from the centre of the town to a quiet walk heading to the suburb where she lived. Here the streets seemed strangely silent, and Brooks walked hat in hand, heedless of the rain which was still sprinkling. "Oh, this is good," he murmured. "How one wearies of these crowds."

"All the same," she answered, smiling, "I think that your place just now is amongst them, and I shall not let you take me further than the top of the hill."

Brooks looked down at her and laughed.

"What a very determined person you are," he said. "I will take you to the top of the hill—and then we will see."

CHAPTER X
A TEMPTING OFFER

The small boy brought in the card and laid it on Brooks' desk with a flourish.

"He's outside, sir—in Mr. Barton's room. Shall I show him in?"

Brooks for a moment hesitated. He glanced at a letter which lay open upon the desk before him, and which he had read and re-read many times. The boy repeated his inquiry.

"Yes, of course," he answered. "Show him in at once."

Lord Arranmore, more than usually immaculate, strolled in, hat in hand, and carefully selecting the most comfortable chair, seated himself on the other side of the open table at which Brooks was working.

"How are you, Brooks?" he inquired, tersely. "Busy, of course. An aftermath of work, I suppose."

"A few months ago," Brooks answered, "I should have considered myself desperately busy. But after last week anything ordinary in the shape of work seems restful."

Lord Arranmore nodded.

"I must congratulate you, I suppose," he remarked. "You got your man in."

"We got him in all right," Brooks assented. "Our majority was less than we had hoped for, though."

Lord Arranmore shrugged his shoulders.

"It was large enough," he answered, "and after all it was a clear gain of a seat to your party, wasn't it?"

"It was a seat which we Radicals had a right to," Brooks declared. "Now that the storm of Imperialism is quieting down and people are beginning to realize that matters nearer home need a little attention, I cannot see how the manufacturing centres can do anything save return Radicals. We are the only party with a definite home policy."

Lord Arranmore nodded.

"Just so," he remarked, indifferently. "I needn't say that I didn't come here to talk politics. There was a little matter of business which I wished to put before you."

Brooks looked up in some surprise.

"Business!" he repeated, a little vaguely.

"Yes. As you are aware, Mr. Morrison has had the control of the Enton estates for many years. He was a very estimable man, and he performed his duties so far as I know quite satisfactorily. Now that he is dead, however, I intend to make a change. The remaining partners in his firm are unknown to me, and I at once gave them notice of my intention. Would you care to undertake the legal management of my estates in this part of the world?"

Brooks felt the little colour he had leave his cheeks. For a moment he was quite speechless.

"I scarcely know how to answer, or to thank you, Lord Arranmore," he said at last. "This is such a surprising offer. I scarcely see how you can be in earnest. You know so little of me."

Lord Arranmore shrugged his shoulders.

"Really," he said, "I don't see anything very surprising in it. Morrisons have a large practice, and without the old man I scarcely see how they could continue to give my affairs the attention they require. You, on the other hand, are only just starting, and you would be able to watch over my interests more closely. Then—although I cannot pretend that I am much influenced by sentimental reasons—still, I knew your father, and the strangeness of our few years of life as neighbours inclines me to be of service to you provided I myself am not the sufferer. As to that I am prepared to take the risk. You see mine is only the usual sort of generosity—the sort which provides for an adequate quid pro quo. Of course, if you think that the undertaking of my affairs would block you in other directions do not hesitate to say so. This is a matter of business between us, pure and simple."

Brooks had recovered himself. The length of Lord Arranmore's speech and his slow drawl had given him an opportunity to do so. He glanced for a moment at the letter which lay upon his desk, and hated it.

"In an ordinary way, Lord Arranmore," he answered, "there could be only one possible reply to such an offer as you have made me—an immediate and prompt acceptance. If I seem to hesitate, it is because, first—I must tell you something. I must make something—in the nature of a confession."

Lord Arranmore raised his eyebrows, but his face remained as the face of a Sphinx. He sat still, and waited.

"On the occasion of my visit to you," Brooks continued, "you may remember the presence of a certain Mr. Lacroix? He is the author, I believe, of several books of travel in Western Canada, and has the reputation of knowing that part of the country exceedingly well."

Brooks paused, but his visitor helped him in no way. His face wore still its passive expression of languid inquiry.

"He spoke of his visit to you," Brooks went on "in Canada, and he twice reiterated the fact that there was no other dwelling within fifty miles of you. He said this upon his own authority, and upon the authority of his Indian guide. Now it is only a few days ago since you spoke of my father as living for years within a few miles of you."

Lord Arranmore nodded his head thoughtfully.

"Ah! And you found the two statements, of course, irreconcilable. Well, go on!"

Brooks found it difficult. He was grasping a paperweight tightly in one hand, and he felt the rising colour burn his cheeks.

"I wrote to Mr. Lacroix," he said.

"A perfectly natural thing to do," Lord Arranmore remarked, smoothly.

And his answer is here!

"Suppose you read it to me," Lord Arranmore suggested.

Brooks took up the letter and read it.

"TRAVELLERS' CLUB, December 10.

"DEAR SIR,

"Replying to your recent letter, I have not the slightest hesitation in reaffirming the statement to which you refer. I am perfectly convinced that at the time of my visit to Lord Arranmore on the bank of Lake Quo, there was no Englishman or dwelling-place of any sort within a radius of fifty miles. The information which you have received is palpably erroneous.

"Why not refer to Lord Arranmore himself? He would certainly confirm what I say, and finally dispose of the matter.

"Yours sincerely,

"VICTOR LACROIX."

"A very interesting letter," Lord Arranmore remarked. "Well?"

Brooks crumpled the letter up and flung it into the waste-paper basket.

"Lord Arranmore," he said, "I made this inquiry behind your back, and in a sense I am ashamed of having done so. Yet I beg you to put yourself in my position. You must admit that my father's disappearance from the world was a little extraordinary. He was a man whose life was more than exemplary—it was saintly. For year after year he worked in the police-courts amongst the criminal classes. His whole life was one long record of splendid devotion. His health at last breaks down, and he is sent by his friends for a voyage to Australia. He never returns. Years afterwards his papers and particulars of his death are sent home from one of the loneliest spots in the Empire. A few weeks ago you found me out and told me of his last days. You see what I must believe. That he wilfully deserted his wife and son—myself. That he went into lonely and inexplicable solitude for no apparent or possible reason. That he misused the money subscribed by his friends in order that he might take this trip to Australia. Was ever anything more irreconcilable?"

"From your point of view—perhaps not," Lord Arranmore answered. "You must enlarge it."

"Will you tell me how?" Brooks demanded.

Lord Arranmore stifled a yawn. He had the air of one wearied by a profitless discussion.

"Well," he said, "I might certainly suggest a few things. Who was your trustee or guardian, or your father's man of business?"

"Mr. Ascough, of Lincoln's Inn Fields."

"Exactly. Your father saw him, of course, prior to his departure from England."

"Yes."

"Well, is it not a fact that instead of making a will your father made over by deed of gift the whole of his small income to your mother in trust for you?"

"Yes, he did that," Brooks admitted.

Lord Arranmore shrugged his shoulders.

"Think that over," he remarked. "Doesn't that suggest his already half-formed intention never to return?"

"It never struck me in that way," Brooks answered. "Yet it is obvious," Lord Arranmore said. "Now, I happen to know from your father himself that he never intended to go to Australia, and he never intended to return to England. He sailed instead by an Allan liner from Liverpool to Quebec under the name of Francis. He went straight to Montreal, and he stayed there until he had spent the greater part of his money. Then he drifted out west. There is his history for you in a few words."

A sudden light flashed in Brooks' eyes.

"He told you that he left England meaning never to return? Then you have the key to the whole thing. Why not? That is what I want to know. Why not?"

"I do not know," Lord Arranmore answered, coolly. "He never told me."

Brooks felt a sudden chill of disappointment. Lord Arranmore rose slowly to his feet.

"Mr. Brooks," he said, "I have told you all that I know. You have asked me a question which I have not been able to answer. I can, however, give you some advice which I will guarantee to be excellent—some advice which you will do well to follow. Shall I go on?"

"If you please!"

"Do not seek to unravel any further what may seem to you to be the mystery of your father's disappearance from the world. Depend upon it, his action was of his own free will, and he had excellent reasons for it. If he had wished you to know them he would have communicated with you. Remember, I was with your father during his last days—and this is my advice to you."

Brooks pointed downward to the crumpled ball of paper.

"That letter!" he exclaimed.

Lord Arranmore shrugged his shoulders.

"I scarcely see its significance," he said. "It is not even my word against Lacroix'. I sent you all your father's papers, I brought back photographs and keepsakes known to belong to him. In what possible way could it benefit me to mislead you?"

The telephone on Brooks' table rang, and for a moment or two he found himself, with mechanical self-possession, attending to some unimportant question. When he replaced the receiver Lord Arranmore had resumed his seat, but was drawing on his gloves.

"Come," he said, "let us resume our business talk. I have made you an offer. What have you to say?"

Brooks pointed to the waste-paper basket.

"I did a mean action," he said. "I am ashamed of it. Do you mean that your offer remains open?"

"Certainly," Lord Arranmore answered. "That little affair is not worth mentioning. I should probably have done the same."

"Well, I am not altogether a madman," Brooks declared, smiling, "so I will only say that I accept your offer gratefully—and I will do my very best to deserve your confidence."

Lord Arranmore rose and stood with his hands behind him, looking out of the window.

"Very good," he said. "I will send for Ascough to come down from town, and we must meet one day next week at Morrisons' office, and go into matters thoroughly. That reminds me. Busher, my head bailiff, will be in to see you this afternoon. There are half-a-dozen leases to be seen to at once, and everything had better come here until the arrangements are concluded."

"I shall be in all the afternoon," Brooks answered, still a little dazed.

"And Thursday," Lord Arranmore concluded, "you dine and sleep at Enton. I hope we shall have a good day's sport. The carriage will fetch you at 6:30. Good-morning."

Lord Arranmore walked out with a little nod, but on the threshold he paused and looked back.

"By the bye, Brooks," he said, "do you remember my meeting you in a little tea-shop almost the day after I first called upon you?"

"Quite well," Brooks answered.

"You had a young lady with you."

"Yes. I was with Miss Scott."

Lord Arranmore's hand fell from the handle. His eyes seemed suddenly full of fierce questioning. He moved a step forward into the room.

"Miss Scott? Who is she?"

Brooks was hopelessly bewildered, and showed it.

"She lives with her uncle in Medchester. He is a builder and timber merchant."

Lord Arranmore was silent for a moment.

"Her father, then, is dead?" he asked.

"He died abroad, I think," Brooks answered, "but I really am not sure. I know very little of any of them."

Lord Arranmore turned away.

"She is the image of a man I once knew," he remarked, "but after all, the type is not an uncommon one. You won't forget that Busher will be in this afternoon. He is a very intelligent fellow for his class, and you may find it worth your while to ask him a few questions. Until Thursday, then."

"Until Thursday," Brooks repeated, mechanically.

CHAPTER XI
WHO THE DEVIL IS BROOKS?

"To be tired," declared Sydney Molyneux, sinking into a low couch, "to be downright dead dog-tired is the most delightful thing in the world. Will some one give me some tea?"

Brooks laughed softly from his place in front of the open fire. A long day in the fresh north wind had driven the cobwebs from his brain, and brought the burning colour to his cheeks. His eyes were bright, and his laughter was like music.

"And you," he exclaimed, "are fresh from electioneering. Why, fatigue like this is a luxury."

Molyneux lit a cigarette and looked longingly at the tea-tray set out in the middle of the hall.

"That is all very well," he said, "but there is a wide difference between the two forms of exercise. In electioneering one can use one's brain, and my brain is never weary. It is capable of the most stupendous exertions. It is my legs that fail me sometimes. Here comes Lady Caroom at last. Why does she look as though she had seen a ghost?"

That great staircase at Enton came right into the hall. A few steps from the bottom Lady Caroom had halted, and her appearance was certainly a little unusual. Every vestige of colour had left her cheeks. Her right hand was clutching the oak banisters, her eyes were fixed upon Brooks. He was for a moment embarrassed, but he stepped forward to meet her.

"How do you do, Lady Caroom?" he said. "We are all in the shadows here, and Mr. Molyneux is crying out for his tea."

She resumed her progress and greeted Brooks graciously. Almost at the same moment a footman brought lamps, and the tea was served. Lady Caroom glanced again with a sort of curious nervousness at the young man who stood by her side.

"You are a little earlier than we expected," she remarked, seating herself before the tea-tray. "Here comes Sybil. She is dying to congratulate you, Mr. Brooks. Is Arranmore here?"

"We left him in the gun-room," Molyneux answered. "He is coming directly."

Sybil Caroom, in a short skirt and a jaunty hat, came towards Brooks with outstretched hand.

"Delightful!" she exclaimed. "I only wish that it had been nine thousand instead of nine hundred. You deserved it."

Brooks laughed heartily.

"Well, we were satisfied to win the seat," he declared.

Molyneux leaned forward tea-cup in hand.

"Well, you deserved it," he remarked. "Our old man opened his mouth a bit, but yours knocked him silly. Upon my word, I didn't think that any one man had cheek stupendous enough to humbug a constituency like Henslow did. It took my breath away to read his speeches."

"Do you really mean that?" asked Brooks.

"Mean it? Of course I do. What I can't understand is how people can swallow such stuff, election after election. Doesn't every Radical candidate get up and talk in the same maudlin way—hasn't he done so for the last fifty years? And when he gets into Parliament is there a more Conservative person on the face of the earth than the Radical member pledged to social reform? It's the same with your man Henslow. He'll do nothing! He'll attempt nothing! Silly farce, politics, I think."

Lady Caroom laughed softly.

"I have never heard you so eloquent in my life, Sydney," she exclaimed. "Do go on. It is most entertaining. When you have quite finished I can see that Mr. Brooks is getting ready to pulverize you."

Brooks shook his head.

"Lady Sybil tells me that Mr. Molyneux is not to be taken seriously," he answered.

Molyneux brought up his cup for some more tea.

"Don't you listen to Lady Sybil, Brooks," he retorted. "She is annoyed with me because I have been spoken of as a future Prime Minister, and she rather fancies her cousin for the post. Two knobs, please, and plenty of cream. As a matter of fact I am in serious and downright earnest. I say that Henslow won his seat by kidding the working classes. He promised them a sort of political Arabian Nights. He'll go up to Westminster, and I'm open to bet what you like that he makes not one serious practical effort to push forward one of the startling measures he talked about so glibly. I will trouble you for the toast, Brooks. Thanks!"

"He is always cynical like this," Sybil murmured, "when his party have lost a seat. Don't take any notice of him, Mr. Brooks. I have great faith in Mr. Henslow, and I believe that he will do his best."

Molyneux smiled.

"Henslow is a politician," he remarked, "a professional politician. What you Radicals want is Englishmen who are interested in politics. Henslow knows how to get votes. He's got his seat, and he'll keep it—till the next election."

Brooks shook his head.

"Henslow has rather a platform manner," he said, "but he is sound enough. I believe that we are on the eve of important changes in our social legislation, and I believe that Henslow will have much to say about them. At any rate, he is not a rank hypocrite. We have shown him things in Medchester which he can scarcely forget in a hurry. He will go to Westminster with the memory of these things before him, with such a cry in his ears as no man can stifle. He might forget if he would—but he never will. We have shown him things which men may not forget."

Lord Arranmore, who had now joined the party, leaned forward with his arm resting lightly upon Lady Caroom's shoulder. An uneasy light flashed in his eyes.

"There are men," he said, "whom you can never reach, genial men with a ready smile and a prompt cheque-book, whose selfishness is an armour more potent than the armour of my forefather there, Sir Ronald Kingston of Arranmore. And, after all, why not? The thoroughly selfish man is the only person logically who has the slightest chance of happiness."

"It is true," Molyneux murmured. "Delightfully true."

"Lord Arranmore is always either cynical or paradoxical," Sybil Caroom declared. "He really says the most unpleasant things with the greatest appearance of truth of any man I know."

"This company," Lord Arranmore remarked lightly, "is hostile to me. Let us go and play pool."

Lady Caroom rose up promptly. Molyneux groaned audibly.

"You shall play me at billiards instead," she declared. "I used to give you a good game once, and I have played a great deal lately. Ring for Annette, will you, Sybil? She has my cue."

Sybil Caroom made room for Brooks by her side.

"Do sit down and tell me more about the election," she said. "Sydney is sure to go to sleep. He always does after shooting."

"You shall ask me questions," he suggested. "I scarcely know what part of it would interest you."

They talked together lightly at first, then more seriously. From the other end of the hall came the occasional click of billiard balls. Lady Caroom and her host were playing a leisurely game interspersed with conversation.

"Who is this young Mr. Brooks?" she asked, pausing to chalk her cue.

"A solicitor from Medchester," he answered. "He was Parliamentary agent for Henslow, and I am going to give him a management of my estates."

"He is quite a boy," she remarked.

"Twenty-six or seven," he answered. "How well you play those cannons."

"I ought to. I had lessons for years. Is he a native of Medchester?"

Lord Arranmore was blandly puzzled. She finished her stroke and turned towards him.

"Mr. Brooks, you know. We were talking of him."

"Of course we were," he answered. "I do not think so. He is an orphan. I met his father in Canada."

"He reminds me of some one," she remarked, in a puzzled tone. "Just now as I was coming downstairs it was almost startling. He is a good-looking boy."

"Be careful not to foul," he admonished her. "You should have the spider-rest."

Lady Caroom made a delicate cannon from an awkward place, and concluded her break in silence. Then she leaned with her back against the table, chalking her cue. Her figure was still the figure of a girl she was a remarkably pretty woman. She laid her slim white fingers upon his coat-sleeve.

"I wonder," she said, softly, "whether you will ever tell me."

"If you look at me like that," he answered, smiling, "I shall tell you—a great many things."

Her eyes fell. It was too absurd at her age, but her cheeks were burning.

"You don't improve a bit," she declared. "You were always too apt with your tongue."

"I practiced in a good school," he answered.

"Dear me," she sighed. "For elderly people what a lot of rubbish we talk."

He shivered.

"What a hideous word," he remarked. "You make me feel that my chest is padded and my hair dyed. If to talk sense is a sign of youth, let us do it."

"By all means. When are you going to find me a husband for Sybil?"

"Well—is there any hurry?" he asked.

"Lots! We are going to Fernshire next week, and the place is always full of young men. If you have anything really good in your mind I don't want to miss it."

He took up his cue and scored an excellent break. She followed suit, and he broke down at an easy cannon. Then he came over to her side.

"How do you like Mr. Brooks?" he asked, quietly.

"He seems a nice boy," she answered, lightly. He remained silent. Suddenly she looked up into his face, and clutched the sides of the table.

"You—you don't mean that?" she murmured, suddenly pale to the lips.

He led her to a chair. The game was over.

"Some day," he whispered, "I will tell you the whole story."

* * * * *

"Even to think of these things," Sybil said, softly, "makes us feel very selfish."

"No one is ever hopelessly selfish who is conscious of it," he answered, smiling. "And, after all, it would not do for every one to be always brooding upon the darker side of life."

"In another minute," Molyneux exclaimed, waking up with a start, "I should have been asleep. Whatever have you two been talking about? It was the most soothing hum I ever heard in my life."

"Mr. Brooks was telling me of some new phases of life," she answered. "It is very interesting, even if it is a little sad."

Molyneux eyed them both for a moment in thoughtful silence.

"H'm!" he remarked. "Dinner is the next phase of life which will interest me. Has the dressing-bell gone yet?"

"You gross person," she exclaimed. "You ate so much tea you had to go to sleep."

"It was the exercise, he insisted.

"You have been standing about all day. I heard you ask for a place without any walking, and where as few people as possible could see you miss your birds."

"Your ears are a great deal too sharp," he said. "It was the wind, then."

"Never mind what it was," she answered, laughing. "You can go to sleep again if you like."

Molyneux put up his eyeglass and looked from one to the other. He saw that Sybil's interest in her companion's conversation was not assumed, and for the first time he appreciated Brooks' good looks. He shook off his sleepiness at once and stood by Sybil's side.

"Have you been trying to convert Lady Sybil?" he asked.

"It is unnecessary," she answered, quickly. "Mr. Brooks and I are on the same side."

He laughed softly and strolled away. Lord Arranmore was standing thoughtfully before the marking-board. He laid his hand upon his arm.

"I say, Arranmore," he asked, "who the devil is Brooks?"

CHAPTER XII
MR. BULLSOM GIVES A DINNER-PARTY

"God bless my soul!" Mr. Bullsom exclaimed. "Listen to this." Mrs. Bullsom, in a resplendent new dress, looking shinier and fatter than ever, was prepared to listen to anything which might relieve the tension of the moment. For it was the evening of the dinner-party, and within ten minutes of the appointed time. Mr. Bullsom stood under the incandescent light and read aloud "The shooting-party at Enton yesterday consisted of the Marquis of Arranmore, the Hon. Sydney Molyneux, Mr. Hennibul, K.C., and Mr. Kingston Brooks. Notwithstanding the high wind an excellent bag was obtained."

"What! Our Mr. Kingston Brooks?" Selina exclaimed.

"It's Brooks, right enough," Mr. Bullsom exclaimed. "I called at his office yesterday, and they told me that he was out for the day. Well, that licks me."

Mary, who was reading a magazine in a secluded corner, looked up.

"I saw Mr. Brooks in the morning," she remarked. "He told me that he was going to Enton to dine and sleep."

Selina looked at her cousin sharply.

"You saw Mr. Brooks?" she repeated. "Where?"

"I met him," Mary answered, coolly. "He told me that Lord Arranmore had been very kind to him."

"Why didn't you tell us?" Louise asked.

"I really didn't think of it," Mary answered. "It didn't strike me as being anything extraordinary."

"Not when he's coming here to dine to-night," Selina repeated, "and is a friend of papa's! Why, Mary, what nonsense."

"I really don't see anything to make a fuss about," Mary said, going back to her magazine.

Mr. Bullsom drew himself up, and laid down the paper with the paragraph uppermost.

"Well, it is most gratifying to think that I gave that young man his first start," he remarked. "I believe, too, that he is not likely to forget it."

"The bell!" Mrs. Bullsom exclaimed, with a little gasp. "Some one has come."

"Well, if they have, there's nothing to be frightened about," Mr. Bullsom retorted. "Ain't we expecting them to come? Don't look so scared, Sarah! Take up a book, or something. Why, bless my soul, you're all of a tremble."

"I can't help it, Peter," Mrs. Bullsom replied, nervously. "I don't know these people scarcely a bit, and I'm sure I shall do something foolish. Selina, be sure you look at me when I'm to come away, and—"

"Mr. Kingston Brooks."

Brooks, ushered in by a neighbouring greengrocer, entered upon a scene of unexpected splendour. Selina and her sister were gorgeous in green and pink respectively. Mr. Bullsom's shirt-front was a thing to wonder at. There was an air of repressed excitement about everybody, except Mary, who welcomed him with a quiet smile.

"I am not much too early, I hope," Brooks remarked.

"You're in the nick of time," Mr. Bullsom assured him.

Brooks endeavoured to secure a chair near Mary, which attempt Selina adroitly foiled.

"We've been reading all about your grandeur, Mr. Brooks," she exclaimed. "What a beautiful day you must have had at Enton."

Brooks looked puzzled.

"It was very enjoyable," he declared. "I wanted to see you, Miss Scott," he added, turning to Mary. "I think that we can arrange that date for the lecture now. How would Wednesday week do?"

"Admirably!" Mary answered.

"Do you know whom you take in, Mr. Brooks?" Selina interrupted.

Brooks glanced at the card in his hand.

"Mrs. Seventon," he said. "Yes, thanks."

Selina looked up at him with an arch smile.

"Mrs. Seventon is most dreadfully proper," she said. "You will have to be on your best behaviour. Oh, here comes some one. What a bother!"

There was an influx of guests. Mrs. Bullsom, reduced to a state of chaotic nervousness, was pushed as far into the background as possible by her daughters, and Mr. Bullsom, banished from the hearth where he felt surest of himself, plunged into a conversation with Mr. Seventon on the weather. Brooks leaned over towards Mary.

"Wednesday week at eight o'clock, then," he said. "I want to have a chat with you about the subject."

"Not now," she interposed. "You know these people, don't you, and the Huntingdons? Go and talk to them, please."

Brooks laughed, and went to the rescue. He won Mrs. Bullsom's eternal gratitude by diverting Mrs. Seventon's attention from her, and thereby allowing her a moment or two to recover herself. Somehow or other a buzz of conversation was kept up until the solemn announcement of dinner. And when she was finally seated in her place, and saw a couple of nimble waiters, with the greengrocer in the back, looking cool and capable, she felt that the worst was over.

The solemn process of sampling doubtful-looking entries and eating saddle of mutton to the tune of a forced conversation was got through without disaster. Mrs. Bullsom felt her fat face break out into smiles. Mr. Bullsom, though he would like to have seen everybody go twice for everything, began to expand. He had already recited the story of Kingston Brooks' greatness to both of his immediate neighbours, and in a casual way mentioned his early patronage of that remarkable young man. And once meeting his eye he raised his glass.

"Not quite up to the Enton vintage, Brooks, eh? but all right, I hope."

Brooks nodded back, and resumed his conversation. Selina took the opportunity to mention casually to her neighbour, Mr. Huntingdon, that Mr. Brooks was a great friend of Lord Arranmore's, and Louise, on her side of the table, took care also to disseminate the same information. Everybody was properly impressed. Mr. Bullsom decided to give a dinner-party every month, and to double the greengrocer's tip, and by the time Selina's third stage whisper had reached her mother and the ladies finally departed, he was in a state of geniality bordering upon beatitude. There was a general move to his end of the table. Mr. Bullsom started the port, and his shirt-front grew wider and wider. He lit a cigar, and his thumb found its way to the armhole of his waistcoat. At that moment Mr. Bullsom would not have changed places with any man on earth.

"What sort of a place is Enton to stay at, Brooks, eh?" he inquired, in a friendly manner. "Keeps it up very well, don't he, the present Marquis?"

Brooks sighed.

"I really don't know much about it," he answered, "I was only there one night."

"Good day's sport?"

"Very good indeed," Brooks answered. "Lord Arranmore is a wonderful shot."

"A remarkable man in a great many ways, Lord Arranmore," Dr. Seventon remarked. "He disappeared from London when he was an impecunious young barrister with apparently no earthly chance of succeeding to the Arranmore estates, and from that time till a few years ago, when he was advertised for, not a soul knew his whereabouts. Even now I am told that he keeps the story of all these years absolutely to himself. No one knew where he was, or how he supported himself."

"I can tell you where he was for some time, at any rate," Brooks said. "He was in Canada, for he met my father there, and was with him when he died."

"Indeed," Dr. Seventon remarked. "Then I should say that you are one of the only men in England to whom he has opened his lips on the subject. Do you know what he was doing there?"

"Fishing and shooting, I think." Brooks answered. "It was near Lake Ono, right out west, and there would be nothing else to take one there."

"It was always supposed too that he had spent most of the time in a situation in New York," Mr. Huntingdon said.

"I know a man," Mr. Seaton put in, "who can swear that he met him as a sergeant in the first Australian contingent of mounted infantry sent to the Cape."

"There are no end of stories about him," Dr. Seventon remarked. "If I were the man I would put a stop to them by telling everybody exactly where I was during those twenty years or so. It is a big slice of one's life to seal up."

"Still, there is not the slightest reason why he should take the whole world into his confidence, is there?" Brooks expostulated. "He is not a public man."

"A peer of England with a seat in the House of Lords must always be a public man to some extent," Mr. Huntingdon remarked.

"I am not sure," Brooks remarked, "that the lives of all our hereditary legislators would bear the most searching inquiry."

"That's right, Brooks," Mr. Bullsom declared. "Stick up for your pals."

Brooks looked a little annoyed.

"The only claim I have upon Lord Arranmore's acquaintance," he remarked, "is his kindness to my father. I hope, Dr. Seventon, that you are going to press the matter of that fever hospital home. I have a little information which I think you might make use of."

Brooks changed his place, wine-glass in hand, and the conversation drifted away. But he found the position of social star one which the Bullsoms were determined to force upon him, for they had no sooner entered the drawing-room than Selina came rushing across the room to him and drew him confidentially on one side.

"Mr. Brooks," she said, "do go and talk to Mrs. Huntingdon. She is so anxious to hear about the Lady Caroom who is staying at Enton."

"I know nothing about Lady Caroom," Brooks replied, without any overplus of graciousness.

Selina looked at him in some dismay.

"But you met her at Enton, didn't you?" she asked.

"Oh, yes, I met her there," Brooks answered, impatiently. "But I certainly don't know enough of her to discuss her with Mrs. Huntingdon. I rather wanted to speak to your cousin."

Selina's thin little lips became compressed, and for a moment she forgot to smile. Her cousin indeed! Mary, who was sitting there in a plain black gown without a single ornament, and not even a flower, looking for all the world like the poor relation she was! Selina glanced downwards at the great bunch of roses and maidenhair fern in her bosom, at the fancy and beaded trimming which ran like a nightmare all over her new gown, and which she was absolutely certain had come from Paris; at the heavy gold bracelets which concealed some part of her thin arms; she remembered suddenly the aigrette in her hair, such a finish to her costume, and her self-confidence returned.

"Oh, don't bother about Mary now. Mrs. Huntingdon is dying to have you talk to her. Please do and if you like—I will give you one of my roses for your button-hole."

Brooks stood the shock gallantly, and bowed his thanks. He had met Mrs. Huntingdon before, and they talked together for a quarter of an hour or so.

"I wish I knew why you were here," was almost her first question. "Isn't it all funny?

"Mr. Bullsom has always been very decent to me," he answered. "It is through him I was appointed agent to Mr. Henslow."

"Oh, business! I see," she answered, shrugging her shoulders. "Same here. I'm a doctor's wife, you know. Did you ever see such awful girls! and who in the name of all that's marvellous can be their dressmaker?"

"Bullsom is a very good sort indeed," Brooks answered. "I have a great respect for him."

She made a little face.

"Who's the nice-looking girl in black with her hair parted in the middle?" she asked. "Mr. Bullsom's niece. She is quite charming, and most intelligent."

"Dear me!" Mrs. Huntingdon remarked. "I had no idea she had anything to do with the family. Sort of a Cinderella look about her now you mention it. Couldn't you get her to come over and talk to me? I'm horribly afraid of Mrs. Bullsom. She'll come out of that dress if she tries to talk, and I know I shall laugh."

"I'm sure I can," Brooks answered, rising with alacrity. "I'll bring her over in a minute."

Mary had just finished arranging a card-table when Brooks drew her on one side.

"About that subject!" he began.

"We shall scarcely have time to talk about it now, shall we?" she answered. "You will be wanted to play cards or something. We shall be quite content to leave it to you."

"I should like to talk it over with you," he said. "Do tell me when I may see you."

She sat down, and he stood by her chair. "Really, I don't know," she answered. "Perhaps I shall be at home when you pay your duty call."

"Come and have some tea at Mellor's with me to-morrow."

She seemed not to hear him. She had caught Mrs. Seventon's eye across the room, and rose to her feet.

"You have left Mrs. Seventon alone all the evening," she said. "I must go and talk to her."

He stood before her—a little insistent.

"I shall expect you at half-past four," he said.

She shook her head.

Oh, no. I have an engagement."

"The next day, then."

"Thank you! I would rather you did not ask me. I have a great deal to do just now. I will bring the girls to the lecture."

"Wednesday week," he protested, "is a long way off."

"You can go over to Enton," she laughed, "and get some more cheques from your wonderful friend."

"I wonder," he remarked, "why you dislike Lord Arranmore so much."

"Instinct perhaps—or caprice," she answered, lightly.

"The latter for choice," he answered. "I don't think that he is a man to dislike instinctively. He rather affected me the other way."

She was suddenly graver.

"It is foolish of me," she remarked. "You will think so too, when I tell you that my only reason is because of a likeness."

"A likeness!" he repeated.

She nodded.

"He is exactly like a man who was once a friend of my father's, and who did him a great deal of harm. My father was much to blame, I know, but this man had a great influence over him, and a most unfortunate one. Now don't you think I'm absurd?"

"I think it is a little rough on Lord Arranmore," he answered, "don't you?"

"It would be if my likes or dislikes made the slightest difference to him," she answered. "As it is, I don't suppose it matters."

"Was this in England?" he asked.

She shook her head.

"No, it was abroad—in Montreal. I really must go to Mrs. Seventon. She looks terribly bored."

Brooks made no effort to detain her. He was looking intently at a certain spot in the carpet. The coincidence—it was nothing more, of course—was curious.

CHAPTER XIII
CHARITY THE "CRIME"

There followed a busy time for Brooks, the result of which was a very marked improvement in his prospects. For the younger Morrison and his partner, loth to lose altogether the valuable Enton connection, offered Brooks a partnership in their firm. Mr. Ascough, who was Lord Arranmore's London solicitor, and had been Brooks' guardian, after careful consideration advised his acceptance, and there being nothing in the way, the arrangements were pushed through almost at once. Mr. Ascough, on the morning of his return to London, took the opportunity warmly to congratulate Brooks.

"Lord Arranmore has been marvellously kind to me," Brooks agreed. "To tell you the truth, Mr. Ascough, I feel almost inclined to add incomprehensibly kind."

The older man stroked his grey moustache thoughtfully.

"Lord Arranmore is eccentric," he remarked. "Has always been eccentric, and will remain so, I suppose, to the end of the chapter. You are the one who profits, however, and I am very glad of it."

"Eccentricity," Brooks remarked, "is, of course, the only obvious explanation of his generosity so far as I am concerned. But it has occurred to me, Mr. Ascough, to wonder whether the friendship or connection between him and my father was in any way a less slight thing than I have been led to suppose."

Mr. Ascough shrugged his shoulders.

"Lord Arranmore," he said, "has told you, no doubt, all that there is to be told."

Brooks sat at his desk, frowning slightly, and tapping the blotting-paper with a pen-holder.

"All that Lord Arranmore has told me," he said, "is that my father occupied a cabin not far from his on the banks of Lake Ono, that they saw little of each other, and that he only found out his illness by accident. That my father then disclosed his name, gave him his papers and your address. There was merely the casual intercourse between two Englishmen coming together in a strange country."

"That is what I have always understood," Mr. Ascough agreed. "Have you any reason to think otherwise?"

"No definite reason—except Lord Arranmore's unusual kindness to me," Brooks remarked. "Lord Arranmore is one of the most self-centred men I ever knew—and the least impulsive. Why, therefore, he should go out of his way to do me a kindness I cannot understand."

"If this is really an enigma to you," Mr. Ascough answered, "I cannot help you to solve it. Lord Arranmore has been the reverse of communicative to me. I am afraid you must fall back upon his lordship's eccentricity."

Mr. Ascough rose, but Brooks detained him.

"You have plenty of time for your train," he said. "Will you forgive me if I go over a little old ground with you—for the last time?"

The lawyer resumed his seat.

"I am in no hurry," he said, "if you think it worth while."

"My father came to you when he was living at Stepney—a stranger to you."

"A complete stranger," Mr. Ascough agreed. "I had never seen him before in my life. I did a little trifling business for him in connection with his property."

"He told you nothing of his family or relatives?"

"He told me that he had not a relation in the world."

"You knew him slightly, then?" Brooks continued, "all the time he was in London? And when he left for that voyage he came to you."

"Yes."

"He made over his small income then to my mother in trust for me. Did it strike you as strange that he should do this instead of making a will?"

"Not particularly," Mr. Ascough declared. "As you know, it is not an unusual course."

"It did not suggest to you any determination on his part never to return to England?"

"Certainly not."

"He left England on friendly terms with my mother?"

"Certainly. She and he were people for whom I and every one who knew anything of their lives had the highest esteem and admiration."

"You can imagine no reason, then, for my father leaving England for good?"

"Certainly not!"

"You know of no reason why he should have abandoned his trip to Australia and gone to Canada?"

"None!"

"His doing so is as inexplicable to you as to me?"

"Entirely."

"You have never doubted Lord Arranmore's story of his death?"

"Never. Why should I?"

"One more question," Brooks said. "Do you know that lately I have met a traveller—a man who visited Lord Arranmore in Canada, and who declared to his certain knowledge there was no other human dwelling-house within fifty miles of Lord Arranmore's cabin?"

"He was obviously mistaken."

You think so?

"It is certain."

Brooks hesitated.

"My question," he said, "will have given you some idea of the uncertainty I have felt once or twice lately, owing to the report of the traveller Lacroix, and Lord Arranmore's unaccountable kindness to me. You see, he isn't an ordinary man. He is not a philanthropist by any means, nor in any way a person likely to do kindly actions from the love of them. Now, do you know of any facts, or can you suggest anything which might make the situation clearer to me?"

"I cannot, Mr. Brooks," the older man answered, without hesitation. "If you take my advice, you will not trouble yourself any more with fancies which seem to me—pardon me—quite chimerical. Accept Lord Arranmore's kindness as the offshoot of some sentimental feeling which he might well have entertained towards a fellow-countryman by whose death-bed he had stood in that far-away, lonely country. You may even yourself be mistaken in Lord Arranmore's character, and you can remember, too, that after all what means so much to you costs him nothing—is probably for his own advantage."

Brooks rose and took up his hat.

"I am very much obliged to you, Mr. Ascough," he said. "Yours, after all, is the common-sense view of the affair. If you like I will walk up to the station. I am going that way...."

So Brooks, convinced of their folly, finally discarded certain uncomfortable thoughts which once or twice lately had troubled him. He dined at Enton that night, and improved his acquaintance with Lady Caroom and her daughter, who were still staying there. Although this was not a matter which he had mentioned to Mr. Ascough, there was something which he found more inexplicable even than Lord Arranmore's transference of the care of his estates to him, and that was the apparent encouragement which both he and Lady Caroom gave to the friendship between Sybil and himself. They had lunched with him twice in Medchester, and more often still the Enton barouche had been kept waiting at his office whilst Lady Caroom and Sybil descended upon him with invitations from Lord Arranmore. After his talk with Mr. Ascough he put the matter behind him, but it remained at times an inexplicable puzzle.

On the evening of this particular visit he found Sybil alone in a recess of the drawing-room with a newspaper in her hand. She greeted him with obvious pleasure.

"Do come and tell me about things, Mr. Brooks," she begged. "I have been reading the local paper. Is it true that there are actually people starving in Medchester?"

"There is a great deal of distress," he admitted, gravely. "I am afraid that it is true."

She looked at him with wide-open eyes.

"But I don't understand," she said. "I thought that there were societies who dealt with all that sort of thing, and behind, the—the workhouse."

"So there are, Lady Sybil," he answered, "but you must remember that societies are no use unless people will subscribe to them, and that there are a great many people who would sooner starve than enter the workhouse."

"But surely," she exclaimed, "there is no difficulty about getting money—if people only understand."

He watched her for a moment in silence—suddenly appreciating the refinement, the costly elegance which seemed in itself to be a part of the girl, and yet for which surely her toilette was in some way also responsible. Her white satin dress was cut and fashioned in a style which he was beginning to appreciate as evidence of skill and costliness. A string of pearls around her throat gleamed softly in the firelight. A chain of fine gold studded with opals and diamonds reached almost to her knees. She wore few rings indeed, but they were such rings as he had never seen before he had come as a guest to Enton. And there were thousands like her. A momentary flash of thought carried him back to the days of the French Revolution. There was a print hanging in his room of a girl as fair and as proud as this one, surrounded by a fierce rabble mad with hunger and the pent-up rage of generations, tearing the jewels from her fingers, tearing even, he thought, the trimming from her gown.

"You do not answer me, Mr. Brooks," she reminded him.

He recovered himself with a start.

"I beg your pardon, Lady Sybil. Your question set me thinking. We have tried to make people understand, and many have given most generously, but for all that we cannot cope with such distress as there is to-day in Medchester. I am secretary for one of the distribution societies, and I have seen things which are enough to sadden a man for life, only during the last few days."

"You have seen people—really hungry?" she asked, with something like timidity in her face.

He laughed bitterly.

"That we see every moment of the time we spend down amongst them," he answered. "I have seen worse things. I have seen the sapping away of character—men become thieves and women worse—to escape from starvation. That, I think, is the greatest tragedy of all. It makes one shudder when one thinks that on the shoulders of many people some portion of the responsibility at any rate for these things must rest."

Her lips quivered. She emptied the contents of a gold chain purse into her hands.

"It is we who are wicked, Mr. Brooks," she said, "who spend no end of money and close our ears to all this. Do take this, will you; can it go to some of the women you know, and the children? There are only five or six pounds there, but I shall talk to mamma. We will send you a cheque."

He took the money without hesitation.

"I am very glad," he said, earnestly, "that you have given me this, that you have felt that you wanted to give it me. I hope you won't think too badly of me for coming over here to help you spend a pleasant evening, and talking at all of such miserable things."

"Badly!" she repeated. "No; I shall never be able to thank you enough for telling me what you have done. It makes one feel almost wicked to be sitting here, and wearing jewelry, and feeling well off, spending money on whatever you want, and to think that there are people starving. How they must hate us."

"It is the wonderful part of it," he answered. "I do not believe that they do. I suppose it is a sort of fatalism—the same sort of thing, only much less ignoble, as the indifference which keeps our rich people contented and deaf to this terribly human cry."

"You are young," she said, looking at him, "to be so much interested in such serious things."

"It is my blood, I suppose," he answered. "My father was a police-court missionary, and my mother the matron of a pauper hospital."

"They are both dead, are they not?" she asked, softly.

"Many years ago," he answered.

Lady Caroom and Lord Arranmore came in together. A certain unusual seriousness in Sybil's face was manifest.

"You two do not seem to have been amusing yourselves," Lady Caroom remarked, giving her hand to Brooks.

"Mr. Brooks has been answering some of my questions about the poor people," Sybil answered, "and it is not an amusing subject."

Lord Arranmore laughed lightly, and there was a touch of scorn in the slight curve of his fine lips and his raised eyebrows. He stood away from the shaded lamplight before a great open fire of cedar logs, and the red glow falling fitfully upon his face seemed to Brooks, watching him with more than usual closeness, to give him something of a Mephistopheles aspect. His evening clothes hung with more than ordinary precision about his long slim body, his black tie and black pearl stud supplied the touch of sombreness so aptly in keeping with the mirthless, bitter smile which still parted his lips.

"You must not take Mr. Brooks too seriously on the subject of the poor people," he said, the mockery of his smile well matched in his tone. "Brooks is an enthusiast—one, I am afraid, of those misguided people who have barred the way to progress for centuries. If only they could be converted!"

Lady Caroom sighed.

"Oh, dear, how enigmatic!" she exclaimed. "Do be a little more explicit."

"Dear lady," he continued, turning to her, "it is not worth while. Yet I sometimes wonder whether people realize how much harm this hysterical philanthropy—this purely sentimental faddism, does; how it retards the natural advance of civilization, throws dust in people's eyes, salves the easy conscience of the rich man, who bargains for immortality with a few strokes of the pen, and finds mischievous occupation for a good many weak minds and parasitical females. Believe me, that all personal charity is a mistake. It is a good deal worse than that. It is a crime."

Sybil rose up, and a little unusual flush had stained her cheeks.

"I still do not understand you in the least, Lord Arranmore," she said. "It seems to me that you are making paradoxical and ridiculous statements, which only bewilder us. Why is charity a crime? That is what I should like to hear you explain."

Lord Arranmore bowed slightly.

"I had no idea," he said, leaning his elbow upon the mantelpiece, "that I was going to be inveigled into a controversy. But, my dear Sybil, I will do my best to explain to you what I mean, especially as at your age you are not likely to discover the truth for yourself. In the first place, charity of any sort is the most insidious destroyer of moral character which the world has ever known. The man who once accepts it, even in extremes, imbibes a poison from which his system can never be thoroughly cleansed. You let him loose upon society, and the evil which you have sown in him spreads. He is like a man with an infectious disease. He is a source of evil to the community. You have relieved a physical want, and you have destroyed a moral quality. I do not need to point out to you that the balance is on the wrong side."

Sybil glanced across at Brooks, and he smiled back at her.

"Lord Arranmore has not finished yet," he said. "Let us hear the worst."

Their host smiled.

"After all," he said, "why do I waste my breath? From the teens to the thirties sentiment smiles. It is only later on in life that reason has any show at all. Yet you should ask yourselves, you eager self-denying young people, who go about with a healthy moral glow inside because you have fed the poor, or given an hour or so of your time to the distribution of reckless charity-you should ask yourselves: What is the actual good of ministering to the outward signs of an internal disease? You are simply trying to renovate the outside when the inside is filthy. Don't you see, my dear young people, that to give a meal to one starving man may be to do him indeed good, but it does nothing towards preventing another starving man from taking his place to-morrow. You stimulate the disease, you help it to spread. Don't you see where instead you should turn—to the social laws, the outcome of which is that starving man? You let them remain unharmed, untouched, while you fall over one another in frantic efforts to brush away to-day's effect of an eternal cause. Let your starving man die, let the bones break through his skin and carry him up—him and his wife and their children, and their fellows—to your House of Commons. Tell them that there are more to-morrow, more the next day, let the millions of the lower classes look this thing in the face. I tell you that either by a revolution, which no doubt some of us would find worse than inconvenient, or by less drastic means, the thing would right itself. You, who work to relieve the individual, only postpone and delay the millennium. People will keep their eyes closed as long as they can. It is you who help them to do so."

"Dinner is served, my lord," the butler announced.

Lord Arranmore extended his arm to Lady Caroom.

"Come," he said, "let us all be charitable to one another, for I too am starving."

CHAPTER XIV
AN AWKWARD QUESTION

"You think they really liked it, then?"

"How could they help it? It was such a delightful idea of yours, and I am sure all that you said was so simple and yet suggestive. Good-night, Mr. Brooks."

They stood in the doorway of the Secular Hall, where Brooks had just delivered his lecture. It seemed to him that her farewell was a little abrupt.

"I was going to ask," he said, "whether I might not see you home."

She hesitated.

"Really," she said, "I wish you would not trouble. It is quite a long way, and I have only to get into a car."

"The further the better," he answered, "and besides, if your uncle is at home I should like to come in and see him."

She made no further objection, yet Brooks fancied that her acquiescence was, to some extent, involuntary. He walked by her side in silence for a moment or two, wondering whether there was indeed any way in which he could have offended her.

"I have not seen you," he remarked, "since the evening of your dinner-party."

"No!"

"You were out when I called."

"I have so many things to do—just now. We can get a car here."

He looked at it.

"It is too full," he said. "Let us walk on for a little way. I want to talk to you."

The car was certainly full, so after a moment's hesitation she acquiesced.

"You will bring your girls again, I hope?" he asked.

"They will come I have no doubt," she answered. "So will I if I am in Medchester."

"You are going away?"

"I hope so," she answered. "I am not quite sure."

"Not for good?" Possibly."

"Won't you tell me about it?" he asked.

"Well—I don't know!"

She hesitated for a moment.

"I will tell you if you like," she said, doubtfully. "But I do not wish anything said about it at present, as my arrangements are not complete."

"I will be most discreet," he promised.

"I have been doing a little work for a woman's magazine in London, and they have half promised me a definite post on the staff. I am to hear in a few days as to the conditions. If they are satisfactory—that is to say, if I can keep myself on what they offer—I shall go and live in London."

He was surprised, and also in a sense disappointed. It was astonishing to find how unpleasant the thought of her leaving Medchester was to him.

"I had no idea of this," he said, thoughtfully. "I did not know that you went in for anything of the sort."

"My literary ambitions are slight enough," she answered. "Yet you can scarcely be surprised that I find the thought of a definite career and a certain amount of independence attractive."

He stole a sidelong glance at her. In her plainly made clothes and quiet hat she was scarcely, perhaps, a girl likely to attract attention, yet he was conscious of certain personal qualities, which he had realized and understood from the first. She carried herself well, she walked with the free graceful movements of a well-bred and healthy girl. In her face was an air of quiet thought, the self-possession of the woman of culture and experience. Her claim to good looks was, after all, slight enough, yet on studying her he came to the conclusion that she could if she chose appear to much greater advantage. Her hair, soft and naturally wavy, was brushed too resolutely back; her smile, which was always charming, she suffered to appear only at the rarest intervals. She suggested a life of repression, and with his knowledge of the Bullsom menage he was able to surmise some glimmering of the truth.

"You are right," he declared. "I think that I can understand what your feeling must be. I am sure I wish you luck."

The touch of sympathy helped her to unbend. She glanced towards him kindly.

"Thank you," she said. "Of course there will be difficulties. My uncle will not like it. He is very good-natured and very hospitable, and I am afraid his limitations will not permit him to appreciate exactly how I feel about it. And my aunt is, of course, merely his echo."

"He will not be unreasonable," Brooks said. "I am sure of that. For a man who is naturally of an obstinate turn of mind I think your uncle is wonderful. He makes great efforts to free himself from all prejudices."

"Unfortunately," she remarked, "he is very down on the independent woman. He would make housekeepers and cooks of all of us."

"Surely," he protested, with a quiet smile, "your cousins are more ambitious than that. I am sure Selina would never wear a cooking-apron, unless it had ribbon and frilly things all over it."

She laughed.

"After all, they have been kind to me," she said. "My mother was the black sheep of the family, and when she died Mr. Bullsom paid my passage home, and insisted upon my coming to live here as one of the family. I should hate them to think that I am discontented, only the things which satisfy them do not satisfy me, so life sometimes becomes a little difficult."

"Have you friends in London?" he asked.

"None! I tried living there when I first came back for a few weeks, but it was impossible."

"You will be very lonely, surely. London is the loneliest of all great cities."

"Why should I not make friends?"

"That is what I too asked myself years ago when I was articled there," he answered. "Yet it is not so easy as it sounds. Every one seems to have their own little circle, and a solitary person remains so often just outside. Yet if you have friends—and tastes—London is a paradise. Oh, how fascinating I used to find it just at first—before the chill came. You, too, will feel that. You will be content at first to watch, to listen, to wonder! Every type of humanity passes before you like the jumbled-up figures of a kaleidoscope. You are content even to sit before a window in a back street—and listen. What a sound that is—the roar of London, the voices of the street, the ceaseless hum, the creaking of the great wheel of humanity as it goes round and round. And then, perhaps, in a certain mood the undernote falls upon your ear, the bitter, long-drawn-out cry of the hopeless and helpless. When you have once heard it, life is never the same again. Then, if you do not find friends, you will know what misery is."

They were both silent for a few minutes. A car passed them unnoticed. Then she looked at him curiously.

"For a lawyer," she remarked, "you are a very imaginative person."

He laughed.

"Ah, well, I was talking just then of how I felt in those days. I was a boy then, you know. I dare say I could go back now to my old rooms and live there without a thrill."

She shook her head.

"What one has once felt," she murmured, "comes back always."

"Sometimes only the echo," he answered, "and that is weariness."

They walked for a little way in silence. Then she spoke to him in an altered tone.

"I have heard a good deal about you during the last few weeks," she said. "You are very much to be congratulated, they tell me. I am sure I am very glad that you have been so fortunate."

"Thank you," he answered. "To tell you the truth, it all seems very marvellous to me. Only a few months ago your uncle was almost my only client of importance."

"Lord Arranmore was your father's friend though, was he not?"

"They came together abroad," he answered, "and Lord Arranmore was with my father when he died in Canada."

She stopped short.

Where?

"In Canada, on the banks of Lake Ono, if you know where that is," he answered, looking at her in surprise.

She resumed her usual pace, but he noticed that she was pale.

"So Lord Arranmore was in Canada?" she said. "Do you know how long ago?"

"About ten years, I suppose," he answered. "How long before that I do not know."

She was silent for several minutes, and they found themselves in the drive leading to the Bullsom villa. Brooks was curious.

"I wonder," he asked, "whether you will tell me why you are interested in Lord Arranmore—and Canada?"

"I was born in Montreal," she answered, "and I once saw some one very much like Lord Arranmore there. But I am convinced that it could only have been a resemblance."

"You mentioned it before—when we saw him in Mellor's," he remarked.

"Yes, it struck me then," she admitted. "But I am sure that Lord Arranmore could not have been the person whom I am thinking about. It is ridiculous of me to attach so much importance to a mere likeness."

They stood upon the doorstep, but she checked him as he reached out for the bell.

"You have seen quite a good deal of him," she said. "Tell me what you think of Lord Arranmore." His hand fell to his side. He stood under the gas-bracket, and she could see his face distinctly. There was a slight frown upon his forehead, a look of trouble in his grey eyes.

"You could not have asked me a more difficult question," he admitted. "Lord Arranmore has been very kind to me, although my claim upon him has been of the slightest. He is very clever, almost fantastic, in some of his notions; he is very polished, and his manners are delightful. He would call himself, I believe, a philosopher, and he is, although it sounds brutal for me to say so, very selfish. And behind it all I haven't the faintest idea what sort of a man he is. Sometimes he gives one the impression of a strong man wilfully disguising his real characteristics, for hidden reasons; at others, he is like one of those brilliant Frenchmen of the last century, who toyed and juggled with words and phrases, esteeming it a triumph to remain an unread letter even to their intimates. So you see, after all," he wound up, "I cannot tell you what I think of Lord Arranmore."

"You can ring the bell," she said. "You must come in for a few minutes."

Their entrance together seemed to cause the little family party a certain amount of disturbed surprise. The girls greeted Brooks with a great show of pleasure, but they looked doubtfully at Mary.

"Did you meet at the front door?" Selina asked. "I thought I heard voices." Brooks was a little surprised.

"Your cousin brought her class of factory girls to my lecture to-night at the Secular Hall."

Selina's eyes narrowed a little, and she was silent for a moment. Then she turned to her cousin.

"You might have told us, Mary," she exclaimed, reproachfully. "We should so much have liked to come, shouldn't we, Louise?"

"Of course we should," Louise answered, snappishly. "I can't think why Mary should go off without saying a word."

Mary looked at them both and laughed. "Well," she said, "I have left the house at precisely the same time on 'Wednesday evenings all through the winter, and neither of you have said anything about coming with me."

"This is quite different," Selina answered, cuttingly. "We should very much have enjoyed Mr. Brooks' lecture. Do tell us what it was about."

"Don't you be bothered, Brooks," Mr. Bullsom exclaimed, hospitably. "Sit down and try one of these cigars. We've had supper, but if you'd like anything—"

"Nothing to eat, thanks," Brooks protested. "I'll have a cigar if I may."

"And a whisky-and-soda, then," Mr. Bullsom insisted. "Say when!"

Brooks turned to Selina. Mary had left the room. "You were asking about the lecture," he said. "Really, it was only a very unpretentious affair, and to tell you the truth, only intended for people whose opportunities for reading have not been great. I am quite sure it would not have been worth your while to come down. We just read a chapter or so from A Tale of Two Cities, and talked about it."

"We should have liked it very mulch," Selina declared. "Do tell us when there is another one, will you?"

"With pleasure," he answered. "I warn you, though, that you will be disappointed."

"We will risk that," Selina declared, with a smile. "Have you been to Enton this week?"

"I was there on Sunday," he answered.

"And is that beautiful girl, Lady Sybil Caroom, still staying there?

"Yes," he answered. "Is she very beautiful, by the bye?"

"Well, I thought men would think so," Selina said, hastily. "I think that she is just a little loud, don't you, Louise?"

Louise admitted that the idea had occurred to her.

"And her hair—isn't it badly dyed?" Selina remarked. "Such a pity. It's all in patches."

"I think girls ought not to make up in the street, either," Louise remarked, primly. "A little powder in the house is all very well"—(Louise had a nose which gave her trouble)—"but I really don't think it looks respectable in the street."

"I suppose," Selina remarked, "you men admire all that sort of thing, don't you?"

"I really hadn't noticed it with Lady Sybil," Brooks admitted.

Selina sighed.

"Men are so blind," she remarked. "You watch next time you are close to her, Mr. Brooks."

"I will," he promised. "I'll get her between me and a window in a strong north light."

Selina laughed.

"Don't be too unkind," she said. "That's the worst of you men. When you do find anything out you are always so severe."

"After all, though," Louise remarked, with a sidelong glance, "it must be very, very interesting to meet these sort of people, even if one doesn't quite belong to their set. I should think you must find every one else quite tame, Mr. Brooks."

"I can assure you I don't," he answered, coolly. "This evening has provided me with quite as pleasant society as ever I should wish for."

Selina beamed upon him.

"Oh, Mr. Brooks, you are terrible. You do say such things!" she declared, archly.

Louise laughed a little hardly.

"We mustn't take too much to ourselves, dear," she said. "Remember that Mr. Brooks walked all the way up from the Secular Hall with Mary."

Mr. Bullsom threw down his paper with a little impatient exclamation.

"Come, come!" he said. "I want to have a few words with Brooks myself, if you girls'll give me a chance. Heard anything from Henslow lately, eh?"

Brooks leaned forward.

"Not a word!" he answered.

Mr. Bullsom grunted.

"H'm! He's taken his seat, and that's all he does seem to have done. To have heard his last speech here before polling time you would have imagined him with half-a-dozen questions down before now. He's letting the estimates go by, too. There are half-a-dozen obstructors, all faddists, but Henslow, with a real case behind him, is sitting tight. 'Pon my word, I'm not sure that I like the fellow."

"I ventured to write to him the other evening," Brooks said, "and I have sent him all the statistics we promised, he seems to have regarded my letter as an impertinence, though, for he has never answered it."

"You mark my words," Mr. Bullsom said, doubling the paper up and bringing it down viciously upon his knee, "Henslow will never sit again for Medchester. There was none too mulch push about him last session, but he smoothed us all over somehow. He'll not do it again. I'm losing faith in the man, Brooks."

Brooks was genuinely disturbed. His own suspicions had been gathering strength during the last few weeks. Henslow had been pleasant enough, but a little flippant after the election. From London he had promised to write to Mr. Bullsom, as chairman of his election committee, mapping out the course of action which, in pursuance of his somewhat daring pledges, he proposed to embark upon. This was more than a month ago, and there had come not a single word from him. All that vague distrust which Brooks had sometimes felt in the man was rekindled and increased, and with it came a flood of bitter thoughts. Another opportunity then was to be lost. For seven years longer these thousands of pallid, heart-weary men and women were to suffer, with no one to champion their cause. He saw again that sea of eager faces in the market-place, lit with a sudden gleam of hope as they listened to the bold words of the man who was promising them life and hope and better things. Surely if this was a betrayal it was an evil deed, not passively to be borne.

Mr. Bullsom had refreshed himself with whisky-and-water, and decided that pessimism was not a healthy state of mind.

"I tell you what it is, Brooks," he said, more cheerfully. "We mustn't be too previous in judging the fellow. Let's write him civilly, and if nothing comes of it in a week or two, we will run up to London, you and me, eh? and just haul him over the coals."

"You are right, Mr. Bullsom," Brooks said. "There is nothing we can do for the present."

"Please don't talk any more horrid politics," Selina begged. "We want Mr. Brooks to give us a lesson at billiards. Do you mind?"

Brooks rose at once.

"I shall be charmed!" he declared.

Mr. Bullsom rose also.

"Pooh, pooh!" he said. "Brooks and I will have a hundred up and you can watch us. That'll be lesson enough for you."

Selina made a little grimace, but they all left the room together. In the hall a housemaid was speaking at the telephone, and a moment afterwards she laid the receiver down and came towards them.

"It is a message for Mr. Brooks, sir, from the Queen's Hotel. Lord Arranmore's compliments, and the ladies from Enton are at the theatre this evening, and would be glad if Mr. Brooks would join them at the Queen's Hotel for supper at eleven o'clock."

Brooks hesitated, but Mr. Bullsom spoke up at once.

"Off you go, Brooks," he said, firmly. "Don't you go refusing an invitation like that. Lord Arranmore is a bit eccentric, they say, and he isn't the sort of man to like refusals. You've just got time."

"They had the message two hours ago, and have been trying everywhere to find Mr. Brooks," the housemaid added.

Selina helped him on with his coat.

"Will you come another evening soon and play billiards with us?" she asked, dropping her voice a little.

"With pleasure," Brooks answered. "Do you mind saying good-bye to your cousin for me? I am sorry not to see her again."

CHAPTER XV
A SUPPER-PARTY AT THE "QUEEN'S"

Brooks was shown into a private room at the Queen's Hotel, and he certainly had no cause to complain of the warmth of his welcome. Lady Sybil, in fact, made room for him by her side, and he fancied that there was a gleam of reproach in her eyes as she looked up at him.

"Is Medchester really so large a place that one can get lost in it?" she asked. "Lord Arranmore has been sending messengers in every direction ever since we decided upon our little excursion."

"I telephoned to your office, sent a groom to your rooms and to the club, and at last we had given you up," Lord Arranmore remarked.

"And I," Sybil murmured, "was in a shocking bad temper."

"It is very good of you all," Brooks remarked, cheerfully. "I left the office rather early, and have been giving a sort of lecture to-night at the Secular Hall. Then I went up to have a game of billiards with Mr. Bullsom. Your telephone message found me there. You must remember that even if Medchester is not a very large place I am a very unimportant person."

"Dear me, what modesty," Lady Caroom remarked, laughing. "To us, however, you happened to be very important. I hate a party of three."

Brooks helped himself to a quail, and remembered that he was hungry.

"This is very unusual dissipation, isn't it?" he asked. "I never dreamed that you would be likely to come into our little theatre."

"It was Sybil's doings," Lady Caroom answered. "She declared that she was dull, and that she had never seen A /Message from Mars./ I think that all that serious talk the other evening gave her the blues."

"I am always dull in the winter when there is no hunting," Sybil remarked. "This frost is abominable. I have not forgotten our talk either. I feel positively wicked every time I sip champagne."

"Our young philanthropist will reassure you," Arranmore remarked, drily.

Lady Caroom sighed.

"I wonder how it is," she murmured, "that one's conscience and one's digestion both grow weaker as one grows old. You and I, Arranmore, are content to accept the good things of the earth as they come to us."

"With me," he answered, "it is the philosophy of approaching old age, but you have no such excuse. With you it must be sheer callousness. You are in an evil way, Lady Caroom. Do have another of these quails."

"You are very rude," she answered, "and extremely unsympathetic. But I will have another quail."

"I do not Want to destroy your appetite, Mr. Brooks," Lady Sybil said, "but this is—if not a farewell feast, something like it."

He looked at her with sudden interest.

"You are going away?" he exclaimed.

"Very soon," she assented. "We were so comfortable at Enton, and the hunting has been so good, that we cut out one of our visits. Mamma developed a convenient attack of influenza. But the next one is very near now, and our host is almost tired of us."

Lord Arranmore was for a moment silent.

"You have made Enton," he said, "intolerable for a solitary man. When you go I go."

"I wish you could say whither instead of when," Lady Caroom answered. "How bored you would be at Redcliffe. It is really the most outlandish place we go to."

"Why ever do we accept, mamma?" Sybil asked. "Last year I nearly cried my eyes out, I was so dull. Not a man fit to talk to, or a horse fit to ride. The girls bicycle, and Lord Redcliffe breeds cattle and talks turnips."

"And they all drink port after dinner," Lady Caroom moaned; "but we have to go, dear. We must live rent free somewhere during these months to get through the season."

Sybil looked at Brooks with laughter in her eyes.

"Aren't we terrible people?" she whispered. "You are by way of being literary, aren't you? You should write an article on the shifts of the aristocracy. Mamma and I could supply you with all the material. The real trouble, of course, is that I don't marry."

"Fancy glorying in your failure," Lady Caroom said, complacently. "Three seasons, Arranmore, have I had to drag that girl round. I've washed my hands of her now. She must look after herself. A girl who refuses one of the richest young men in England because she didn't like his collars is incorrigible."

"It was not his collars, mother," Sybil objected. "It was his neck. He was always called 'the Giraffe.' He had no head and all neck—the most fatuous person, too. I hate fools."

"That is where you lack education, dear," Lady Caroom answered. "A fool is the most useful person—for a husband."

Sybil glanced towards Brooks with a little sigh, and, catching a glimpse of his expression, burst out laughing.

"Mother, you must really not let your tongue run away with you. Mr. Brooks is believing every word you say. You needn't," she murmured in a discreet undertone. "Mother and I chaff one another terribly, but we're really very nicely-behaved persons—for our station in life."

"Lady Caroom has such a delightfully easy way of romancing," Brooks said.

Sybil nodded.

"It's quite true," she answered. "She ought to write the prospectuses for gold mines and things."

Arranmore smiled across the table at Brooks.

"This," he said, "is what I have had to endure for the last six weeks. Do you wonder that I am getting balder, or that I set all my people to work tonight to try and find some one to suffer with me?"

"He'll be so dull when we've gone," Lady Caroom sighed.

"You've no idea how we've improved him," Sybil murmured. "He used to read Owen Meredith after dinner, and go to sleep. By the bye, where are you going when we leave Enton?"

Lord Arranmore hesitated.

"Well, I really am not sure," he said. "You have alarmed me. Don't go."

Lady Caroom laughed.

"My dear man," she said, "we must! I daren't offend the Redcliffes. He's my trustee, and he'll never let me overdraw a penny unless I'm civil to him. If I were you I should go to the Riviera. We'll lend you our cottage at Lugiano. It has been empty for a year."

"Come and be hostess," he said. "I promise you that I will not hesitate then."

She shook her head towards Sybil.

"How can I marry that down there?" she demanded. "No young men who are really respectable go abroad at this time of the year. They are all hunting or shooting. The Riviera is thronged with roues and invalids and adventurers, and we don't want any of them. Dear me, what sacrifices a grown-up daughter does entail. This coming season shall be your last, Sybil. I won't drag on round again. I'm really getting ashamed of it."

"Isn't she dreadful?" Sybil murmured to Brooks. "I hope you will come to Enton before we leave."

"It is very kind of you, Lady Sybil," Brooks said, "but you must remember that I am not like most of the men you meet. I have to work hard, especially just now."

"And if I were you I would be thankful for it," she said, warmly. "From our point of view, at any rate, there is nothing so becoming to a man as the fact that he is a worker. Sport is an excellent thing, but I detest young men who do nothing else but shoot and hunt and loaf about. It seems to me to destroy character where work creates it. All the same, I hope you will find an opportunity to come to Enton and say good-bye to us."

Brooks was suddenly conscious that it would be no pleasant thing to say good-bye to Lady Sybil. He had never known any one like her, so perfectly frank and girlish, and yet with character enough underneath in her rare moments of seriousness. More than ever he was struck with the wonderful likeness between mother and daughter.

"I will come at any time I am asked," he answered, quietly, "but I am sorry that you are going."

They had finished supper, and had drawn their chairs around the fire. Arranmore was smoking a cigarette, and Brooks took one from his case. The carriage was ordered in a quarter of an hour. Brooks found that he and Sybil were a little apart from the others.

"Do you know, I am sorry too," she declared. "Of course it has been much quieter at Enton than most of the houses we go to, and we only came at first, I think, because many years ago my mother and Lord Arranmore were great friends, and she fancied that he was shutting himself up too much. But I have enjoyed it very much indeed."

He looked at her curiously. He was trying to appreciate what a life of refined pleasure which she must live would really be like—how satisfying— whether its limitations ever asserted themselves. Sybil was a more than ordinarily pretty girl, but her face was as smooth as a child's. The Joie de vivre seemed to be always in her eyes. Yet there were times, as he knew, when she was capable of seriousness.

"I am glad," he said, "Lord Arranmore will miss you."

She laughed at him, her eyebrows raised, a challenge in her bright eyes.

"May I add that I also shall?" he whispered.

"You may," she answered. "In fact, I expected it. I am not sure that I did not ask for it. And that reminds me. I want you to do me a favour, if you will."

"Anything I can do for you," he answered, "you know will give me pleasure."

She laughed softly.

"It is wonderful how you have improved," she murmured. "I want you to go and see Lord Arranmore as often as you can. We are both very fond of him really, mamma especially, and you know that he has a very strange disposition. I am convinced that solitude is the very worst thing for him. I saw him once after he had been alone for a month or two, and really you would not have known him. He was as thin as a skeleton, strange in his manner, and he had that sort of red light in his eyes sometimes which always makes me think of mad people. He ought not to be alone at all, but the usual sort of society only bores him. You will do what you can, won't you?"

"I promise you that most heartily," Brooks declared. "But you must remember, Lady Sybil, that after all it is entirely in his hands. He has been most astonishingly kind to me, considering that I have no manner of claim upon him. He has made me feel at home at Enton, too, and been most thoughtful in every way. For, after all, you see I am only his man of business. I have no friends much, and those whom I have are Medchester people. You see I am scarcely in a position to offer him my society. But all the same, I will take every opportunity I can of going to Enton if he remains there."

She thanked him silently. Lady Caroom was on her feet, and Sybil and she went out for their wraps. Lord Arranmore lit a fresh cigarette and sent for his bill.

"By the bye, Brooks," he remarked, "one doesn't hear much of your man Henslow."

"Mr. Bullsom and I were talking about it this evening," Brooks answered. "We are getting a little anxious.

"You have had seven years of him. You ought to know what to expect."

"The war has blocked all legislation," Brooks said. "It has been the usual excuse. Henslow was bound to wait. He would have done the particular measures which we are anxious about more harm than good if he had tried to force them upon the land. But now it is different. We are writing to him. If nothing comes of it, Mr. Bullsom and I are going up to see him."

Arranmore smiled.

"You are young to politics, Brooks," he remarked, "yet I should scarcely have thought that you would have been imposed upon by such a man as Henslow. He is an absolute fraud. I heard him speak once, and I read two of his speeches. It was sufficient. The man is not in earnest. He has some reason, I suppose, for wishing to write M.P. after his name, but I am perfectly certain that he has not the slightest idea of carrying out his pledges to you. You will have to take up politics, Brooks."

He laughed—a little consciously.

"Some day," he said, "the opportunity may come. I will confess that it is amongst my ambitions. But I have many years' work before me yet."

Lord Arranmore paid the bill, and they joined the women. As Brooks stood bareheaded upon the pavement Arranmore turned towards him.

"We must have a farewell dinner," he said. "How would to-morrow suit you—or Sunday?"

"I should like to walk over on Sunday, if I might," Brooks answered, promptly.

"We shall expect you to lunch. Good-night."

The carriage drove off. Brooks walked thoughtfully through the silent streets to his rooms.

CHAPTER XVI
UNCLE AND NIECE

Mr. Bullsom was an early riser, and it chanced that, as was frequently the case, on the morning following Brooks' visit he and Mary sat down to breakfast together. But when, after a cursory glance through his letters, he unfolded the paper, she stopped him.

"Uncle," she said, "I want to talk to you for a few minutes, if I may."

"Go ahead," he answered. "No fear of our being interrupted. I shall speak to those girls seriously about getting up. Now, what is it?"

"I want to earn my own living, uncle," she said, quietly.

He looked over his spectacles at her.

"Eh?"

"I want to earn my own living," she repeated. "I have been looking about for a means of doing so, and I think that I have succeeded."

Mr. Bullsom took off his spectacles and wiped them carefully.

"Earn your own living, eh!" he repeated. "Well! Go on!"

Mary leaned across the table towards him.

"Don't think that I am not grateful for all you have done for me, uncle," she said. "I am, indeed. Only I have felt lately that it was my duty to order my life a little differently. I am young and strong, and able to work. There is no reason why I should be a burden upon any one."

She found his quietness ominous, but she did not flinch.

"I am not accomplished enough for a governess, or good-tempered enough for a companion," she continued, "but I believe I have found something which I can do. I have written several short stories for a woman's magazine, and they have made me a sort of offer to do some regular work for them. What they offer would just keep me. I want to accept."

"Where should you live?" he asked.

"In London!"

"Alone?"

"There is a girls' club in Chelsea somewhere. I should go there at first, and then try and share rooms with another girl."

"How much a week will they give you?"

"Twenty-eight shillings, and I shall be allowed to contribute regularly to the magazine at the usual rates. I ought to make at least forty shillings a week."

Mr. Bullsom sighed.

"Is this owing to any disagreement between you and the girls?" he asked, sharply.

"Certainly not," she answered.

"You ain't unhappy here? Is there anything we could do? I don't want to lose you."

Mary was touched. She had expected ridicule or opposition. This was more difficult.

"Of course I am not unhappy," she answered. "You and aunt have been both of you most generous and kind to me. But I do feel that a busy life—and I'm not a bit domestic, you know would be good for me. I believe, uncle, if you were in my place you would feel just like me. If you were able to, I expect you'd want to earn your own living."

"You shall go!" he said, decidedly. "I'll help you all I can. You shall have a bit down to buy furniture, if you want it, or an allowance till you feel your way. But, Mary, I'm downright sorry. No, I'm not blaming you. You've a right to go. I—I don't believe I'd live here if I were you.

"You are very good, uncle," Mary said, gratefully. "And you must remember it isn't as though I were leaving you alone. You have the girls."

Mr. Bullsom nodded.

"Yes," he said, "I have the girls. Look here, Mary," he added, suddenly, looking her in the face, "I want to have a word with you. I'm going to talk plainly. Be honest with me."

"Of course," she murmured.

"It's about the girls. It's a hard thing to say, but somehow—I'm a bit disappointed with them."

She looked at him in something like amazement.

"Yes, disappointed," he continued. "That's the word. I'm an uneducated man myself—any fool can see that—but I did all I could to have them girls different. They've been to the best school in Medchester, and they've been abroad. They've had masters in most everything, and I've had 'em taught riding and driving, and all that sort of thing, properly. Then as they grew up I built this 'ouse, and came up to live here amongst the people whom I reckoned my girls'd be sure to get to know. And the whole thing's a damned failure, Mary. That's the long and short of it."

"Perhaps—a little later on" Mary began, hesitatingly.

"Don't interrupt me," he said, brusquely. "This is the first honest talk I've ever had about it, and it's doing me good. The girls'd like to put it down to your mother and me, but I don't believe it. I'm ashamed to say it, but I'm afraid it's the girls themselves. There's something not right about them, but I'm blessed if I know what it is. Their mother and I are a bit vulgar, I know, but I've done my best to copy those who know how to behave—and I believe we'd get through for what we are anywhere without giving offence. But my girls oughtn't to be vulgar. It's education as does away with that, and I've filled em chock-full of education from the time they were babies. It's run out of them, Mary, like the sands through an hour-glass. They can speak correctly, and I dare say they know all the small society tricks. But that isn't everything. They don't know how to dress. They can spend just as much as they like, and then you can come into the room in a black gown as you made yourself, and you look a lady, and they don't. That's the long and short of it. The only decent people who come to this house are your friends, and they come to see you. There's young Brooks, now. I've no son, Mary, and I'm fond of young men. I never knew one I liked as I like him. My daughters are old enough to be married, and I'd give fifty thousand pounds to have him for a son-in-law. And, of course, he won't look at 'em. He sees it. He'll talk to you. He takes no more notice of them than is civil. They fuss round him, and all that, but they might save themselves the pains. It's hard lines, Mary. I'm making money as no one knows on. I could live at Enton and afford it. But what's the good of it? If people don't care to know us here, they won't anywhere. Mary, how was it education didn't work with them girls? Your mother was my own sister, and she married a gentleman. He was a blackguard, but hang it, Mary, if I were you I'd sooner be penniless and as you are than be my daughters with five thousand apiece."

There was an embarrassed silence. Then Mary faced the situation boldly.

"Uncle," she said, "you are asking my advice. Is that it?"

"If there's any advice you can give, for God's sake let's have it. But I don't know as you can make black white."

"Selina and Louise are good girls enough," she said, "but they are a little spoilt, and they are a little limited in their ideas. A town like this often has that effect. Take them abroad, uncle, for a year, or, better still, if you can find the right person, get a companion for them—a lady—and let her live in the house."

"That's sound!" he answered. "I'll do it."

"And about their clothes, uncle. Take them up to London, go to one of the best places, and leave the people to make their things. Don't let them interfere. Down here they've got to choose for themselves. They wouldn't care about taking advice here, but in London they'd probably be content to leave it. Take them up to town for a fortnight. Stay at one of the best hotels, the Berkeley or the Carlton, and let them see plenty of nice people. And don't be discouraged, uncle."

"Where the devil did you get your common-sense from?" he inquired, fiercely. "Your mother hadn't got it, and I'll swear your father hadn't."

She laughed heartily.

"Above all, be firm with them, uncle," she said. "Put your foot down, and stick to it. They'll obey you.

"Obey me? Good Lord, I'll make 'em," Mr. Bullsom declared, vigorously. "Mary, you're a brick. I feel quite cheerful. And, remember this, my girl. I shall make you an allowance, but that's nothing. Come to me when you want a bit extra, and if ever the young man turns up, then I've got a word or two to say. Mind, I shall only be giving you your own. My will's signed and sealed."

She kissed him fondly.

"You're a good sort, uncle," she said. "And now will you tell me what you think of this letter?"

"Read it to me, dear," he said. "My eyes aren't what they were."

She obeyed him.

"41, BUCKLESBURY, LONDON, E. C.

"DEAR MADAM,

"We have received a communication from our agents at Montreal, asking us to ascertain the whereabouts of Miss Mary Scott, daughter of Richard Scott, at one time a resident in that city.

"We believe that you are the young lady in question, and if you will do us the favour of calling at the above address, we may be able to give you some information much to your advantage.

"We are, dear madam,

"Yours respectfully,

"JONES AND LLOYD."

Mr. Bullsom stroked his chin thoughtfully.

"Sounds all right," he remarked. "Of course you'll go. But I always understood that your father's relations were as poor as church mice."

"Poorer, uncle! His father—my grandfather, that is—was a clergyman with barely enough to live on, and his uncle was a Roman Catholic priest. Both of them have been dead for years."

"And your father—well, I know there was nothing there," Mr. Bullsom remarked, thoughtfully.

"You cabled out the money to bring me home," Mary reminded him.

"Well, well!" Mr. Bullsom declared. "You must go and see these chaps. There's no harm in that, at any rate. We must all have that trip to London. I expect Brooks will be wanting to go and see Henslow. We'll have to give that chap what for, I know."

Selina sailed into the room in a salmon-coloured wrapper, which should long ago have been relegated to the bath-room. She pecked her father on the cheek and nodded to Mary.

"Don't you see Mr. Brooks, dear?" her father remarked, with a twinkle in his eye and something very much like a wink to Mary.

Selina screamed, and looked fearfully around the room.

"What do you mean, papa?" she exclaimed. "There is no one here."

"Serve you right if there had been," Mr. Bullsom declared, gruffly. "A pretty state to come down in the morning at past nine o'clock."

Selina tossed her head.

"I am going to dress directly after breakfast," she remarked.

"Then if you'll allow me to say so," her father declared, "before breakfast is the time to dress, and not afterwards. You're always the same, Selina, underdressed when you think there's no one around to see you, and overdressed when there is."

Selina poured herself out some coffee and yawned.

"La, papa, what do you know about it?" she exclaimed.

"What my eyes tell me," Mr. Bullsom declared, sternly. "You've no allowance to keep to. You've leave to spend what you want, and you're never fit to be seen. There's Mary there taking thirty pounds a year from me, and won't have a penny more, though she's heartily welcome to it, and she looks a lady at any moment of the day."

Selina drew herself up, and her eyes narrowed a little.

"You're talking about what, you don't understand, pa," she answered with dignity. "If you prefer Mary's style of dress"—she glanced with silent disparagement at her cousin's grey skirt and plain white blouse—"well, it's a matter of taste, isn't it?

"Taste!" Mr. Bullsom replied, contemptuously. "Taste! What sort of taste do you call that beastly rug on your shoulders, eh? Or your hair rolled round and just a pin stuck through it? Looks as though it hadn't been brushed for a week. Faugh! When your mother and I lived on two pounds a week she never insulted me by coming down to breakfast in such a thing."

Selina eyed her father in angry astonishment.

"Thing indeed!" she repeated. "This wrapper cost me four guineas, and came from Paris. That shows how much you know about it."

"From Paris, did it?" Mr. Bullsom retorted, fiercely. "Then up-stairs you go and take it off. You girls have had your own way too much, and I'm about tired of it."

"I shall change it—after breakfast," Selina said, doubtfully.

Mr. Bullsom threw open the door.

"Up-stairs," he repeated, "and throw it into the rag-bag."

Selina hesitated. Then she rose, and with scarlet cheeks and a poor show of dignity, left the room. Mr. Bullsom drew himself up and beamed upon Mary.

"I'll show 'em a bit," he declared, with great good-humour. "I may be an ignorant old man, but I'm going to wake these girls up."

Mary struggled for a moment, but her sense of humour triumphed. She burst out laughing.

"Oh, uncle, uncle," she exclaimed, "you're a wonderful man."

He beamed upon her.

"You come shopping with us in London," he said. "We'll have some fun."

CHAPTER XVII
FIFTEEN YEARS IN HELL

"Really," Lady Caroom exclaimed, "Enton is the cosiest large house I was ever in. Do throw that Bradshaw away, Arranmore. The one o'clock train will do quite nicely."

Lord Arranmore obeyed her literally. He jerked the volume lightly into a far corner of the room and came over to her side. She was curled up in a huge easy-chair, and her face caught by the glow of the dancing firelight almost startled him by its youth. There was not a single sign of middle age in the smooth cheeks, not a single grey hair, no sign of weariness in the soft full eyes raised to his.

She caught his glance and smiled.

"The firelight is so becoming!" she murmured.

"Don't go!" he said.

"My dear Arranmore. The Redcliffes would never forgive me, and we must go some time."

"I don't see the necessity," he answered, slowly. "You like Enton. Make it your home."

She raised her eyebrows.

"How improper!" "Not necessarily," he answered. "Take me too."

She sat up in her chair and regarded him steadily.

"Am I to regard this," she asked, "as an offer of marriage?"

"Well, it sounds like it," he admitted.

"Dear me. You might have given me a little more notice," she said. "Let me think for a moment, please."

Perhaps their thoughts travelled back in the same direction. He remembered his cousin and his playfellow, the fairest and daintiest girl he had ever seen, his best friend, his constant companion. He remembered the days when she had first become something more to him, the miseries of that time, his hopeless ineligibility—the separation. Then the years of absence, the terrible branding years of his life, the horrible pit, the time when night and day his only prayer had been the prayer for death. The self-repression of years seemed to grow weaker and weaker. He held out his hands. But she hesitated.

"Dear," she said, "you make me very happy. It is wonderful to think this may come after all these years. But there is something which I wish to say to you first."

"Well?"

"You are very, very dear to me now—as you are—but you are not the man I loved years ago. You are a very different person indeed. Sometimes I am almost afraid of you."

"You have no cause to be," he said. "Indeed, you have no cause to be. So far as you are concerned I have never changed. I am the same man."

She took one of his hands in hers.

"Philip," she said, "you must not think hardly of me. You must not think of me as simply afflicted with the usual woman's curiosity. I am not curious at all. I would rather not know. But remember that for nearly twenty years you passed out of my life. You have come back again wonderfully altered. You do not wish to keep the story of those years for ever a sort of Bluebeards chamber in our lives?"

"Not I," he answered. "I would have you do as I have done, rip them out page and chapter, annihilate them utterly. What have they to do with the life before us? To you they would seem evil enough, to me they are thronged with horrible memories, with memories which, could I take them with me, would poison heaven itself. So let us blot them out for ever. Come to me, Catherine, and help me to forget."

She looked at him with strained eyes.

"Philip," she said, "I must understand you. I must understand what has made you the man you are."

"Fifteen years in hell has done it," he answered, fiercely. "Not even my memory shall ever take me back."

"If I marry you," she said, "remember that I marry your past as well as your future. And there are things—which need explanation."

"Well?"

"You have been married."

"She is dead."

"You have a son."

He reeled as though he had been struck, and the silence between them was as the silence of tragedy.

"You see," she continued, "I am bound to ask you to lift the curtain a little. Fate or instinct, or whatever you may like to call it, has led me a little way. I am not afraid to know. I have seen too much of life to be a hard judge. But you must hold out your hand and take me a little further."

"I cannot."

She held him tightly. Her voice trembled a little. "Dear, you must. I am not an exacting woman, and I love you too well to be a hard judge of anything you might have to tell me. Ignorance is the only thing which I cannot bear. Remember how greatly you are changed, you are almost a stranger to me in some of your moods. I could not have you wandering off into worlds of which I knew nothing. Sit down by my side and talk to me. I will ask no questions. You shall tell me your own way, and what you wish to leave out—leave it out. Come, is this so hard a task?"

He seemed frozen into inanition. His face was like the cast of a dead man's. His voice was cold and hopeless.

"The key," he said, "is gone. I shall never seek for it, I shall never find it. I have known what madness is, and I am afraid. Shall we go into the hall? I fancy that they are serving tea."

She looked at him, half terrified, half amazed.

"You mean this as final?" she said, deliberately. "You refuse to offer any explanation, the explanation which common decency even would require of these things?"

"I expected too much," he answered. "I know it very well. Forgive me, and let us forget."

She rose to her feet.

"I do not know that you will ever regret this," she said. "I pray that you may."

To Brooks she seemed the same charming woman as usual, as he heard her light laugh come floating across the hall, and bowed over her white fingers. But Sybil saw the over-bright eyes and nervous mouth and had hard work to keep back the tears. She piled the cushions about a dark corner of the divan, and chattered away recklessly.

"This is a night of sorrows," she exclaimed, pouring out the tea. "Mr. Brooks and I were in the midst of a most affecting leave-taking—when the tea came. Why do these mundane things always break in upon the most sacred moments?"

"Life," Lady Caroom said, helping herself recklessly to muffin, "is such a wonderful mixture of the real and the fanciful, the actual and the sentimental, one is always treading on the heels of the other. The little man who turns the handle must have lots of fun."

"If only he has a sense of humour," Brooks interposed. "After all, though, it is the grisly, ugly things which float to the top. One has to probe always for the beautiful, and it requires our rarest and most difficult sense to apprehend the humorous."

Lord Arranmore stirred his tea slowly. His face was like the face of a carved image. Only Brooks seemed still unconscious of the shadow which was stalking amongst them.

"We talk of life so glibly," he said. "It is a pity that we cannot realize its simplest elements. Life is purely subjective. Nothing exists except in our point of view. So we are continually making and marring our own lives and the lives of other people by a word, an action, a thought."

"Dear me!" Lady Caroom murmured. "How-ever shall I be able to play bridge after tea if you all try to addle my brain by paradoxes and subtle sayings beforehand! What does Arranmore mean?"

He put down his cup.

"Do not dare to understand me," he said. "It is the most sincere unkindness when one talks only to answer. And as for bridge—remember that this is a night of mourning. Bridge is far too frivolous a pursuit."

"Bridge a frivolous pursuit?" Sybil exclaimed. "Heavens, what sacrilege. What ought we to do, Lord Arranmore?"

"Sit in sackcloth and ashes, and hear Brooks lecture on the poor," he answered, lightly. "Brooks is a mixture of the sentimentalist and the hideous pessimist, you know, and it is the privilege of his years to be sometimes in earnest. I know nothing more depressing than to listen to a man who is in earnest."

"You are getting positively light-headed," Sybil laughed. "I can see no pleasure in life save that which comes from an earnest pursuit of things, good or evil."

"My dear child," Lord Arranmore answered, "when you are a little older you will know that to take life seriously is a sheer impossibility. You may think that you are doing it, but you are not."

"There must be exceptions," Sybil declared.

"There are none," Lord Arranmore answered, lightly, "outside the madhouse. For the realization of life comes only hand in hand with insanity. The people who have come nearest to it carry the mark with them all their life. For the fever of knowledge will scorch even those who peer over the sides of the cauldron."

Lady Caroom helped herself to some more tea.

"Really, Arranmore," she drawled, "for sheer and unadulterated pessimism you are unsurpassed. You must be a very morbid person."

He shrugged his shoulders.

"One is always called morbid," he remarked, "who dares to look towards the truth."

"There are people," Lady Caroom answered, "who look always towards the clouds, even when the sun is shining."

"I am in the minority," Lord Arranmore said, smiling. "I feel myself becoming isolated. Let us abandon the subject."

"No, let us convert you instead," Sybil declared. "We want to look at the sun, and we want to take you with us. You are really a very stupid person, you know. Why do you want to stay all alone amongst the shadows?" Arranmore smiled faintly.

"The sun shines," he said, "only for those who have eyes to see it."

"Blindness is not incurable," she answered.

"Save when the light in the eyes is dead," he answered. "Come, shall we play a game at fourhanded billiards?"

It resolved itself into a match between Lady Caroom and Lord Arranmore, who were both players far above the average. Sybil and Brooks talked, but for once her attention wandered. She seemed listening to the click of the billiard-balls, and watching the man and the woman between whom all conversation seemed dead. Brooks noticed her absorption, and abandoned his own attempts to interest her.

"Your mother and Lord Arranmore," he remarked, "are very old friends."

"They have known one another all their lives," she murmured. "Lord Arranmore has changed a good deal though since his younger days."

Brooks made no reply. The girl suddenly bent her head towards him.

"Are you a judge of character?" she asked.

He shook his head.

"Scarcely. I have not had enough experience. It is a fascinating study."

"Very. Now I want to ask you something. What do you think of Lord Arranmore?"

Her tone betokened unusual seriousness. His light answer died away on his lips.

"It is very hard for me to answer that question," he said. "Lord Arranmore has been most unnecessarily kind to me."

"His character?"

"I do not pretend to be able to understand it. I think that he is often wilfully misleading. He does not wish to be understood. He delights in paradoxy and moral gymnastics."

"He may blind your judgment. How do you personally feel towards him?"

"That," he answered, "might be misleading. He has shown me so much kindness. Yet I think—I am sure—that I liked him from the first moment I saw him."

She nodded.

"I like him too. I cannot help it. Yet one can be with him, can live in the same house for weeks, even months, and remain an utter stranger to him. He has self-repression which is marvellous—never at fault—never a joint loose. One wonders so much what lies beyond. One would like to know."

"Is it wise?" he asked. "After all, is it our concern?"

"Not ours. But if you were a woman would you be content to take him on trust?"

"It would depend upon my own feelings," he answered, hesitatingly.

"Whether you cared for him?"

"Yes!"

She beat the floor with her foot.

"You are wrong," she said, "I am sure that you are wrong. To care for one is to wish ever to believe the best of them. It is better to keep apart for ever than to run any risks. Supposing that unknown past was of evil, and one discovered it. To care for him would only make the suffering keener."

"It may be so," he admitted. "May I ask you something?"

"Well?"

"You speak—of yourself?"

Her eyes met his, and he looked hastily downwards.

"Absurd," she murmured, and inclined her head towards the billiard-table. "They have been—attached to one another always. Come over here to the window, and I will tell you something."

They walked towards the great circular window which overlooked the drive. As they stood there together a four-wheeled cab drove slowly by, and a girl leaned forward and looked at them. Brooks started as he recognized her.

"Why, that must be some one for me," he exclaimed, in a puzzled tone. "Whatever can have happened to old Bullsom?"

She looked at him politely bewildered.

"It is the niece of a man whom I know very well in Medchester," he exclaimed. "Something must have happened to her uncle. It is most extraordinary."

CHAPTER XVIII
MARY SCOTT PAYS AN UNEXPECTED CALL

Brooks met the butler entering the room with a card upon his salver. He stretched out his hand for it mechanically, but the man only regarded him in mild surprise. "For his lordship, sir. Excuse me."

The man passed on. Brooks remained bewildered. Lord Arranmore took the card from the tray and examined it leisurely.

"Miss Mary Scott," he repeated aloud. "Are you sure that the young lady asked to see me?"

"Quite sure, your lordship," the servant answered.

"Scott. The name sounds familiar, somehow!" Lord Arranmore said. "Haven't I heard you mention it, Brooks?"

"Miss Scott is the niece of Mr. Bullsom, one of my best clients, a large builder in Medchester," Brooks answered. "Why?"

He stopped suddenly short. Arranmore glanced towards him in polite unconcern.

"You saw her with me at Mellon's, in Medchester. You asked me her name."

Lord Arranmore bent the card in his forefinger, and dropped his eyeglass.

"So that is the young lady," he remarked. "I remember her distinctly. But I do not understand what she can want within me. Is she by any chance, Brooks, one of those young persons who go about with a collecting-card—who want money for missions and that sort of thing? If so, I am afraid she has wasted her cab fare."

"She is not in the least that sort of person," Brooks answered, emphatically. "I have no idea what she wants to see you about, but I am convinced that her visit has a legitimate object."

Lord Arranmore stuck the card in his waistcoat pocket and shrugged his shoulders.

"You are my man of affairs, Brooks. I commission you to see her. Find out her business if you can, and don't let me be bothered unless it is necessary."

Brooks hesitated.

"I am not sure that I care to interfere—that my presence might not be likely to cause her embarrassment," he said. "I have seen her lately, and she made no mention of this visit."

Lord Arranmore glanced at him as though surprised. "I should like you to see her," he said, suavely. "It seems to me preferable to asking her to state her business to a servant. If you have any objection to doing so she must be sent back."

Brooks turned unwillingly away. As he had expected, Mary sprang to her feet upon his entrance into the room, and the colour streamed into her cheeks.

"You here!" she exclaimed.

He shook hands with her, and tried to behave as though he thought her presence the most natural thing in the world. "Yes. You see I am Lord Arranmore's man of affairs now, and he keeps me pretty hard at work. He seems to have a constitutional objection to doing anything for himself. He has even sent me to—to—"

"I understand," she interrupted. "To ascertain my business. Well, I can't tell it even to you. It is Lord Arranmore whom I want to see. No one else will do."

Brooks leaned against the table and looked at her with a puzzled smile.

"You see, it's a little awkward, isn't it?" he declared. "Lord Arranmore is very eccentric, and especially so upon this point. He will not see strangers. Write him a line or two and let me take it to him."

She considered for a moment.

"Very well. Give me a piece of paper and an envelope."

She wrote a single line only. Brooks took it back into the great inner hall, where Lord Arranmore had started another game of billiards with Lady Caroom.

"Miss Scott assured me that her business with you is private," he announced. "She has written this note."

Lord Arranmore laid his cue deliberately aside and broke the seal. It was evident that the contents of the note consisted of a few words only, yet after once perusing them he moved a little closer to the light and re-read them slowly. Then with a little sigh he folded the note in the smallest possible compass and thrust it into his waistcoat pocket.

"Your young friend, my dear Brooks," he said, taking up his cue, "does me the honour to mistake me for some one else. Will you inform her that I have no knowledge of the person to whom she alludes, and suggest—as delicately as you choose—that as she is mistaken an interview is unnecessary. It is, I believe, my turn, Catherine." "You decline, then, to see her?" Brooks said.

Lord Arranmore turned upon him with a rare irritation.

"Have I not made myself clear, Brooks?" he said. "If I were to keep open house to all the young women who choose to claim acquaintance with me I should scarcely have a moment to call my own, or a house fit to ask my friends to visit. Be so good as to make my answer sufficiently explicit."

"It is unnecessary, Lord Arranmore. I have come to ask you for it yourself."

They all turned round. Mary Scott was coming slowly towards them across the thick rugs, into which her feet sunk noiselessly. Her face was very pale, and her large eyes were full of nervous apprehension. But about her mouth were certain rigid lines which spoke of determination.

Sybil leaned forward from her chair, and Lady Caroom watched her approach with lifted eyebrows and a stare of well-bred and languid insolence. Lord Arranmore laid down his cue and rose at once to meet her.

"You are Lord Arranmore," she said, looking at him fixedly. "Will you please answer the question—in my note?"

He bowed a little coldly, but he made no remark as to her intrusion. "I have already," he said, "given my answer to Mr. Brooks. The name which you mention is altogether unknown to me, nor have I ever visited the place you speak of. You have apparently been misled by a chance likeness."

"It is a very wonderful one," she said, slowly, keeping her eyes fixed upon him.

He shrugged his shoulders.

"I regret," he said, "that you should have had your journey for nothing. I can, I presume, be of no further use to you."

"I do not regret my journey here," she answered. "I could not rest until I had seen you closely, face to face, and asked you that question. You deny then that you were ever called Philip Ferringshaw?"

"Most assuredly," he answered, curtly.

"That is very strange," she said.

"Strange?"

"Yes. It is very strange because I am perfectly certain that you were."

He took up his cue and commenced chalking it in a leisurely manner.

"My dear young lady," he said, "you are; I understand, a friend of Mr. Brooks, and are therefore entitled to some amount of consideration from me. But I must respectfully remind you that your presence here is, to put it mildly, unsought, and that I do not find it pleasant to be called a liar under my own roof and before my friends."

"Pleasant!" she eyed him scornfully; "nor did my father find it pleasant to be ruined and murdered by you, a debauched gambler, a common swindler."

Lord Arranmore, unruffled, permitted himself to smile.

"Dear me," he said, "this is getting positively melodramatic. Brooks, for her own sake, let me beg of you to induce the young woman to leave us. In her calmer moments she will, I am sure, repent of these unwarranted statements to a perfect stranger."

Brooks was numbed—for the moment speechless. Sybil had risen to her feet as though with the intention of leaving the room. But Lord Arranmore interposed. If he were acting it was marvellously done.

"I beg," he said, "that you will none of you desert me. These accusations of—Miss Scott, I believe are unnerving. A murderer, a swindler and a rogue are hard names, young lady. May I ask if your string of invectives is exhausted, or is there any further abuse which you feel inclined to heap upon me?"

The girl never flinched.

"I have called you nothing," she said, "which you do not deserve. Do you still deny that you were in Canada—in Montreal—sixteen years ago?"

"Most assuredly I do deny it," he answered.

Brooks started, and turned suddenly towards Lord Arranmore as though doubtful whether he had heard rightly. This was a year before his father's death. The girl was unmoved.

"I see that I should come here with proofs," she exclaimed. "Well, they are easy enough to collect. You shall have them. But before I go, Lord Arranmore, let me ask you if you know who I am."

"I understand," Lord Arranmore answered, "that you are the daughter or niece of a highly respectable tradesman in Medchester, who is a client of our young friend here, Mr. Brooks. Let me tell you, young lady, that but for that fact I should not—tolerate your presence here."

"I am Mr. Bullsom's niece," the girl answered, "but I am the daughter of Martin Scott Cartnell!"

It seemed to Brooks that a smothered exclamation of some sort broke from Lord Arranmore's tightly compressed lips, but his face was so completely in the shadow that its expression was lost. But he himself now revealed it, for touching a knob in the wall a shower of electric lamps suddenly glowed around the room. He leaned forward and looked intently into the face of the girl who had become his accuser. She met his gaze coldly, without flinching, the pallor of her cheeks relieved by a single spot of burning colour, her eyes bright with purpose.

"It is incredible," he said, softly, "but it is true. You are the untidy little thing with a pigtail who used always to be playing games with the boys when you ought to have been at school. Come, I am glad to see you. Why do you come to me like a Cassandra of the Family Herald? Your father was my companion for a while, but we were never intimate. I certainly neither robbed nor murdered him."

"You did both," she answered, fiercely. "You were his evil genius from the first. It was through you he took to drink, through you he became a gambler. You encouraged him to play for stakes larger than he could afford. You won money from him which you knew was not his to lose. He came to you for help. You laughed at him. That night he shot himself."

"It was," Lord Arranmore remarked, "a very foolish thing to do."

"Who or what you were before you came to Montreal I do not know," she continued, "but there you brought misery and ruin upon every one connected with you. I was a child in those days, but I remember how you were hated. You broke the heart of Durran Lapage, an honest man whom you called your friend, and you left his wife to starve in a common lodging house. There was never a man or woman who showed you kindness that did not live to regret it. You may be the Marquis of Arranmore now, but you have left a life behind the memory of which should be a constant torture to you."

"Have you finished, young lady?" he asked, coldly.

"Yes, I have finished," she answered. "I pray Heaven that the next time we meet may be in the police-court. The police of Montreal are still looking for Philip Ferringshaw, and they will find in me a very ready witness."

"Upon my word, this is a most unpleasant young person," Lord Arranmore said. "Brooks, do see her off the premises before she changes her mind and comes for me again. You have, I hope, been entertained, ladies," he added, turning to Sybil and Lady Caroom.

He eyed them carelessly enough to all appearance, yet with an inward searchingness which seemed to find what it feared. He turned to Brooks, but he and Mary Scott had left the room together.

"The girl—was terribly in earnest," Lady Caroom said, with averted eyes. "Were you not—a little cruel to her, Arranmore? Not that I believe these horrid things, of course. But she did. She was honest."

Lord Arranmore shrugged his shoulders. He was looking out of the window, out into the grey windy darkness, listening to the raindrops splashing against the window-pane, wondering how long Brooks would be, and if in his face too he should see the shadow, and it seemed to him that Brooks lingered a very long time.

"Shall we finish our game of billiards, Catherine?" he asked, turning towards her.

"Well—I think not," she answered. "I am a little tired, and it is almost time the dressing bell rang. I think Sybil and I will go up-stairs."

They passed away—he made no effort to detain them. He lit a cigarette, and paced the room impatiently. At last he rang the bell.

"Where is Mr. Brooks?" he asked.

"Mr. Brooks has only just returned, my lord," the man answered. "He went some distance with the young lady. He has gone direct to his room."

Lord Arranmore nodded. He threw himself into his easy-chair, and his head sank upon his hand. He looked steadfastly into the heart of the red coals.

CHAPTER XIX
THE MARQUIS MEPHISTOPHELES

"I am so sorry," she said, softly, "our last evening is spoilt."

He shook his head with an effort at gaiety.

"Let us conspire," he said. "You and I at least will make a struggle."

"I am afraid," she said, "that it would be hopeless. Mother is an absolute wreck, and I saw Lord Arranmore go into the library just now with that terrible white look under his eyes. I saw it once before. Ugh!"

"After all," he said, "it only means that we shall be honest. Cheerfulness to-night could only be forced."

She laughed softly into his eyes.

"How correct!" she murmured. "You are improving fast."

He turned and looked at her, slim and graceful in her white muslin gown, her fair hair brushed back from her forehead with a slight wave, but drooping low over her ears, a delicate setting for her piquant face. The dark brown eyes, narrowing a little towards the lids, met his with frank kindliness, her mouth quivered a little as though with the desire to break away into a laugh. The slight duskiness of her cheeks—she had lived for three years in Italy and never worn a veil—pleased him better than the insipidity of pink and white, and the absence of jewelry—she wore neither bracelet nor rings gave her an added touch of distinction, which restless youth finds something so much harder to wear than sedate middle age. The admiration grew in his eyes. She was charming.

The lips broke away at last.

"After all," she murmured, "I think that I shall enjoy myself this evening. You are looking all sorts of nice things at me."

"My eyes," he answered, "are more daring than my lips."

"And you call yourself a lawyer?"

"Is that a challenge? Well, I was thinking that you looked charming."

"Is that all? I have a looking-glass, you know."

"And I shall miss you—very much."

She suddenly avoided his eyes, but it was for a second only. Yet Brooks was himself conscious of the significance of that second. He set his teeth hard.

"The days here," he said, slowly, "have been very pleasant. It has all been—such a different life for me. A few months ago I knew no one except a few of the Medchester people, and was working hard to make a modest living. Sometimes I feel here as though I were a modern Aladdin. There is a sense of unreality about Lord Arranmore's extraordinary kindness to me. To-night, more than ever, I cannot help feeling that it is something like a dream which may pass away at any moment."

She looked at him thoughtfully.

"Lord Arranmore is not an impulsive person," she said. "He must have had some reason for being so decent to you."

"Yes, as regards the management of his affairs perhaps," Brooks answered. "But why he should ask me here, and treat me as though I were his social equal and all that sort of thing—well, you know that is a puzzle, isn't it?"

"Well, I don't know," she answered. "Lord Arranmore is not exactly the man to be a slave to, or even to respect, the conventional, and your being—what you are, naturally makes you a pleasant companion to him—and his guests. No, I don't think that it is strange."

"You are very flattering," he said, smiling.

"Not in the least," she assured him. "Now-a-days birth seems to be rather a handicap than otherwise to the making of the right sort of people. I am sure there are more impossibilities in the peerage than in the nouveaux riches. I know heaps of people who because their names are in Debrett seem to think that manners are unnecessary, and that they have a sort of God-sent title to gentility."

Brooks laughed.

"Why," he said, "you are more than half a Radical."

"It is your influence," she said, demurely.

"It will soon pass away," he sighed. "To-morrow you will be back again amongst your friends."

She sighed.

"Why do one's friends bore one so much more than other people's?" she exclaimed.

"When one thinks of it," he remarked, "you must have been very bored here. Why, for the last fortnight there have been no other visitors in the house."

"There have been compensations," she said.

"Tell me about them!" he begged.

She laughed up at him.

"If I were to say the occasional visits of Mr. Kingston Brooks, would you be conceited?"

"It would be like putting my vanity in a hothouse," he answered, "but I would try and bear it."

"Well, I will say it, then!"

He turned and looked at her with a sudden seriousness. Some consciousness of the change in his mood seemed to be at once communicated to her. Her eyes no longer met his. She moved a little on one side and took up an ornament from an ormolu table.

"I wish that you meant it," he murmured.

"I do!" she whispered, almost under her breath.

Brooks suddenly forgot many things, but Nemesis intervened. There was the sound of much rustling of silken skirts, and—Lady Caroom's poodle, followed by herself, came round the angle of the drawing-room.

"My dear Sybil," she exclaimed, "do come and tie Balfour's ribbon for me. Marie has no idea of making a bow spread itself out, and pink is so becoming to him. Thanks, dear. Where is our host? I thought that I was late."

Lord Arranmore entered as she spoke. His evening dress, as usual, was of the most severely simple type. To-night its sombreness was impressive. With such a background his pallor seemed almost waxen-like. He offered his arm to Lady Caroom.

"I was not sure," he said, with a lightness which seemed natural enough, "whether to-night I might not have to dine alone whilst you poor people sat and played havoc with the shreds of my reputation. Groves, the cabinet Johannesburg and the '84 Heidsieck—though I am afraid," he added, looking down at his companion, "that not all the wine in my cellar could make this feast of farewells a cheerful one."

"Farewell celebrations of all sorts are such a mistake," Lady Caroom murmured. "We have been so happy here too."

"You brought the happiness with you," Lord Arranmore said, "and you take it away with you. Enton will be a very dull place when you are gone."

"Your own stay here is nearly up, is it not?" Lady Caroom asked. "Very nearly. I expect to go to Paris next week—at latest the week after, in time at any rate for Bernhardt's new play. So I suppose we shall soon all be scattered over the face of the earth."

"Except me," Brooks interposed, ruefully. "I shall be the one who will do the vegetating."

Lady Caroom laughed softly.

"Foolish person! You will be within two hours of London. You none of you have the slightest idea as to the sort of place we are going to. We are a day's journey from anywhere. The morning papers are twenty-four hours late. The men drink port wine, and the women sit round the fire in the drawing-room after dinner and wait—and wait—and wait. Oh, that awful waiting. I know it so well. And it isn't much better when the men do come. They play whist instead of bridge, and a woman in the billiard-room is a lost soul. Our hostess always hides my cue directly I arrive, and pretends that it has been lost. By the bye, what a dear little room this is, Arranmore. We haven't dined here before, have we?"

Lord Arranmore shook his head. He held up his wineglass thoughtfully as though criticizing the clearness of the amber fluid.

"No!" he said. "I ordered dinner to be served in here because over our dessert I propose to offer you a novel form of entertainment."

"How wonderful," Sybil said. "Will it be very engrossing? Will it help us to forget?"

He looked at her with a smile.

"That depends," he said, "how anxious you are to forget."

She looked hastily away. For a moment Brooks met her eyes, and his heart gave an unusual leap. Lady Caroom watched them both thoughtfully, and then turned to their host.

"You have excited our curiosity, Arranmore. You surely don't propose to keep us on tenterhooks all through dinner?"

"It will give a fillip to your appetite."

"My appetite needs no fillip. It is disgraceful to try and make me eat more than I do already. I am getting hideously stout. I found my maid in tears to-night because I positively could not get into my most becoming bodice."

"If you possess a more becoming one than this," Lord Arranmore said, with a bow, "it is well for our peace of mind that you cannot wear it."

"That is a very pretty subterfuge, but a subterfuge it remains," Lady Caroom answered. "Now be candid. I love candour. What are you going to do to amuse us?"

He shook his head.

"Do not spoil my effect. The slightest hint would make everything seem tame. Brooks, I insist upon it that you try my Johannesburg. It was given to my grandfather by the Grand Duke of Shleistein. Groves!"

Brooks submitted willingly enough, for the wine was wonderful. Sybil leaned over so that their heads almost touched.

"Look at our host," she whispered. "What does he remind you of?"

Brooks glanced across the table, brilliant with its burden of old silver, of cut-glass and hothouse flowers. Lord Arranmore's face, notwithstanding his ready flow of conversation, seemed unusually still and white—the skin drawn across the bones, even the lips pallid. The sombreness of his costume, the glitter in his eyes, the icy coldness of his lack of coloring, though time after time he set down his wineglass empty, were curiously impressive. Brooks looked back into her face, his eyes full of question.

"Mephistopheles," she whispered. "He is absolutely weird to-night. If he sat and looked at me and we were alone I should shriek."

Lord Arranmore lifted a glass of champagne to the level of his head and looked thoughtfully around the table.

"Come," he said, "a toast-to ourselves. Singly? Collectively. Lady Caroom, I drink to the delightful memories with which you have peopled Enton. Sybil, may you charm society as your mother has done. Brooks, your very good health. May your entertainment this evening be a welcome one.

"We will drink to all those things," Lady Caroom declared, "with enthusiasm. But I am afraid your good wishes for Sybil are beyond any hope of realization. She is far too honest to flourish in society. She will probably marry a Bishop or a Cabinet Minister, and become engrossed in theology or politics. You know how limiting that sort of thing is. I am in deadly fear that she may become humdrum. A woman who really studies or knows anything about anything can never be a really brilliant woman."

"You—"

"Oh, I pass for being intelligent because I parade my ignorance so, just as Sophie Mills is considered a paragon of morality because she is always talking about running off with one of the boys in her husband's regiment. It is a gigantic bluff, you know, but it comes off. Most bluffs do come off if one is only daring enough."

"You must tell them that up at Redcliffe," Lord Arranmore remarked.

Sybil laughed heartily.

"Redcliffe is the one place where mother is dumb," she declared. "Up there they look upon her as a stupid but well-meaning person. She is absolutely afraid to open her mouth."

"They are so absurdly literal," Lady Caroom sighed, helping herself to an infinitesimal portion of a wonderful savoury. "Don't talk about the place. I know I shall have an attack of nerves there."

"Mother always gets nerves if she mayn't talk," Sybil murmured.

"You're an undutiful daughter," Lady Caroom declared. "If I do talk I never say anything, so nobody need listen unless they like. About this entertainment, Arranmore. Are you going to make the wineglass disappear and the apples fly about the room a la Maskelyne and Cook? I hope our share in it consists in sitting down."

Arranmore turned to the butler behind his chair.

"Have coffee and liqueur served here, Groves, and bring some cigarettes. Then you can send the servants away and leave us alone."

The man bowed.

"Very good, your lordship."

Lord Arranmore looked around at his guests.

"The entertainment," he said, "will incur no greater hardship upon you than a little patience. I am going to tell you a story."

CHAPTER XX
THE CONFIDENCE OF LORD ARRANMORE

The servants had left the room, and the doors were fast closed. Lord Arranmore sat a little forward in his high-backed chair, one hand grasping the arm, the other stretched flat upon the table before him. By his side, neglected, was a cedar-wood box of his favourite cigarettes.

"I am going," he said, thoughtfully, "to tell you a story, of whom the hero is—myself. A poor sort of entertainment perhaps, but then there is a little tragedy and a little comedy in what I have to tell. And you three are the three people in the world to whom certain things were better told."

They bent forward, fascinated by the cold directness of his speech, by the suggestion of strange things to come. The mask of their late gaiety had fallen away. Lady Caroom, grave and sad-eyed, was listening with an anxiety wholly unconcealed. Under the shaded lamplight their faces, dominated by that cold masterly figure at the head of the table, were almost Rembrandtesque.

"You have heard a string of incoherent but sufficiently damaging accusations made against me to-day by a young lady whose very existence, I may say, was a surprise to me. It suited me then to deny them. Nevertheless they were in the main true."

The announcement was no shock. Every one of the three curiously enough had believed the girl.

"I must go a little further back than the time of which she spoke. At twenty-six years old I was an idle young man of good family, but scant expectations, supposed to be studying at the Bar, but in reality idling my time about town. In those days, Lady Caroom, you had some knowledge of me."

"Up to the time of your disappearance—yes. I remember, Arranmore," she continued, her manner losing for a moment some of its restraint, and her eyes and tone suddenly softening, "dancing with you that evening. We arranged to meet at Ranelagh the next day, and, when the next day came, you had vanished, gone as completely as though the earth had swallowed you up. For weeks every one was asking what has become of him. And then—I suppose you were forgotten."

"This," Lord Arranmore continued, "is the hardest part of my narrative, the hardest because the most difficult to make you understand. You will forgive my offering you the bare facts only. I will remind you that I was young, impressionable, and had views. So to continue!"

The manner of his speech was in its way chillingly impressive. He was still sitting in exactly the same position, one hand upon the arm of his high-backed chair, the other upon the table before him. He made use of no gestures, his face remained as white and emotionless as a carved image, his tone, though clear and low, was absolutely monotonous. But there was about him a subtle sense of repression apparent to all of them.

"On my way home that night my hansom knocked down an old man. He was not seriously hurt, and I drove him home. On the way he stared at me curiously. Every now and then he laughed—unpleasantly.

"'I have never seen any one out of your world before,' he said. 'I dare say you have never spoken to any one out of mine except to toss us alms. Come and see where I live.'

"He insisted, and I went. I found myself in a lodging-house, now pulled down and replaced by one of Lord Rowton's tenement houses. I saw a hundred human beings more or less huddled together promiscuously, and the face of every one of them was like the face of a rat. The old man dragged me from room to room, laughing all the time. He showed me children herded together without distinction of sex or clothing, here and there he pointed to a face where some apprehension of the light was fighting a losing battle with the ghouls of disease, of vice, of foul air, of filth. I was faint and giddy when we had looked over that one house, but the old man was not satisfied. He dragged me on to the roof and pointed eastwards. There, as far as the eyes could reach, was a blackened wilderness of smoke-begrimed dwellings. He looked at me and grinned. I can see him now. He had only one tooth, a blackened yellow stump, and every time he opened his mouth to laugh he was nearly choked with coughing. He leaned out over the palisading and reached with both his arms eastward. 'There,' he cried, frantically, 'you have seen one. There are thousands and tens of thousands of houses like this, a million crawling vermin who were born into the world in your likeness, as you were born, my fine gentleman. Day by day they wake in their holes, fill their lungs with foul air, their stomachs with rotten food, break their backs and their hearts over some hideous task. Every day they drop a little lower down. Drink alone keeps them alive, stirs their blood now and then so that they can feel their pulses beat, brings them a blessed stupor. And see over there the sun, God's sun, rises every morning, over them and you. Young man! You see those flaming spots of light? They are gin-palaces. You may thank your God for them, for they alone keep this horde of rotten humanity from sweeping westwards, breaking up your fine houses, emptying your wine into the street, tearing the silk and laces from your beautiful soft-limbed women. Bah! But you have read. It would be the French Revolution over again. Oh, but you are wise, you in the West, your statesmen and your philanthropists, that you build these gin-palaces, and smile, and rub your hands and build more and spend the money gaily. You build the one dam which can keep back your retribution. You keep them stupefied, you cheapen the vile liquor and hold it to their noses. So they drink, and you live. But a day of light may come.'"

Lord Arranmore ceased speaking, stretched out his hand and helped himself to wine with unfaltering fingers.

"I have tried," he continued, "to repeat the exact words which the old man used to me, and I do not find it so difficult as you might imagine, because at that time they made a great impression upon me. But I cannot, of course, hope to reproduce to you his terrible earnestness, the burning passion with which every word seemed to spring from his lips. Their effect upon me at that time you will be able to judge when I tell you this—that I never returned to my rooms, that for ten years I never set foot west of Temple Bar. I first joined a small society in Whitechapel, then I worked for myself, and finally I became a police-court missionary at Southwark Police-Court. The history of those years is the history of a slowly-growing madness. I commenced by trying to improve whole districts-I ended with the individual."

Brooks' wineglass fell with a little crash upon the tablecloth. The wine, a long silky stream, flowed away from him unstaunched, unregarded. His eyes were fixed upon Lord Arranmore. He leaned forward.

"A police-court missionary!" he cried, hoarsely.

Lord Arranmore regarded him for a moment in silence.

"Yes. As you doubtless surmise, I am your father. Afterwards you may ask me questions."

Brooks sat as one stupefied, and then a sudden warm touch upon his hand sent the blood coursing once more through his veins. Sybil's fingers lay for a moment upon his. She smiled kindly at him. Lord Arranmore's voice once more broke the short silence.

"The individual was my greatest disappointment," he continued. "Young and old, all were the same. I took them to live with me, I sent them abroad, I found them situations in this country, I talked with them, read with them, showed them the simplest means within their reach by means of which they might take into their lives a certain measure of beautiful things. Failure would only make me more dogged, more eager. I would spend months sometimes with one man or boy, and at last I would assure myself of success. I would find them a situation, see them perhaps once a week, then less often, and the end was always the same. They fell back. I had put the poison to sleep, but it was always there. It was their everlasting heritage, a gift from father to son, bred in the bone, a part of their blood.

"In those days I married a lady devoted to charitable works. Our purpose was to work together, but we found it impracticable. There was, I fear, little sympathy between us. The only bond was our work—and that was soon to be broken. For there came a time, after ten breathless years, when I paused to consider."

He raised his glass to his lips and drained it. The wine was powerful, but it brought no tinge of colour to his cheeks, nor any lustre to his eyes. He continued in the same firm, expressionless tone.

"There came a night when I found myself thinking, and I knew then that a new terror was stealing into my life. I made my way up to the roof of the house where that old man had first taken me, and I leaned once more over the palisading and looked eastwards. I fancied that I could still hear the echoes of his frenzied words, and for the first time I heard the note of mockery ringing clearly through them. There they stretched—the same blackened wilderness of roofs sheltering the same horde of drinking, filthy, cursing, parasitical creatures; there flared the gin-palaces, more of them, more brilliantly lit, more gorgeously decorated. Ten years of my life, and what had I done? What could any one do? The truth seemed suddenly written across the sky in letters of fire. I, a poor human creature, had been fighting with a few other fanatics against the inviolable, the unconquerable laws of nature. The hideous mistake of all individual effort was suddenly revealed to me. 'We were like a handful of children striving to dam a mighty torrent with a few handfuls of clay. Better a thousand times that these people rotted—and died in their holes, that disease should stalk through their streets, and all the evil passions born of their misery and filth should be allowed to blaze forth that the whole world might see, so the laws of the world might intervene, the great natural laws by which alone these things could be changed. I looked down at myself, then wasted to the bone, a stranger to the taste of wine or tobacco, to all the joys of life, a miserable heart-broken wretch, and I cursed that old man and the thought of him till my lips were dry and my throat ached. I walked back to my miserable dwelling with a red fire before my eyes, muttering, cursing that power which stood behind the universe, and which we call God, that there should be vomited forth into the world day by day, hour by hour, this black stream of human wretchedness, an everlasting mockery to those who would seek for the joy of life.

"They took me to the hospital, and they called my illness brain-fever. But long before they thought me convalescent I was conscious, lying awake and plotting my escape. With cunning I managed it. Of my wife and child I never once thought. Every trace of human affection seemed withered up in my heart. I took the money subscribed for me with a hypocrite's smile, and I slunk away from England. I went to Montreal in Canada, and I deliberately entered upon a life of low pleasures. Pardon me!"

He bent forward and with a steady hand readjusted the shade of a lamp which was in danger of burning. Lady Caroom leaned back in her chair with an indrawn sobbing breath. The action at such a moment seemed grotesque. His own coolness, whilst with steady fingers he probed away amongst the wounded places of his life, was in itself gruesome.

"My money," he continued, "was no large sum, but I eked it out with gambling. The luck was always on my side. It's quite true that I ruined the father of the young lady who paid me a visit to-day. After a somewhat chequered career he was settling down in a merchant's office in Montreal when I met him. His luck at cards was as bad as mine was good. I won all he had, and more. I believe that he committed suicide. A man there was kind to me, asked me to his house—I persuaded his wife to run away with me. These are amongst the slightest of my delinquencies. I steeped myself in sin. I revelled in it. I seemed to myself in some way to be showing my defiance for the hidden powers of life which I had cursed. I played a match with evil by day and by night until I was glutted. And then I stole away from the city, leaving behind a hideous reputation and not a single friend. Then a new mood came to me. I wanted to get to a place where I should see no human beings at all, and escape in that way from the memories which were still like a clot upon my brain. So I set my face westwards. I travelled till at last civilization lay behind. Still I pushed onward. I had stores in plenty, an Indian servant who chanced to be faithful, and whom I saw but twice a day. At last I reached Lake Ono. Here between us we built a hut. I sent my Indian away then, and when he fawned at my feet to stay I kicked him. This was my third phase of living, and it was true that some measure of sanity came back to me. Oh, the blessed relief of seeing the face of neither man nor woman. It was the unpeopled world of Nature— uncorrupted, fresh, magnificent, alive by day and by night with everlasting music of Nature. The solitudes of those great forests were like a wonderful balm. So the fevers were purged out of me, and I became once more an ordinary human being. I was content, I think, to die there, for I had plenty to eat and drink, and the animals and birds who came to me morning and evening kept me from even the thought of loneliness. The rest is obvious. I lost two cousins in South Africa, an uncle in the hunting-field. A man in Montreal had recognized me. I was discovered. But before I returned I killed Brooks, the police-court missionary. This girl has forced me to bring him to life again."

It was a strange silence which followed. Brooks sat back in his chair, pale, bewildered, striving to focus this story properly, to attain a proper comprehension of these new strange things. And behind all there smouldered the slow burning anger of the child who has looked into the face of a deserted mother. Lady Caroom was white to the lips, and in her eyes the horror of that story so pitilessly told seemed still to linger.

Lord Arranmore spoke again. Still he sat back in his high-backed chair, and still he spoke in measured, monotonous tones. But this time, if only their ears had been quick enough to notice it, there lay behind an emotion, held in check indeed, but every now and then quivering for expression. He had turned to Lady Caroom.

"Chance," he said, "has brought together here at the moment when the telling of these things has become a necessity, the two people who have in a sense some right to hear them, for from each I have much to ask. Sybil is your daughter, and from her there need be no secrets. So, Catherine, I ask you again, now that you know everything, are you brave enough to be my wife?"

She raised her eyes, and he saw the horror there. But he made no sign. She rose and held out her hand for Sybil.

"Arranmore," she said, "I am afraid."

He looked down upon his plate.

"So let it be, then," he said. "It would need a brave woman indeed to join her lot with mine after the things which I have told you. At heart, Catherine, I am almost a dead man. Believe me, you are wise."

He rose, and the two women passed from the room. Then he resumed his former seat, and attitude, and Brooks, though he tried to speak, felt his tongue cleave to the roof of his mouth, a dry and nerveless thing.

For in these doings there was tragedy.

"There remains to me you, Philip Kingston, my son," Lord Arranmore said, in the same measured tone. "You also have before you the story of my life, you are able from it to form some sort of idea as to what my future is likely to be. I do not wish to deceive you. My early enthusiasms are extinct. I look upon the ten or twenty years or so which may be left to me of life as merely a space of time to be filled with as many amusements and new sensations as may be procurable without undue effort. I have no wish to convert, or perhaps pervert you, to my way of thinking. You live still in Utopia, and to me Utopia does not exist. So make your choice deliberately. Do you care to come to me?"

Then Brooks found words of a sort.

"Lord Arranmore," he said, "forgive me if what I must say sounds undutiful. I know that you have suffered. I can realize something of what you have been through. But your desertion of my mother and me was a brutality. What you call your creed of life sounds to me hideous. You and I are far apart, and so far as I am concerned, God grant that we may remain so."

For the first time Lord Arranmore smiled. He poured out with steady hand yet another glass of wine, and he nodded towards the door.

"I am obliged to you," he said, "for your candour. I have met with enough hypocrisy in life to be able to appreciate it. Be so good as to humour my whim—and to leave me alone."

Brooks rose from his seat, hesitated for a single moment, and left the room. Lord Arranmore leaned back in his high-backed chair and looked round at the empty places. The cigarette burned out between his fingers, his wine remained untasted. The evening's entertainment was over.

PART II

CHAPTER I
LORD ARRANMORE'S AMUSEMENTS

"The domestic virtues," Lord Arranmore said softly to himself, "being denied to me, the question remains how to pass one's time."

He rose wearily from his seat, and walking to the window looked out upon St. James's Square. A soft rain hung about the lamp-posts, the pavements were thick with umbrellas. He returned to his chair with a shrug of the shoulders.

"The only elucidation from outside seems to be a change of climate," he mused. "I should prefer to think of something more original. In the meantime I will write to that misguided young man in Medchester."

He drew paper and pen towards him and began to write. Even his handwriting seemed a part of the man—cold, shapely, and deliberate.

"My DEAR BROOKS,

"I have been made acquainted through Mr. Ascough with your desire to leave the new firm of Morrison and Brooks, and while I congratulate you very much upon the fact itself, I regret equally the course of reasoning which I presume led to your decision. You will probably have heard from Mr. Ascough by this time on a matter of business. You are, by birth, Lord Kingston of Ross, and the possessor of the Kingston income, which amounts to a little over two thousand a year. Please remember that this comes to you not through any grace or favour of mine, but by your own unalienable right as the eldest son of the Marquis of Arranmore. I cannot give it to you. I cannot withhold it from you. If you refuse to take it the amount must accumulate for your heirs, or in due time find its way to the Crown. Leave the tithe alone by all means, if you like, but do not carry quixotism to the borders of insanity by declining to spend your own money, and thereby cramp your life.

"I trust to hear from Mr. Ascough of your more reasonable frame of mind, and while personally I agree with you that we are better apart, you can always rely upon me if I can be of any service to you.

"Yours sincerely,

"ARRANMORE."

He read the letter through thoughtfully and folded it up.

"I really don't see what the young fool can kick about in that," he said, throwing it into the basket. "Well, Hennibul, how are you?"

Mr. Hennibul, duly ushered in by a sedate butler, pronounced himself both in words and appearance fit and well. He took a chair and a cigarette, and looked about him approvingly.

"Nice house, yours, Arranmore. Nice old-fashioned situation, too. Why don't you entertain?"

"No friends, no inclination, no womankind!"

Mr. Hennibul smiled incredulously.

"Your card plate is chock-full," he said, "and there are a dozen women in town at least of your connections who'd do the polite things by you. As to inclination—well, one must do something."

"That's about the most sensible thing you have said, Hennibul," Arranmore remarked. "I've just evoked the same fact out of my own consciousness. One must do something. It's tiresome, but it's quite true." Politics?

"Hate 'em! Not worth while anyway."

"Travel."

"Done all I want for a bit, but I keep that in reserve.

"Hunt."

"Bad leg, but I do a bit at it."

"Society."

"Sooner go on the County Council."

"City."

"Too much money already."

"Write a book." "No one would read it."

"Start a magazine."

"Too hard work."

Mr. Hennibul sighed.

"You're rather a difficult case," he admitted. "You'd better come round to the club and play bridge."

"I never played whist—and I'm bad-tempered."

"Bit of everything then."

Lord Arranmore smiled.

"That's what it'll end in, I suppose."

"Pleasant times we had down at Enton," Mr. Hennibul remarked. "How's the nice young lawyer—Brooks his name was, I think?"

"All right, I believe."

"And the ladies?

"I believe that they are quite well. They were in Scotland last time I heard of them."

Mr. Hennibul found conversation difficult.

"I saw that you were in Paris the other week," he remarked.

"I went over to see Bernhardt's new play," Arranmore continued.

"Good?"

"It disappointed me. Very likely though the fault was with myself."

Mr. Hennibul looked across at his host shrewdly.

"What did you see me for?" he asked, suddenly. "You're bored to death trying to keep up a conversation."

Lord Arranmore laughed.

"Upon my word, I don't know, Hennibul," he answered. "For the same old reason, I suppose. One must see some one, do something. I thought that you might amuse me."

"And I've failed," Hennibul declared, smiling. "Come to supper at the Savoy to-night. The two new American girls from the Lyric and St. John Lyttleton are to be there. Moderately respectable, I believe, but a bit noisy perhaps."

Arranmore shook his head.

"You're a good fellow, Hennibul," he said, "but I'm too old for that sort of thing."

Hennibul rose to his feet.

"Well," he said, "I've kept the best piece of advice till last because I want you to think of it. Marry!"

Lord Arranmore did not smile. He did not immediately reply.

"You are a bachelor!" he remarked.

"I am a man of a different disposition," Hennibul answered. "I find pleasure in everything—everything amuses me. My work is fascinating, my playtime is never big enough. I really don't know where a wife would come in. However, if ever I did get a bit hipped, find myself in your position, for instance, I can promise you that I'd take my own medicine. I've thought of it more than once lately."

"Perhaps by that time," Lord Arranmore said, "the woman whom you wanted to marry wouldn't have you."

Hennibul looked serious for a moment. A new idea had occurred to him.

"One must take one's chances!" he said.

"You are a philosopher," Arranmore declared. "Will you have some tea—or a whisky-and-soda?"

"Neither, thanks. In an abortive attempt to preserve my youth I neither take tea nor drinks between meals. I will have one of your excellent cigarettes and get round to the club. Why, this is Enton over again, for here comes Molyneux."

The Hon. Sydney Molyneux shook hands with both of them in somewhat dreary fashion, and embarked upon a few disjointed remarks. Hennibul took his leave, and Arranmore yawned openly.

"What is the matter with you, Sydney?" he asked. "You are duller than ever. I am positively not going to sit here and mumble about the weather. How are the Carooms? Have you heard from them lately?"

"They are up in Yorkshire," Molyneux announced, "staying with the Pryce-Powells. I believe they're all right. I'm beastly fit myself, but I had a bit of a facer last week. I—er—I wanted to ask you a question."

"Well?"

"About that fellow Brooks I met at your place down at Enton. Lawyer at Medchester, isn't he? I thought that he and Sybil seemed a bit thick somehow. Don't suppose there could have been anything in it, eh? He's no one in particular, I suppose. Lady Caroom wouldn't be likely to listen to anything between Sybil and him?"

Arranmore raised his eyebrows.

"Brooks is a very intelligent young man," he said, "and some girls are attracted by brains, you know. I don't know anything about his relations with Sybil Caroom, but he has ample private means, and I believe that he is well-born."

"Fellow's a gentleman, of course," Molyneux declared, "but Lady Caroom is a little ambitious, isn't she? I always seemed to be in the running all right lately. I spent last Sunday with them at Chelsom Castle. Awful long way to go, but I'm fond of Sybil. I thought she was a bit cool to me, but, like a fool, I blundered on, and in the end—I got a facer."

"Very sorry for you," Arranmore yawned.

"What made me think about Brooks was that she was awfully decent to me before Enton," Molyneux continued. "I don't mind telling you that I'm hard hit. I want to know who Brooks is. If he's only a country lawyer, he's got no earthly chance with Lady Caroom, and Sybil'd never go against her mother. They're too great pals for that. Never saw them so thick."

"Was Lady Caroom—quite well?" Arranmore asked, irrelevantly.

"Well, now you mention it," Molyneux said, "I don't think she was quite in her usual form. She was much quieter, and it struck me that she was aging a bit. Wonderful woman, though. She and Sybil were quite inseparable at Chelsom—more like sisters than anything, 'pon my word."

Lord Arranmore looked into the fire, and was silent for several minutes.

"So far as regards Brooks," he said, "I do not think that he would be an acceptable son-in-law to Lady Caroom, but I am not in the least sure. He is by no means an insignificant person. If he were really anxious to marry Sybil Caroom, he would be a rival worth consideration. I cannot tell you anything more."

"Much obliged to you I'm sure. I shall try again when they come to town, of course."

Arranmore rose up.

"I am going down to Christie's to see some old French manuscripts," he said. "Is that on your way?"

Molyneux shook his head.

"Going down to the House, thanks," he answered. "I'll look you up again some time, if I may."

They walked out into the street together. Arranmore stepped into his brougham and was driven off. At the top of St. James's Street he pulled the check-string and jumped out. He had caught a glimpse of a girl's face looking into a shop window. He hastily crossed the pavement and accosted her, hat in hand.

"Miss Scott, will you permit me the opportunity of saying a few words to you?"

Mary turned round, speechless for more than a minute or two.

"I will not detain you for more than a minute or two. I hope that you will not refuse me."

"I will listen to anything you have to say, Lord Arranmore," she said, "but let me tell you that I have been to see Mr. Ascough. He told me that he had your permission to explain to me fully the reasons of your coming to Montreal and the story of your life before."

"Well?"

She hesitated. He stood before her, palpably anxiously waiting for her decision.

"I was perhaps wrong to judge so hastily, Lord Arranmore," she said, "and I am inclined to regret my visit to Enton. If you care to know it, I do not harbour any animosity towards you. But I cannot possibly accept this sum of money. I told Mr. Ascough so finally."

"It is only justice, Miss Scott," he said, in a low tone. "I won the money from your father fairly in one sense, but unfairly in another, for I was a good player and he was a very poor one. You will do me a great, an immeasurable kindness, if you will allow me to make this restitution."

She shook her head.

"If my forgiveness is of any value to you, Lord Arranmore," she said, "you may have it. But I cannot accept the money."

"You have consulted no one?"

"No one."

You have a guardian or friends?

"I have been living with my uncle, Mr. Bullsom. He has been very kind to me, and I have—"

"Mary!"

They both turned round. Selina and Mr. Bullsom had issued from the shop before which they stood, Both were looking at Lord Arranmore with curiosity, in Selina's case mixed with suspicion.

"Is this your uncle?" he asked. "Will you introduce me?"

Mary bit her lip.

"Uncle, this is Lord Arranmore," she said. "Mr. Bullsom, my cousin, Miss Bullsom."

Mr. Bullsom retained presence of mind enough to remove a new and very shiny silk hat, and to extend a yellow, dog-skinned gloved hand.

"Very proud to meet your lordship," he declared. "I—I wasn't aware—"

Lord Arranmore extricated his hand from a somewhat close grasp, and bowed to Selina.

"We are neighbours, you know, Mr. Bullsom," he said, "at Medchester. I met your niece there, and recognized her at once, though she was a little slip of a girl when I knew her last. Her father and I were in Montreal together."

"God bless my soul," Mr. Bullsom exclaimed, in much excitement. "It's your lawyers, then, who have been advertising for Mary?"

Lord Arranmore bowed.

"That is so," he admitted. "I am sorry to say that I cannot induce your niece to look upon a certain transaction between her father and myself from a business-like point of view. I think that you and I, Mr. Bullsom, might come to a better understanding. Will you give me an appointment? I should like to discuss the matter with you."

"With the utmost pleasure, my lord," Mr. Bullsom declared heartily. "Can't expect these young ladies to see through a business matter, eh? I will come to your lordship's house whenever you like."

"It would be quite useless, uncle," Mary interposed, firmly. "Lord Arranmore has already my final answer."

Mr. Bullsom was a little excited.

"Tut, tut, child!" he exclaimed. "Don't talk nonsense. I should be proud to talk this matter over with Lord Arranmore. We are staying at the Metropole, and if your lordship would call there to-morrow and take a bit of lunch, eh, about one o'clock—if it isn't too great a liberty."

Selina had never loved her father more sincerely. Lord Arranmore smiled faintly, but good-humoredly.

"You are exceedingly kind," he said. "For our business talk, perhaps, it would be better if you would come to St. James's House at, say, 10:30, if that is convenient. I will send a carriage."

"I'll be ready prompt," Mr. Bullsom declared. "Now, girls, we will say good-afternoon to his lordship and get a four-wheeler."

Selina raised her eyes and dropped them again in the most approved fashion. Mr. Bullsom shook hands as though it were a sacrament; Mary, who was annoyed, did not smile at all.

"This is all quite unnecessary, Lord Arranmore," she said, while her uncle was signalling for a cab. I shall not change my mind, and I am sorry that you spoke to uncle about it at all."

"It is a serious matter to me, Miss Scott," Lord Arranmore said, gravely. "And there is still another point of view from which I might urge it."

"It is wasted time," she declared, firmly.

Selina detached herself from her father, and stood by Lord Arranmore's side.

"I suppose you are often in London, Lord Arranmore?" she asked shyly.

"A great deal too often," he answered.

"We read about your beautiful parties at Enton," she said, with a sigh. "It is such a lovely place."

"I am glad you like it," he answered, absently. "I see your uncle cannot find a four-wheeler. You must take my carriage. I am only going a few steps."

Mary's eager protest was drowned in Selina's shrill torrent of thanks. Lord Arranmore beckoned to his coachman, and the brougham, with its pair of strong horses, drew up against the pavement. The footman threw open the door. Selina entered in a fever for fear a cab which her father was signalling should, after all, respond to his summons. Mr. Bullsom found his breath taken away.

"We couldn't possibly take your lordship's carriage," he protested.

"I have only a few steps to go, Mr. Bullsom, and it would be a kindness, for my horses are never more than half exercised. At 10:30 to-morrow then."

He stood bareheaded upon the pavement for a moment, and Selina's eyes and smile had never worked harder. Mary leaned back, too angry to speak. Selina and Mr. Bullsom sat well forward, and pulled both windows down.

CHAPTER II
THE HECKLING OF HENSLOW

"The long and short of it is, then, Mr. Henslow, that you decline to fulfil your pledges given at the last election?" Brooks asked, coldly.

"Nothing of the sort," Mr. Henslow declared, testily. "You have no right to suggest anything of the sort."

"No right!"

"Certainly not. You are my agent, and you ought to work with me instead—"

"I have already told you," Brooks interrupted, "that I am nothing of the sort. I should not dream of acting for you again, and if you think a formal resignation necessary, I will post you one to-morrow. I am one of your constituents, nothing more or less. But as I am in some measure responsible for your presence here, I consider myself within my rights in asking you these questions."

"I'm not going to be hectored!" Mr. Henslow declared.

"Nobody wants to hector you! You gave certain pledges to us, and you have not fulfilled one of them."

"They won't let me. I'm not here as an independent Member. I'm here as a Liberal, and Sir Henry himself struck out my proposed question and motion. I must go with the Party."

"You know quite well," Brooks said, "that you are within your rights in keeping the pledges you made to the mass meeting at Medchester."

Henslow shook his head.

"It would be no good," he declared. "I've sounded lots of men about it. I myself have not changed. I believe in some measure of protection. I am a firm believer in it. But the House wouldn't listen to me. The times are not ripe for anything of the sort yet."

"How do you know until you try?" Brooks protested. "Your promise was to bring the question before Parliament in connection with the vast and increasing number of unemployed. You are within your rights in doing so, and to speak frankly we insist upon it, or we ask for your resignation."

"Are you speaking with authority, young man?" Mr. Henslow asked.

"Of course I am. I am the representative of the Liberal Parliamentary Committee, and I am empowered to say these things to you, and more.

"Well, I'll do the best I can to get a date," Mr. Henslow said, grumblingly, "but you fellows are always in such a hurry, and you don't understand that it don't go up here. We have to wait our time month after month sometimes."

"I don't see any motion down in your name at all yet," Brooks remarked.

"I told you that Sir Henry struck it through."

"Then I shall call upon him and point out that he is throwing away a Liberal seat at the next election," Brooks replied. "He isn't the sort of man to encourage a Member to break his election pledges."

"You'll make a mess of the whole thing if you do anything of the sort," Henslow declared. "Look here, come and have a bit of dinner with me, and talk things over a bit more pleasantly, eh? There's no use in getting our rags out."

"Please excuse me," Brooks said. "I have arranged to dine elsewhere. I do not wish to seem dictatorial or unreasonable, but I have just come from Medchester, where the distress is, if anything, worse than ever. It makes one's heart sick to walk the streets, and when I look into the people's faces I seem to always hear that great shout of hope and enthusiasm which your speech in the market-place evoked. You see, there is only one real hope for these people, and that is legislation, and you are the man directly responsible to them for that."

"I'll tell you what I'll do!" Mr. Henslow said, in a burst of generosity. "I'll send another ten guineas to the Unemployed Fund."

"Take my advice and don't," Brooks answered, dryly. "They might be reminded of the people who clamoured for bread and were offered a stone. Do your duty here. Keep your pledges. Speak in the House with the same passion and the same eloquence as when you sowed hope in the heart of those suffering thousands. Some one must break away from this musty routine of Party politics. The people will be heard, Mr. Henslow. Their voice has dominated the fate of every nation in time, and it will be so with ours."

Mr. Henslow was silent for a few minutes. This young man who would not drink champagne, or be hail-fellow-well-met, and who was in such deadly earnest, was a nuisance.

"I tell you what I'll do," he said at last. "I'll have a few words with Sir Henry, and see you tomorrow at what time you like."

"Certainly," Brooks answered, rising. "If you will allow me to make a suggestion, Mr. Henslow, I would ask you to run through in your memory all your speeches and go through your pledges one by one. Let Sir Henry understand that your constituents will not be trifled with, for it is not a question of another candidate, it is a question of another party. You have set the ball rolling, and I can assure you that the next Member whom Medchester sends here, whether it be you or any one else, will come fully pledged to a certain measure of Protection."

Mr. Henslow nodded.

"Very well," he said, gloomily. "Where are you staying?"

"At the Metropole. Mr. Bullsom is there also."

"I will call," Mr. Henslow promised, "at three o'clock, if that is convenient."

Brooks passed out across the great courtyard and through the gates. He had gone to his interview with Henslow in a somewhat depressed state of mind, and its result had not been enlivening. Were all politics like this? Was the greatest of causes, the cause of the people, to be tossed about from one to the other, a joke with some, a juggling ball with others, never to be dealt with firmly and wisely by the brains and generosity of the Empire? He looked back at the Houses of Parliament, with their myriad lights, their dark, impressive outline. And for a moment the depression passed away. He thought of the freedom which had been won within those walls, of the gigantic struggles, the endless, restless journeying onward towards the truths, the great truths of the world. All politicians were not as this man Henslow. There were others, more strenuous, more single-hearted. He himself—and his heart beat at the thought—why should he not take his place there? The thought fascinated him,—every word of Lord Arranmore's letter which he had recently received, seemed to stand out before him. His feet fell more blithely upon the pavement, he carried himself with a different air. Here were ample means to fill his life,—means by which he could crush out that sweet but unhappy tangle of memories which somehow or other had stolen the flavour out of life for the last few weeks.

At the hotel he glanced at the clock. It was just eight, and he was to accompany the Bullsoms to the theatre. He met them in the hall, and Selina looked with reproach at his morning clothes. She was wearing a new swansdown theatre cloak, with a collar which she had turned up round her face like a frame. She was convinced that she had never looked so well in her life.

"Mr. Brooks, how naughty of you," she exclaimed, shaking her head in mock reproach. "Why, the play begins at 8:15, and it is eight o'clock already. Have you had dinner?"

"Oh, I can manage with something in my room while I change," he answered cheerily. "I'm going to take you all out to supper after the theatre, you know. Don't wait for me—I'll come on. His Majesty's, isn't it?"

"I'll keep your seat," Selina promised him, lowering her voice. "That is, if you are very good and come before it is half over. Do you know that we met a friend of yours, and he lent us his carriage, and I think he's charming."

Brooks looked surprised. He glanced at Mary, and saw a look in her face which came as a revelation to him.

"You don't mean—"

"Lord Arranmore!" Selina declared, triumphantly. "He was so nice, he wouldn't let us come home in a cab. He positively made us take his own carriage."

Mr. Bullsom came hurrying up.

"Cab waiting," he announced. "Come on, girls."

"See you later, then, Brooks."

Brooks changed his clothes leisurely, and went into the smoking-room for some sandwiches and a glass of wine. A small boy shouting his number attracted his attention. He called him, and was handed a card.

"Lord Arranmore!"

"You can show the gentleman here," Brooks directed.

Arranmore came in, and nodded a little wearily to Brooks, whom he had not seen since the latter had left Enton.

"I won't keep you," he remarked. "I just wanted a word with you about that obstinate young person Miss—er—Scott."

Brooks wheeled an easy-chair towards him.

"I am in no great hurry," he remarked.

Arranmore glanced at the clock.

"More am I," he said, "but I find I am dining with the Prime Minister at nine o'clock. It occurs to me that you may have some influence with her."

"We are on fairly friendly terms," Brooks admitted.

"Just so. Well, she may have told you that my solicitors approached her, as the daughter of Martin Scott, with the offer of a certain sum of money, which is only a fair and reasonable item, which I won from her father at a time when we were not playing on equal terms. It was through that she found me out."

"Yes, I knew as much as that."

"So I imagined. But the hot-headed young woman has up to now steadily refused to accept anything whatever from me. Quite ridiculous of her. There's no doubt that I broke up the happy home, and all that sort of thing, and I really can't see why she shouldn't permit me the opportunity of making some restitution."

"You want her to afford you the luxury of salving your conscience," Brooks remarked, dryly.

Lord Arranmore laughed hardly.

"Conscience," he repeated. "You ought to know me better, Brooks, than to suppose me possessed of such a thing. No; I have a sense of justice, that is all—a sort of weakness for seeing the scales held fairly. Now, don't you think it is reasonable that she should accept this money from me?"

"It depends entirely upon how she feels," Brooks answered. "You have no right to press it upon her if she has scruples. Nor have you any right to try and enlist her family on your side, as you seem to be doing."

Will you discuss it with her?

"I should not attempt to influence her," Brooks answered.

"Be reasonable, Brooks. The money can make no earthly difference to me, and it secures for her independence. The obligation, if only a moral one, is real enough. There is no question of charity. Use your influence with her."

Brooks shook his head.

"I have great confidence in Miss Scott's own judgment," he said. "I prefer not to interfere."

Arranmore sat quite still for a moment. Then he rose slowly to his feet.

"I am sorry to have troubled you," he said. "The world seems to have grown more quixotic since I knew it better. I am almost afraid to ask you whether my last letter has yet received the favour of your consideration."

Brooks flushed a little at the biting sarcasm in Arranmore's tone, but he restrained himself.

"I have considered—the matter fully," he said; "and I have talked it over with Mr. Ascough. There seems to be no reason why I should refuse the income to which I seem to be entitled."

Lord Arranmore nodded and lit a cigarette.

"I am thankful," he said, dryly, "for so much common-sense. Mr. Ascough will put you in possession of a banking account at any moment. Should you consider it—well—intrusive on my part if I were to inquire as to your plans?"

Brooks hesitated.

"They are as yet not wholly formed," he said, "but I am thinking of studying social politics for some time here in London with the intention of entering public life."

"A very laudable ambition," Lord Arranmore answered. "If I can be of any assistance to you, I trust that you will not fail to let me know."

"I thank you," Brooks answered. "I shall not require any assistance from you."

Lord Arranmore winced perceptibly. Brooks, who would not have believed him capable of such a thing, for a moment doubted his eyes.

"I am much obliged for your candour," Lord Arranmore said, coldly, and with complete self-recovery. "Don't trouble to come to the door. Good-evening."

Brooks was alone. He sat down in one of the big easy-chairs, and for a moment forgot that empty stall next to Selina. He had seen the first sign of weakness in a man whom he had judged to be wholly and entirely heartless.

CHAPTER III
MARY SCOTT'S TWO VISITORS

"I AM sure," he said, "that Selina would consider this most improper."

"You are quite right," Mary assured him, laughing. "It was one of the first things she mentioned. When I told her that I should ask any one to tea I liked she was positively indignant."

"It is hard to believe that you are cousins," he remarked.

"We were brought up very differently."

He looked around him. He was in a tiny sitting-room of a tiny flat high up in a great building. Out of the window he seemed to look down upon the Ferris wheel. Inside everything was cramped but cosy. Mary Scott sat behind the tea-tray, and laughed at his expression.

"I will read your thoughts," she exclaimed. "You are wondering how you will get out of this room without knocking anything over."

"On the contrary," he answered, "I was wondering how I ever got in."

"You were really very clever. Now do have some more tea, and tell me all the news."

"I will have the tea, if you please," he answered, "and you shall have the news, such as it is."

"First of all then," she said, "I hear that you are leaving Medchester, giving up your business and coming to live in London, and that you have had some money left you. Do you know that all this sounds very mysterious?"

"I admit it," he answered, slowly stirring his tea. "Yet in the main—it is true."

"How nice to hear all about it," she sighed, contentedly. "You know I have scarcely had a word with you while my uncle and cousins were up. Selina monopolized you most disgracefully."

He looked at her with twinkling eyes.

"Selina was very amusing," he said.

"You seemed to find her so," she answered. "But Selina isn't here now, and you have to entertain me. You are really going to live in London?"

He nodded.

"I have taken rooms!"

"Delightful. Whereabouts?" "In Jermyn Street!"

"And are you going to practise?"

He shook his head.

"No, I shall have enough to live on. I am going to study social subjects and politics generally."

"You are going into Parliament?" she exclaimed, breathlessly.

"Some day, perhaps," he answered, hesitatingly. "If I can find a constituency."

She was silent for a moment.

"Do you know, I think I rather dislike you," she said. "I envy you most hideously."

He laughed.

"What an evil nature!"

"Well, I've never denied it. I'm dreadfully envious of people who have the chance of doing things, whose limitations are not chalked out on the blackboard before them."

"Oh, well, you yourself are not at Medchester now," he reminded her. "You have kicked your own limitation away. Literature is as wide a field as politics."

"That is true enough," she answered. "I must not grumble. After Medchester this is elysium. But literature is a big name to give my little efforts. I'm just a helper on a lady's threepenny paper, and between you and me I don't believe they think much of my work yet."

He laughed.

"Surely they haven't been discouraging you?"

"No, they have been very kind. But they keep on assuring me that I am bound to improve, and the way they use the blue pencil! However, it's only the journalist's part they go for. The little stories are all right still."

"I should think so," he declared, warmly. "I think they are charming."

"How nice you are," she sighed. "No wonder Selina didn't like going home."

He looked at her in amused wonder.

"Do you know," he said, "you are getting positively frivolous. I don't recognize you. I never saw such a change."

She leaned back in her chair, laughing heartily, her eyes bright, her beautiful white teeth in delightful evidence.

"Oh, I suppose it's the sense of freedom," she exclaimed. "It's delightful, isn't it? Medchester had got on my nerves. I hated it. One saw nothing but the ugly side of life, day after day. It was hideously depressing. Here one can breathe. There's room for every one."

"The change agrees with you!"

"Why not. I feel years younger. Think how much there is to do, and see, even for a pauper like myself—picture galleries, the shops, the people, the theatres."

He looked at her thoughtfully.

"Don't think me a prig, will you?" he said, "but I want to understand you. In Medchester you used to work for the people—it was the greater part of your life. You are not giving that up altogether, are you?"

She laughed him to scorn.

"Am I such a butterfly? No, I hope to get some serious work to do, and I am looking forward to it. I have a letter of introduction to a Mrs. Capenhurst, whom I am going to see on Sunday. I expect to learn a lot from her. I was very, very sorry to leave my own girls. It was the only regret I had in leaving Medchester. By the bye, what is this about Mr. Henslow?"

"We are thinking of asking him to resign," Brooks answered. "He has been a terrible disappointment to us."

She nodded.

"I am sorry. From his speeches he seemed such an excellent candidate."

"He was a magnificent candidate," Brooks said ruefully, "but a shocking Member. I am afraid what I heard in the City the other day must have some truth in it. They say that he only wanted to be able to write M.P. after his name for this last session to get on the board of two new companies. He will never sit for Medchester again."

"He was at the hotel the other day, wasn't he?" Mary asked, "with you and uncle? What has he to say for himself?"

"Well, he shelters himself behind the old fudge about duty to his Party," Brooks answered. "You see the Liberals only just scraped in last election because of the war scandals, and their majority is too small for them to care about any of the rank and file introducing any disputative measures. Still that scarcely affects the question. He won his seat on certain definite pledges, and if he persists in his present attitude, we shall ask him at once to resign."

You still keep up your interest in Medchester, then?"

"Why, yes!" he answered. "Between ourselves, if I could choose, I would rather, when the time comes, stand for Medchester than anywhere."

"I am glad! I should like to see you Member for Medchester. Do you know, even now, although I am so happy, I cannot think about the last few months there without a shudder. It seemed to me that things were getting worse and worse. The people's faces haunt me sometimes."

He looked up at her sympathetically.

"If you have once lived with them," he said, "once really understood, you never can forget. You can travel or amuse yourself in any way, but their faces are always coming before you, their voices seem always in your ears. It is the one eternal sadness of life. And the strangest part of it is, that just as you who have once really understood can never forget, so it is the most difficult thing in the world to make those people understand who have not themselves lived and toiled amongst them. It is a cry which you cannot translate, but if once you have heard it, it will follow you from the earth to the stars."

"You too, then," she said, "have some of the old aim at heart. You are not going to immerse yourself wholly in politics?"

"My studies," he said, "will be in life. It is not from books that I hope to gain experience. I want to get a little nearer to the heart of the thing. You and I may easily come across one another, even in this great city."

"You," she said, "are going to watch, to observe, to trace the external only that you may understand the internal. But I am going to work on my hands and knees."

"And you think that I am going to play the dilettante?"

"Not altogether. But you will want to pass from one scheme to another to see the inner workings of all. I shall be content to find occupation in any one.

"I shall be coming to you," he said, "for information and help."

"I doubt it," she answered, cheerfully. "Never mind! It is pleasant to build castles, and we may yet find ourselves working side by side."

He suddenly looked at her.

"I have answered all your questions," he said. "There is something about you which I should like to know."

"I am sure you shall."

"Lord Arranmore came to me when I was staying at the Metropole with your uncle and cousin. He wished me to use my influence with you to induce you to accept a certain sum of money which it seemed that you had already declined."

"Well?"

"Of course I refused. In the first place, as I told him, I was not aware that I possessed any influence over you. And in the second I had every confidence in your own judgment."

She was suddenly very thoughtful.

"My own judgment," she repeated. "I am afraid that I have lost a good deal of faith in that lately."

"Why?"

"I have learned to repent of that impulsive visit of mine to Enton."

"Again why?"

"I was mad with rage against Lord Arranmore. I think that I was wrong. It was many years ago, and he has repented."

Brooks smiled faintly. The idea of Lord Arranmore repenting of anything appealed in some measure to his sense of humour.

"Then I am afraid that I did him some great harm in accusing him like that—openly. He has seemed to me since like an altered man. Tell me, those others who were there—they believed me?"

"Yes."

"It did him harm—with the lady, the handsome woman who was playing billiards with him?"

"Yes."

"Was he engaged to her?

"No! He proposed to her afterwards, and she refused him."

Her eyes were suddenly dim.

"I am sorry," she said.

"I think," he said, quietly, "that you need not be. You probably saved her a good deal of unhappiness."

She looked at him curiously.

"Why are you so bitter against Lord Arranmore?" she asked.

"I?" he laughed. "I am not bitter against him. Only I believe him to be a man without heart or conscience or principles."

"That is your opinion—really?"

"Really! Decidedly."

"Then I don't agree with you," she answered.

"Why not?"

"Simply that I don't."

"Excellent! But you have reasons as well as convictions?

"Perhaps. Why, for instance, is he so anxious for me to have this money? That must be a matter of conscience?"

"Not necessarily. An accident might bring his Montreal career to light. His behaviour towards you would be an excellent defence."

She shook her head.

"He isn't mean enough to think so far ahead for his own advantage. Villain or paragon, he is on a large scale, your Lord Arranmore."

"He has had the good fortune," Brooks said, with a note of satire in his tone, "to attract your sympathies."

"Why not? I struck hard enough at him, and he has borne me no ill-will. He even made friends with Selina and my uncle to induce me to accept his well, conscience money."

"I need not ask you what the result was," Brooks said. "You declined it, of course."

She looked at him thoughtfully.

"I refused it at first, as you know," she said. "Since then, well, I have wavered."

He looked at her blankly.

"You mean—that you have contemplated—accepting it?"

"Why not? There is reason in it. I do not say that I have accepted it, but at any rate I see nothing which should make you look upon my possible acceptance as a heinous thing."

He was silent for a moment.

"May I ask you then what the position is?"

"I will tell you. Lord Arranmore is coming to me perhaps this afternoon for my answer. I asked him for a few days to think it over."

"And your decision—is it ready?"

"No, I don't think it is," she admitted. "To tell you the truth, I shall not decide until he is actually here—until I have heard just how he speaks of it."

He got up and stood for a moment looking out of the window. Then he turned suddenly towards her with outstretched hand.

"I am going—Miss Scott. Good-afternoon." She rose and held out her hand.

"Aren't you—a little abrupt?" she asked.

"Perhaps I am. I think that it is better that I should go away now. There are reasons why I do not want to talk about Lord Arranmore, or discuss this matter with you, and if I stayed I might do both. Will you dine with me somewhere on Friday night? I will come and fetch you."

"Of course I will. Do be careful how you walk. About 7:30."

"I will be here by then," he answered.

On the last flight of stone steps he came face to face with Lord Arranmore, who nodded and pointed upwards with his walking-stick.

"How much of this sort of thing?" he asked, dryly.

"Ten storeys," Brooks answered, and passed out into the street.

Lord Arranmore looked after him—watched him until he was out of sight. Then he stood irresolute for several moments, tapping his boots.

"Damned young fool!" he muttered at last; and began the ascent.

CHAPTER IV
A MARQUIS ON MATRIMONY

"My dear Miss Scott," Lord Arranmore said, settling himself in the most comfortable of her fragile easy-chairs, and declining tea. "I cannot fail to perceive that my cause is hopeless. The united efforts of myself and your worthy relatives appear to be powerless to unearth a single grain of common-sense in your—er—pardon me—singularly obstinate disposition."

A subdued smile played at the corners of her mouth.

"I am delighted that you are convinced, Lord Arranmore," she said. "It will save us both a good deal of time and breath."

"Well—as to that I am not so sure," he answered, deliberately. "You forget that there is still an important matter to be decided."

She looked at him questioningly.

"The disposal of the money, of course," he said.

"The disposal of it? But that has nothing to do with me!" she declared. "I refuse to touch it—to have anything to do with it."

He shook his head.

"You see," he explained, "I have placed it, or rather my solicitors have, in trust. Actually you may decline, as you are doing, to have anything to do with it—legally you cannot avoid your responsibilities. That money cannot be touched without your signature."

She laughed a little indignantly.

"Then you had better withdraw it from trust, or whatever you call it, at once. If it was there until I was eighty I should never touch it."

"I understand that perfectly," Lord Arranmore said. "You have refused it. Very well! What are we going to do with it?"

"Put it back where it came from, of course," she answered.

"Well," he said, "by signing several papers that might be managed. In that case I should distribute it amongst the various public-houses in the East End to provide drinks for the thirstiest of their customers."

"If you think that," she said, scornfully, "a reputable use to make of your money."

He held out his hand.

"My dear Miss Scott. Our money!"

"The money," she exclaimed. "I repeat, the money. Well, there is nothing more to be said about it."

"Will you sign the papers which authorize me to distribute the money in this way?"

She thought for a moment.

"No; I will not."

"Exactly. You would be very foolish and very untrue to your principles if you did. So you see, this sum is not to be foisted altogether upon me, for there is no doubt that I should misuse it. Now I believe that if you were to give the matter a little consideration you could hit upon a more reasonable manner of laying out this sum. Don't interrupt me, please. My own views as to charity you know. You however look at the matter from an altogether different point of view. Let us leave it where it is for the moment. Something may occur to you within the next few months. Don't let it be a hospital, if you can help it—something altogether original would be best. Set your brain to work. I shall be at your service at any moment."

He rose to his feet and began slowly to collect his belongings. Then their eyes met, and she burst out laughing—he too smiled.

"You are very ingenious, Lord Arranmore," she said.

"It is my conscience," he assured her. "It is out of gear to the tune of three thousand."

"I don't believe in the conscience," she answered. 'This is sheer obstinacy. You have made up your mind that I should be interested in that money somehow, and you can't bear to suffer defeat."

"I am an old man," he said, "and you are a young woman. Let us leave it where it is for a while. I have an idea of the sort of life which you are planning for yourself. Believe me, that before you have lived here for many months you will be willing to give years of your life, years of your labour and your youth, to throw yourself into a struggle which without money is hopeless. Remember that there was a time when I too was young. I too saw these things as you and Brooks see them to-day. I do not wish to preach pessimism to you. I fought and was worsted. So will you be. The whole thing is a vast chimera, a jest of the God you have made for yourself. But as long as the world lasts the young will have to buy knowledge—as I have bought it. Don't go into the fray empty-handed—it will only prolong the suffering."

"You speak," she protested, gently, "as though it were impossible to do good."

"It is absolutely and entirely impossible to do good by any means which you and Brooks and the whole army of your fellow-philanthropists have yet evoked," he answered, with a sudden fierce note in his tone. "Don't think that I speak to you as a cynic, one who loiters on the edge of the cauldron and peers in to gratify cravings for sensation. I have been there, down in the thick of it, there where the mud is as black as hell—bottomless as eternity. I was young—as you—mad with enthusiasm. I had faith, strength, belief. I meant to cleanse the world. I worked till the skin hung on my bones. I gave all that I had—youth—gifts—money. And, do you know what I was doing? I was swimming against the tide of natural law, stronger than all mankind, unconquerable, eternal. There wasn't the smallest corner of the world the better for my broken life. There wasn't a child, a man, or a woman content to grasp my hand and climb out. There were plenty who mocked me. But they fell back again. They fell back always."

"Oh, but you can't tell that," she cried. "You can't be sure."

"You can be as sure of it as of life itself," he answered. "Come, take my advice. I know. I can save you a broken youth—a broken heart. Keep away from there."

He pointed out of the window eastwards.

"You can be charitable like the others, subscribe to societies, visit the sick, read the Bible, play at it as long as you like—but keep away from the real thing. If you feel the fever in your veins—fly. Go abroad, study art, literature, music—anything. Only don't listen to that cry. It will draw you against your will even. But not you nor the whole world of women, or the world full of gold, will ever stop it. It is the everlasting legacy to the world of outraged nature."

He went swiftly and silently, leaving her motionless. She saw him far down on the pavement below step into his brougham, pausing for a moment to light a cigarette. And half-an-hour later he walked with elastic tread into Mr. Ascough's office.

Mr. Ascough greeted him with an inquiring smile. Lord Arranmore nodded and sat down.

"You were quite right," he announced. "The tongues of men or of angels wouldn't move her. Never mind. She's going to use the money for charity."

"Well, that's something, at any rate," Mr. Ascough remarked.

"The eloquence," Lord Arranmore said, lazily, "which I have wasted upon that young woman would entrance the House of Lords. By the bye, Ascough, I am going to take my seat next week."

"I am delighted to hear it, your lordship."

"Yes, it's good news for the country, isn't it?" Lord Arranmore remarked. "I have not quite decided what my particular line shall be, but I have no doubt but that the papers will all be calling me a welcome addition to that august assembly before long. I believe that's what's the matter with me. I want to make a speech. Do you remember me at the Bar, Ascough? Couldn't keep me down, could they?"

Mr. Ascough smiled.

"You were rather fond of being on your feet!" he admitted.

Lord Arranmore sighed regretfully.

"And to think that I might have been Lord High Chancellor by now," he remarked. "Good-bye, Ascough."

* * * * *

Later, at the reception of a Cabinet Minister, Lord Arranmore came across Hennibul talking with half-a-dozen other men. He detached himself at once.

"This is odd," he remarked, with a whimsical smile. "What the dickens are you doing in this respectable household, Arranmore? You look like a lost sheep."

Lord Arranmore shrugged his shoulders.

"I've decided to go in for something," he said; "politics or society or something of that sort. What do you recommend?"

"Supper!" Mr. Hennibul answered, promptly.

"Come on then," Lord Arranmore assented. "One of those little tables in the far room, eh?"

"The pate here is delicious," Mr. Hennibul said; "but for Heaven's sake leave the champagne alone." "There's some decent hock. You'll excuse my pointing out these little things to you, but, of course, you don't know the runs yet. I'll give you a safe tip while I'm about it. The Opposition food is beastly, but the wine is all right—Pommery and Heidsieck, most of it, and the right years. The Government food now is good, but the wine, especially the champagne, is positively unholy."

"One should eat then with the Government, and drink with the Opposition," Lord Arranmore remarked.

"Or, better still," Mr. Hennibul said, "do both with the Speaker. By the bye, did you know that they are going to make me a judge?"

"I heard that your friends wanted to get rid of you!" Arranmore answered.

"To make yourself obnoxious—thoroughly obnoxious," Mr. Hennibul murmured, "is the sure road to advancement."

"That's right, give me a few tips," Lord Arranmore begged, sipping his wine.

"My dear fellow, I don't know what you're going in for yet."

"Neither do I. What about the stage? I used to be rather good at private theatricals. Elderly Wyndhamy parts, you know."

Mr. Hennibul shook his head.

"Twenty years too late," he declared. "Even the suburbs turn up their noses at a lord now."

"I must do something," Arranmore declared, meditatively.

"Don't see the necessity," Hennibul remarked.

Lord Arranmore lifted his glass and looked thoughtfully at the wine for a moment.

"Ah, well," he said, "you were born lazy, and I was born restless. That is the reason you have done something, and I haven't."

"If you want my advice—my serious advice," the K. C. said, quietly, "you will make yourself a nuisance to that right woman, whoever she is, until she marries you—if only to get rid of you."

"All sorts of things in the way," Lord Arranmore declared. "You see, I was married abroad."

Mr. Hennibul looked up quickly.

"Nonsense!"

"Quite true, I assure you."

"Is she alive?"

"No—but her son is.

"Great Heavens. Why, he's Lord Kingston?"

"Of course he is."

"How old is he?"

"Twenty-eight—or somewhere thereabouts."

"What is he doing? Where is he? Why don't we know him?"

"He doesn't approve of me," Lord Arranmore said. "Fact, really! We are scarcely on speaking terms."

"Why not?"

"Says I deserted his mother. So I did! Played the blackguard altogether. Left 'em both to starve, or next door to it!"

Mr. Hennibul fetched out his handkerchief and dabbed his forehead.

"You are serious, Arranmore?"

"Rather! You wouldn't expect me to be frivolous on this hock."

"That young man must be talked to," Mr. Hennibul declared. "He ought to be filling his proper place in the world. It's no use carrying on a grudge against his own father. Let me have a try at him."

"No!" Lord Arranmore said, quietly. "I am obliged to you, Hennibul, but the matter is one which does not admit of outside interference, however kindly. Besides, the boy is right. I wilfully deserted both him and his mother, and she died during my absence. My life, whilst away from them, was the sort one forgets—or tries to—and he knows about it. Further, when I returned to England I was two years before I took the trouble to go and see him. I merely alluded to these domestic matters that you might not wholly misjudge the situation."

Mr. Hennibul went on with his supper in silence. Lord Arranmore. whose appetite had soon failed him, leaned back in his chair and watched the people in the further room.

"This rather puts me off politics," he remarked, after a while. "I don't like the look of the people."

"Oh, you'll get in for the select crushers," Mr. Hennibul said. "This is a rank and file affair. You mustn't judge by appearances. But why must you specialize? Take my advice. Don't go in specially for politics, or society, or sport. Mix them all up. Be cosmopolitan and commonplace."

"Upon my word, Hennibul, you are a genius," Arranmore declared, "and yonder goes my good fairy."

He sprang up and disappeared into the further room.

"Lady Caroom," he exclaimed, bending over her shoulder. "I never suspected it of you."

She started slightly—she was silent perhaps for the fraction of a second. Then she looked up with a bright smile, meeting him on his own ground.

"But of you," she cried, "it is incredible. Come at once and explain."

CHAPTER V
BROOKS ENLISTS A RECRUIT

Brooks had found a small restaurant in the heart of fashionable London, where the appointments and decorations were French, and the waiters were not disposed to patronize. Of the cooking neither he nor Mary Scott in those days was a critic. Nevertheless she protested against the length of the dinner which he ordered.

"I want an excuse," he declared, laying down the carte, "for a good long chat. We shall be too late for the theatre, so we may as well resign ourselves to an hour or so of one another's society."

She shook her head.

"A very apt excuse for unwarrantable greediness," she declared. "Surely we can talk without eating?"

He shook his head.

"You do not smoke, and you do not drink liqueurs," he remarked. "Now I have noticed that it is simply impossible for one to sit before an empty table after dinner and not feel that one ought to go. Let the waiter take your cape. You will find the room warm."

"Do you remember," she asked him, "the first night we dined together?"

He looked at her with twinkling eyes.

"Rather! It was my introduction to your uncle's household. Selina sat on my left, and Louise on my right. You sat opposite, tired and disagreeable."

"I was tired—and I am always disagreeable."

"I have noticed it," he agreed, equably. "I hope you like oysters."

"If Selina were to see us now," she remarked, with a sudden humorous smile, "how shocked she would be."

"What a little far-away world it seems down there," he said thoughtfully. "After all, I am glad that I have not to live in Medchester all my life."

"You have been there this afternoon, haven't you?"

"Yes. Henslow is giving us a lot of trouble. I am afraid we shall lose the seat next election."

"Do you mind?"

"Not much. I am no party politician. I want to see Medchester represented by a man who will go there with a sense of political proportion, and I don't care whether he calls himself Liberal, or Radical, or Conservative, or Unionist."

"Please explain what you mean by that," she begged.

"Why, yes. I mean a man who will understand how enormously more important is the welfare of our own people, the people of whom we are making slaves, than this feverish Imperialism and war cant. Mind, I think our patriotism should be a thing wholly understood. It needn't be talked about. It makes showy fireworks for the platform, but it's all unnecessary and to my mind very undignified. If only people would take that for granted and go on to something worth while."

"Are things any better in Medchester just now?" she asked.

"On the surface, yes, but on the surface only. More factories are running half-time, but after all what does that mean? It's slow starvation. A man can't live and keep a family on fifteen shillings a week, even if his wife earns a little. He can't do it in a dignified manner, and with cleanliness and health. That is what he has a right to. That is what the next generation will demand. He should have room to expand. Cleanliness, air, fresh food. Every man and woman who is born into the world has a God-given right to these, and there are millions in Medchester, Manchester, and all the great cities who are denied all three."

"So all Henslow's great schemes, his Royal Commissions, his Protection Duties, his great Housing Bill, have come to nothing then?" she remarked.

"To less than nothing," he answered, gloomily. "The man was a fraud. He is not worth attempting to bully. He is a puppet politician of a type that ought to have been dead and buried generations ago. Enoch Stone is our only hope in the House now. He is a strong man, and he has hold of the truth."

"Have they decided upon Henslow's successor?" she asked.

"Not yet," he answered.

She looked up at him.

"I heard from uncle this morning," she said, smiling meaningly.

He shook his head.

"Well, it was mentioned," he said, "but I would not hear of it. I am altogether too young and inexperienced. I want to live with the people for a year or two first. That is why I am glad to get to London."

"With the people?" she asked, "in Jermyn Street?"

He laughed good-humouredly.

"I have also lodgings in the Bethnal Green Road," he said. "I took possession of them last week."

"Anywhere near Merry's Corner?" she asked.

"What do you know about Merry's Corner?" he exclaimed, with uplifted eyebrows. "Yes, my rooms are nearly opposite, at the corner of the next street."

"I've been down there once or twice lately," she said. "There's a mission-hall just there, and a girl named Kate Stuart gave me a letter to go three times a week."

He nodded.

"I know the place. Week-night services and hymn-singing and preaching. A cold, desolate affair altogether. I'm thankful I went in there, though, for it's given me an idea."

Yes?

"I'm going to start a mission myself."

"Go on."

"On a new principle. The first thing will be that there will be no religious services whatever. I won't have a clergyman connected with it. It will be intended solely for the benefit of the people from a temporal point of view."

"You are going a long way," she said. "What about Sundays?"

"There will be a very short service for the mission helpers only. No one will be asked from outside at all. If they come it will be as a favour. Directly it is over the usual week-day procedure will go on."

"And what is that to be?"

Brooks smiled a little doubtfully.

"Well," he said, "I've got the main idea in my head, but all the details want thinking out. I want the place to be a sort of help bureau, to give the people living in a certain street or couple of streets somewhere to go for advice and help in cases of emergency. There will be no money given away, under any consideration—only food, clothing, and, if they are asked for, books. I shall have half-a-dozen bathrooms, and the people who come regularly for advice and help will have to use them and to keep their houses clean. There will be no distinction as to character. We shall help the drunkards and the very worst of them just the same as the others if they apply. If we get enough helpers there will be plenty of branches we can open. I should like to have a children's branch, for instance—one or two women will take the children of the neighbourhood in hand and bathe them every day. As we get to know the people better and appreciate their special needs other things will suggest themselves. But I want them to feel that they have some place to fail back upon. We shall be frightfully humbugged, robbed, cheated, and deceived—at first. I fancy that after a time that will wear itself out."

"It is a fascinating idea," she said, thoughtfully, "but to carry it out in any way thoroughly you want a great many helpers and a great deal of money."

"I have enough to start it," he said, "and when it is really going and improving itself I shall go out and ask for subscriptions-big ones, you know, from the right sort of people. You can always get money if you can show that it is to be well spent."

"And what about the helpers?"

"Well, I know of a few," he said, "who I think would come in, and there is one to whom I would have to pay a small salary."

"I could come in the afternoons," she said.

"Capital! But are you sure," he said, after a moment's hesitation, "that it is quite fair to yourself?"

"Oh, I can manage with my morning's salary," she answered, laughing. "I shan't starve. Besides, I can always burn a little midnight oil."

A waiter stood at their table for a moment, deftly carving some new dish, and Brooks, leaning back in his chair, glanced critically at his companion. In his judgment she represented something in womankind essentially of the durable type. He appreciated her good looks, the air with which she wore her simple clothes, her large full eyes, her wide, gently-humorous mouth, and the hair parted in the middle, and rippling away towards her ears. A frank companionable woman, whose eyes had never failed to look into his, in whom he had never at any time seen a single shadow of embarrassment. It occurred to him just at that moment that never since he had known her had he seen her interested to the slightest degree in any man. He looked back at her thoughtfully. She was young, good-looking, too catholic in her views of life and its possibilities to refuse in any way to recognize its inevitable tendencies. Yet he told himself complacently as he sipped his wine and watched her gazing with amused interest at the little groups of people about the place, that there must be in her composition a lack of sentiment. Never for a second in their intercourse had she varied from her usual good-natured cheerfulness. If there had been a shadow she had brushed it away ruthlessly. Even on that terrible afternoon at Enton she had sat in the cab white and silent—she had appealed to him in no way for sympathy.

The waiter retreated with a bow. She shot a swift glance across at him.

"I object to being scrutinized," she declared. "Is it the plainness of my hat or the depth of my wrinkles to which you object?"

"Object!" he repeated.

"Yes. You were looking for something which you did not find. You were distinctly disappointed. Don't deny it. It isn't worth while."

"I won't plead guilty to the disappointment," he answered, "but I'll tell you the truth. I was thinking what a delightfully companionable girl you were, and yet how different from any other girl I have ever met in my life."

"That sounds hackneyed—the latter part of it," she remarked, "but in my case I see that it is not intended to be a compliment. What do I lack that other girls have?

"You are putting me in a tight corner," he declared. "It isn't that you lack anything, but nearly all the girls one meets some time or other seem to expect from one nice little speeches or compliments, just a little sentiment now and then. Now you seem so entirely superior to that sort of thing altogether. It is a ridiculously lame explanation. The thing's in my head all right, but I can't get it out. I can only express it when I say that you are the only girl I have ever known, or known of, in my life with whom sex would never interfere with companionship."

She stirred her coffee absently. At first he thought that she might be offended, for she did not look up for several moments.

"I'm afraid I failed altogether to make you understand what I meant," he said, humbly. "It is the result of an attempt at too great candour."

Then she looked up and smiled at him graciously enough, though it seemed to him that she was a little pale.

"I am sure you were delightfully lucid," she said. "I quite understood, and on the whole I think I agree with you. I don't think that the sentimental side of me has been properly developed. By the bye, you were going to tell me about that pretty girl I saw at Enton—Lady Caroom's daughter, wasn't she?"

His face lit up—she saw his thoughts go flitting away, and the corner of his lips curl in a retrospective smile of pleasure.

"Sybil Caroom," he said, softly. "She is a very charming girl. You would like her, I am sure. Of course she's been brought up in rather a frivolous world, but she's quite unspoilt, very sympathetic, and very intelligent. Isn't that a good character?"

"Very," she answered, with a suspicion of dryness in her tone. "Is this paragon engaged to be married yet?"

He looked at her, keenly surprised by the infusion of something foreign in her tone.

"I—I think not," he answered. "I should like you to meet her very much. She will be coming to London soon, and I know that she will be interested in our new scheme if it comes to anything. We will take her down and give her a few practical lessons in philanthropy."

"Will she be interested?" Mary asked.

"Immensely," he answered, with confidence. "Lady Caroom is an awfully good sort, too."

Mary remembered the well-bred insolence of Lady Caroom's stare, the contemplative incredulity which found militant expression in her beautiful eyes and shapely curving lips, and for a moment half closed her eyes.

"Ah, well," she said, "that afternoon was rather a terrible one to me. Let us talk of something else."

He was profuse at once in apologies for his own thoughtlessness. But she checked him almost at the outset.

"It is I who am to blame for an unusual weakness," she said. "Let us both forget it. And don't you find this place hot? Let us get outside and walk."

They found a soft misty rain falling. The commissionaire called a hansom. She moved her skirts to make room for him.

"I am going down to Stepney to see a man who I think will be interested in my scheme," he said. "When may I come down again and have tea with you?"

"Any afternoon, if you will drop me a line the night before," she said, "but I am not very likely to be out, in any case. Thank you so much for my dinner. My aunt seemed to think that I was coming to London to starve. I think I feel fairly safe this evening, at any rate."

The cab drove off, skirting the gaily-lit crescent of Regent Street. The smile almost at once died away from her lips. She leaned forward and looked at herself in one of the oblong mirrors. Her face was almost colourless, the skin seemed drawn closely round her eyes, giving her almost a strained look. For the rest, her hair, smoothly brushed away from her face, was in perfect order, her prim little hat was at exactly the right angle, her little white tie alone relieved the sombreness of her black jacket. She sighed and suddenly felt a moistening of her hot eyes. She leaned far back into the corner of the cab.

CHAPTER VI
KINGSTON BROOKS, PHILANTHROPIST

"It is my deliberate intention," Lord Arranmore said, leaning over towards her from his low chair, "to make myself a nuisance to you." Lady Caroom smiled at him thoughtfully.

"Thank you for the warning," she said, "but I can take care of myself. I do not feel even obliged to deny myself the pleasure of your society."

"No, you won't do that," he remarked. "You see, so many people bore you, and I don't."

"It is true," she admitted. "You pay me nothing but unspoken compliments, and you devote a considerable amount of ingenuity to conceal the real meaning of everything you say. Now some people might not like that. I adore it."

"Catherine, will you marry me?"

"Certainly not! I'm much too busy looking after Sybil, and in any case you've had your answer, my friend."

"You will marry me," he said, deliberately, "in less than two years—perhaps in less than one. Why can't you make your mind up to it?"

"You know why, Arranmore," she said, quietly. "If you were the man I remember many years ago, the man I have wasted many hours of my life thinking about, I would not hesitate for a moment. I loved that man, and I have always loved him. But, Arranmore, I cannot recognize him in you. If these terrible things which you have suffered, these follies which you have committed, have withered you up so that there remains no trace of the man I once cared for, do you blame me for refusing you? I will not marry a stranger, Arranmore, and I not only don't know you, but I am a little afraid of you."

He sighed.

"Perhaps you are right," he said, softly. "I believe that the only thing I have carried with me from the beginning, and shall have with me to the end, is my love for you. Nothing else has survived."

Her eyes filled with tears. She leaned over to him.

"Dear friend," she said, "listen! At least I will promise you this. If ever I should see the least little impulse or action which seems to me to come from the Philip I once knew, and not Lord Arranmore, anything which will convince me that some part, however slight, of the old has survived, I will come to you."

He sighed.

"You alone," he said, "might work such a miracle."

"Then come and see me often," she said, with a brilliant smile, "and I will try."

He moved his chair a little nearer to her.

"You encourage me to hope," he said. "I remember that one night in the conservatory I was presumptuous enough—to take your hand. History repeats itself, you see, and I claim the prize, for I have fulfilled the condition."

She drew her hand away firmly, but without undue haste.

"If you are going to be frivolous," she said, "I will have all the callers shown in. You know very well that that is not what I mean. There must be some unpremeditated action, some impulse which comes from your own heart. Frankly, Arranmore, there are times now when I am afraid of you. You seem to have no heart—to be absolutely devoid of feeling, to be cold and calculating even in your slightest actions. There, now I have told you just what I feel sometimes, and it doesn't sound nice, does it?"

"It sounds very true," he said, wearily. "Will you tell me where I can buy a new heart and a fresh set of impulses, even a disposition, perhaps? I'd be a customer. I'm willing enough."

"Never mind that," she said, softly. "After all, I have a certain amount of faith. A miracle may happen at any moment."

Sybil came in, dressed in a fascinating short skirt and a toque. Her maid on the threshold was carrying a small green baize box.

"I am going to Prince's, mother, just for an hour, with Mrs. Huntingdon. How do you do, Lord Arranmore? You'll keep mother from being dull, won't you?"

"It is your mother," he said, "who is making me dull."

"Poor old mummy," Sybil declared, cheerfully.

"Never mind. Her bark's a good deal worse than her bite. Good-bye, both of you."

Lord Arranmore rose and closed the door after her.

"Sybil is a remarkably handsome young woman," he said. "Any signs of her getting married yet?"

Lady Caroom shook her head.

"No! Arranmore, that reminds me, what has become of—Mr. Brooks?" Lord

Arranmore smiled a little bitterly. "He is in London."

"I have never seen him, you must remember, since that evening. Is he still—unforgiving?

"Yes! He refuses to be acknowledged. He is taking the bare income which is his by law—it comes from a settlement to the eldest son—and he is studying practical philanthropy in the slums."

"I am sorry," she said. "I like him, and he would be a companion for you."

"He's not to be blamed," Lord Arranmore said. "From his point of view I have been the most scandalous parent upon this earth." Lady Caroom sighed.

"Do you know," she said, "that he and Sybil were very friendly?"

"I noticed it," he answered.

"She has asked about him once or twice since we got back to town, and when she reads about the starting of this new work of his at Stepney she will certainly write to him."

"You mean—"

"I mean that she has sent Sydney to the right-about this time in earnest. She is a queer girl, reticent in a way, although she seems such a chatterbox, and I am sure she thinks about him."

Lord Arranmore laughed a little hardly.

"Well," he said, "I am the last person to be consulted about anything of this sort. If he keeps up his present attitude and declines to receive anything from me, his income until my death will be only two or three thousand a year. He might marry on that down in Stepney, but not in this part of the world."

"Sybil has nine hundred a year," Lady Caroom said, "but it would not be a matter of money at all. I should not allow Sybil to marry any one concerning whose position in the world there was the least mystery. She might marry Lord Kingston of Ross, but never Mr. Kingston Brooks."

"Has—Mr. Brooks given any special signs of devotion?" Lord Arranmore asked.

"Not since they were at Enton. I dare say he has never even thought of her since. Still, it was a contingency which occurred to me."

"He is a young man of excellent principles," Lord Arranmore said, dryly, "taking life as seriously as you please, and I should imagine is too well balanced to make anything but a very safe husband. If he comes to me, if he will accept it without coming to me even, he can have another ten thousand a year and Enton."

"You are generous," she murmured.

"Generous! My houses and my money are a weariness to me. I cannot live in the former, and I cannot spend the latter. I am a man really of simple tastes. Besides, there is no glory now in spending money. One can so easily be outdone by one's grocer, or one of those marvellous Americans."

"Yet I thought I read of you last week as giving nine hundred pounds for some unknown tapestry at Christie's."

"But that is not extravagance," he protested. "That is not even spending money. It is exchanging one investment for another. The purple colouring of that tapestry is marvellous. The next generation will esteem it priceless."

"You must go?" she asked, for he had risen.

"I have stayed long enough," he answered. "In another five minutes you will yawn, and mine would have been a wasted visit. I should like to time my visits always so that the five minutes which I might have stayed seem to you the most desirable five minutes of the whole time."

"You are an epicurean and a schemer," she declared. "I am afraid of you."

* * * * *

He bought an evening paper on his way to St. James's Square, and leaning back in his brougham, glanced it carelessly through. Just as he was throwing it aside a small paragraph at the bottom of the page caught his attention.

**A NOVEL PHILANTHROPIC DEPARTURE.
THE FIRST BUREAU OPENED TO-DAY.**

INTERVIEW WITH MR. KINGSTON BROOKS.

He folded the paper out, and read through every line carefully. A few minutes after his arrival home he re-issued from the house in a bowler hat and a long, loose overcoat. He took the Metropolitan and an omnibus to Stepney, and read the paragraph through again. Soon he found himself opposite the address given.

He recognized it with a little start. It had once been a mission hall, then a furniture shop, and later on had been empty for years. It was brilliantly lit up, and he pressed forward and peered through the window. Inside the place was packed. Brooks and a dozen or so others were sitting on a sort of slightly-raised platform at the end of the room, with a desk in front of each of them. Lord Arranmore pulled his hat over his eyes and forced his way just inside. Almost as he entered Brooks rose to his feet.

"Look here," he said, "you all come up asking the same question and wasting my time answering you all severally. You want to know what this place means. Well, if you'll stay just where you are for a minute, I'll tell you all together, and save time."

"Hear, hear, guv'nor," said a bibulous old costermonger, encouragingly. "Let's hear all about it."

"So you shall," Brooks said. "Now listen. I dare say there are a good many of you who go up in the West End sometimes, and see those big houses and the way people spend their money there, who come back to your own houses here, and think that things aren't exactly dealt out square. Isn't that so?"

There was a hearty and unanimous assent.

"Well," Brooks continued, "it may surprise you to hear that a few of us who have a little money up there have come to the same conclusion. We'd like to do our little bit towards squaring things up. It may not be much, but lots more may come of it."

A modified but a fairly cordial assent.

"We haven't money to give away—not much of it, at any rate," Brooks continued.

"More bloomin' tracks," the costermonger interrupted, and spat upon the floor. "Fair sickens me, it does."

"As for tracts," Brooks continued, calmly, "I don't think I've ever read one in my life, and I don't want to. We haven't such a thing in the place, and I shouldn't know where to go for them, and though that gentleman down there with a herring sticking out of his pocket seems to have done himself pretty well already, I'd rather stand him a glass of beer than offer him such a thing."

A roar of laughter, during which a wag in the crowd quietly picked the costermonger's pocket of the fish with a deftness born of much practice, and sent it flying over the room. It was promptly returned, and found a devious way back to its owner in a somewhat dusty and mauled condition.

"There is just one thing we have to ask for and insist upon," Brooks continued. "When you come to us for help, tell us the truth. If you've been drunk all the week and haven't earned any money, well, we may help you out with a Sunday dinner. If you've been in prison and won't mind owning up to it, we shan't send you away for that reason. We want your women to come and bring us your children, that we can have a look at them, tell us how much you all make a week between you, and what you need most to make you a bit more comfortable. And we want your husbands to come and tell us where they work, and what rent they pay, and if they haven't any work, and can't get it, we'll see what we can do. I tell you I don't care to start with whether you're sober and industrious, or idle, or drunkards. We'll give any one a leg-up if we can. I don't say we shall keep that up always, because of course we shan't. But we'll give any one a fair chance. Now do you want to ask any questions?"

A pallid but truculent-looking young man pushed himself to the front.

"'Ere, guv'nor!" he said. "Supposing yer was to stand me a coat—I ain't 'ad one for two months—should I 'ave to come 'ere on a Sunday and sing bloomin' hymns?"

"If you did," Brooks answered him, "you'd do it by yourself, and you'd stand a fair chance of being run out. There's going to be no preaching or hymn-singing here. Those sorts of things are very well in their way, but they've nothing to do with this show. I'm not sure whether we shall open on Sundays or not. If we do it will be only for the ordinary business. Now let's get to work."

"Sounds a bit of orl right, and no mistake," the young man remarked, turning round to the crowd. "I'm going to stop and 'ave a go for that coat."

A young man in a bright scarlet jersey pushed himself to the front, followed by a little volley of chaff, more or less good-natured.

"There's Salvation Joe wants a new trombone."

"Christian Sall's blown a hole in the old one, eh, Joe?"

Breathless he reached Brooks' side. The sweat stood out in beads upon his forehead. He seemed not to hear a word that was said amongst the crowd. Brooks smiled at him good-humouredly. "Well, sir," he said, "what can I do for you?"

"I happened in, sir, out of curiosity," the young man said, in a strange nasal twang, the heritage of years of outdoor preaching; "I hoped to hear of one more good work begun in this den of iniquity and to clasp hands with another brother in God."

"Glad to see you," Brooks said. "You'll remember we're busy."

"The message of God," the young man answered, "must be spoken at all times."

"Oh, chuck 'im out!" cried the disgusted costermonger, spitting upon the floor. "That sort o' stuff fair sickens me."

The young man continued as though he had not heard.

"Such charity as you are offering," he cried, "is corruption. You are going to dispense things for their carnal welfare, and you do nothing for their immortal souls. You will not let them even shout their thanks to God. You will fill their stomachs and leave their souls hungry."

The costermonger waved a wonderful red handkerchief, and spat once more on the floor. Brooks laid his hand upon the young man's shoulder.

"Look here, my young friend," he said, "you're talking rot. Men and women who live down here in wretchedness, and who are fighting every moment of their time to hang on to life, don't want to be talked to about their souls. They need a leg-up in the world, and we've come to try and give it to them. We're here as friends, not preachers. We'll leave you to look after their souls. You people who've tried to make your religion the pill to go with your charity have done more harm in the world than you know of."

The young man was on fire to speak, but he had no chance. They hustled him out good-naturedly except that the costermonger, running him down the room, took his cap from his head and sent it spinning across the road. Lord Arranmore left the hall at the same time, and turned homewards, walking like a man in a dream.

CHAPTER VII
BROOKS AND HIS MISSIONS

"Now then, please," Brooks said, dipping his pen in the ink.

A lady of ample proportions, who had been standing since the commencement of the proceedings with her hand tightly grasping the leg of Brooks' table, gave a final shove of discomfiture to a meek-faced girl whom she had suspected of an attempt to supersede her, and presented herself before the desk.

"I'm first," she declared, firmly; "been 'ere for four mortal hours."

"What is your name, please?" Brooks asked.

"Mrs. Robert Jones, No. 4, St. Mary's Court, down Fennell Street—leastways you go that way from 'ere. I'm a widow woman with four children, and lost me husband on the railway. What I wants is a suit of clothes for my Tommy, he's five-and-'arf, and stout for his years, and a pair of boots for Selina Ann. And I'm not a saying," she continued, blandly, "as me having waited 'ere so long, and this being a sort of opening ceremony, as a pound of tea for myself wouldn't be a welcome and reasonable gift. And if the suit," she concluded, breathlessly, "has double-seated breeches so much the better."

Brooks maintained the most perfect composure, although conscious of a suppressed titter from behind. He commenced to write rapidly in his book, and Mrs. Jones, drawing her shawl about her, looked around complacently. Suddenly she caught the ripple of mirth, which some of Brooks' helpers were powerless to control. Her face darkened.

"Which is little enough to ask for," she declared, truculently, "considering as it's four mortal hours since I first laid hold of the leg of that table, and neither bite nor sup have I had since, it not being my habit," she continued, slowly, and staring intently at the hang of her neighbour's skirt, "to carry bottles in my pocket."

Brooks looked up.

"Thank you, Mrs. Jones," he said. "I have entered your name and address, and I hope we shall see you again soon. This young lady," he indicated Mary, "will take you over to our clothes department, and if we haven't anything to fit Tommy you must come again on Wednesday, when we shall have a larger supply."

"I'll take the nearest you've got to-day," she decided, promptly. "Wot about the tea?"

"We shall be glad to ask you to accept a small packet," Brooks answered. "By the bye, have you a pension from the railway company?"

"Not a penny, sir," she declared, "and a burning shame it is."

"We must see into it," Brooks said. "You see that gentleman behind me?"

"Him with the squint?" she asked, doubtfully.

Brooks bent over his book.

"Mr. Fellows, his name is," he said. "He is one of our helpers here, and he is a lawyer. You can tell him all about it, and if we think you have a claim we will try and see what we can do for you. Now, if you please, we must get on. Come in any time, Mrs. Jones, and talk to us. Some one is, always here. What is your name, please?"

"Amy Hardinge!"

There was a howl of derision from the rear. The girl, pallid, with large dark eyes, a somewhat tawdry hat and torn skirt, turned angrily around.

"Who yer shouting at, eh? There ain't so many of yer as knows yer own names, I dir say, and 'Ardinge's as good as any other. Leave a body be, won't yer?"

She turned round to Brooks, and disclosed a most alarming rent in her gown.

"Look 'ere, guv'nor," she said, "that's my name, and I 'as a back room behind old Connel's fish-shop next door but one to 'ere. If yer want to give away things to them as wants 'em, wot price a new skirt 'ere, eh?"

A woman from the rear leaned over to Brooks.

"The 'ussy," she said. "Don't you take no notice of 'er, sir. We all knows 'er—and precious little good there is ter know."

Miss Hardinge was not unreasonably annoyed. She turned round with flashing eyes and belligerent attitude.

"Who the 'ell asked you anything?" she exclaimed. "Can't yer keep your bloomin' mouths closed?"

A pale-faced little man pushed his way through the throng. He was dressed in a semi-clerical garb, and he tapped Brooks on the shoulder.

"Can you favour me with one moment's private conversation, sir?" he said. "My name is John Deeling, and I am a minister of the Gospel. The Mission House in Fennell Street is my special charge."

"Glad to know you, Mr. Deeling," Brooks answered, "but I can't spare any time for private conversation now. Can't you speak to me here?"

Mr. Deeling looked doubtfully at the girl who stood still before the desk, silent, but breathing hard. A sullen shade had fallen upon her face. She looked like a creature at bay.

"It is concerning-this unfortunate young person."

"I can assure you," Brooks said, dipping his pen in the ink, "that no recommendation is necessary. I shall do what I can for her."

"You misapprehend me, sir," Mr. Deeling said, with some solemnity. "I regret to say that no recommendation is possible. That young person is outside the pale of all Christian help. I regret to speak so plainly before ladies, sir, but she is a notorious character, a hardened and incurable prostitute."

Brooks looked at him for a moment fixedly.

"Did I understand you to say, sir, that you were a minister of the Gospel?" he asked.

"Certainly! I am well known in the neighbourhood."

"Then if you take my advice," Brooks said, sternly, "you will take off those garments and break stones upon the street. It is to help such unfortunate and cruelly ill-used young women as this that I and my friends have come here. Be off, sir. Miss Hardinge, this young lady will take you to our clothes store in the inner room there. I hope you will permit us to be of some further use to you later on."

The girl, half dazed, passed away. Mr. Deeling, his face red with anger, turned towards the door.

"You may call it a Christian deed, sir," he exclaimed, angrily, "to encourage vice of the worst description. We shall see what the bishop, what the Press, have to say about it."

"I don't care a snap of the fingers what you, or the bishop, or time Press have to say," Brooks rejoined, equably; "but lest there should be those here who agree with your point of view, let them hear this from me at once, to prevent misunderstanding. We are here to help to the best of our ability all who need help, whatsoever their characters. They are equally welcome to what we have to offer, whether they be thieves, or prostitutes, or drunkards, or respectable men and women. But if I were asked what really brought me here, for what class of people in the world my sympathy and the sympathies of my friends have been most warmly kindled, I should say, for such as that young woman who has just presented herself here. If she asks for them, she will have from us food and clothes and the use of our baths and reading-rooms whenever she chooses, and I will guarantee that not one of my women friends here who come in contact with her will ask a single question as to her mode of life, until she invites their confidence. If you think that she is responsible for her present state, you and I differ—if you think that one shadow of blame rests upon her, we differ again. And if there are any more like her in the room, let them come out, and they shall have all that they ask for, that it is within our power to give."

"Hear, hear, guv'nor!"

"That's ginger for 'im."

"Out of this, old white choker. There's beans for you."

They let him pass through. On the threshold he turned and faced Brooks again.

"At least," he said, "I can promise you this. God's blessing will never be upon your work. I doubt whether you will be allowed to continue it in this Christian country."

Brooks rose to his feet.

"Mr. Deeling," he said, "you and your mission system of work amongst the poor have been fighting a losing battle in this country for fifty years and more. A Christian country you call it. Go outside in the streets. Look north and south, east and west, look at the people, look at their children, look at their homes. Is there one shadow of improvement in this labyrinth of horrors year by year, decade by decade? You know in your heart that there is none. Therefore if new means be chosen, do not condemn them too rashly. Your mission houses, many of them, have been nothing but breeding-places for hypocrisy. It is time the old order was changed. Now, sir, you are next. What can we do for you?"

A weary-looking man with hollow eyes and nervously-twitching fingers found himself pushed before the desk. He seemed at first embarrassed and half dazed. Brooks waited without any sign of impatience. When at last he spoke, it was without the slightest trace of any Cockney accent.

"I—I beg your pardon, sir! I ought not perhaps to intrude here, but I don't know who needs help more than I do."

"He's orl right, sir," sung out the costermonger. "He is a bit queer in the 'ead, but he's a scholar, and fair on his uppers. Speak up, Joe."

"You see, my friends are willing to give me a character, sir," the man remarked, with a ghost of a smile. "My name is Edward Owston. I was clerk at a large drapery firm, Messrs. Appleby, Sons, and Dawson, in St. Paul's Churchyard, for fourteen years. I have a verified character from them. They were obliged to cult down their staff, owing to foreign competition, and—I have never succeeded—in obtaining another situation. There is nothing against me, sir. I would have worked for fifteen shillings a week. I walked the streets till my boots were worn through and my clothes hung around me like rags. It was bad luck at first—afterwards it was my clothes. I have been selling matches for a month it has brought me in two shillings a week."

"How old are you?" Brooks asked. "Thirty-four, sir." Brooks nearly dropped his pen.

"What?" he exclaimed.

"Thirty-four, sir. It is four years since I lost my situation."

The man's hair was grey, a little stubbly grey beard was jutting out from his chin. His eyes were almost lost in deep hollows. Brooks felt a lump in his throat, and for a moment pretended to be writing busily. Then he looked up.

"We shall give you a fresh start in life, Edward Owston," he said. "Follow this gentleman at my left. He will find you clothes and food. To-morrow you will go to a cottage which belongs to us at Hastings for one month. Afterwards, if your story is true, we shall find you a suitable situation—if it is partially true, we shall still find you something to do. If it is altogether false we cannot help you, for absolute truth in answering our questions is the only condition we impose." The man never uttered a word. He went out leaning upon the arm of one of Brooks' assistants. Another, who was a doctor, after a glance into the man's face, followed them. When he returned, after about twenty minutes' absence, he leaned forward and whispered in Brooks' ear "You'll never have to find a situation for that poor fellow. A month's about all he's good for." Brooks looked round shocked. "What is it—drink?" he asked. The doctor shook his head.

"Not a trace of it. Starvation and exhaustion. If I hadn't been with him just now he'd have been dead before this. He fainted away."

Brooks half closed his eyes.

"It is horrible!" he murmured.

The costermonger was next. Brooks looked around the room and at the clock.

"Look here," he said. "If I sit here till tomorrow I can't possibly attend to all of you. I tell you what I'll do. If you others will give place to those whose cases are really urgent, I'll be here at seven to-morrow morning till seven at night, and the next day too, if necessary. It's no good deputing any one else to tell me, because however many branches we open—and I hope we shall open a great many—I mean to manage this one myself, and I must know you all personally. Now are you all agreeable?"

"I am for one," declared the costermonger, moving away from before the desk. "I ain't in no 'urry. I've 'ad a bit o' bad luck wi' my barrer, all owing to a plaguing drunken old omnibus-driver, and horl I want is a bit o' help towards the security. Josh Auk wants it before he'll let me out a new one. Tomorrow's horl right for me."

"Well, I expect we'll manage that," Brooks remarked. "Now where are the urgent cases?"

One by one they were elbowed forward. Brooks' pen flew across the paper. It was midnight even then before they had finished. Brooks and Mary Scott left together. They were both too exhausted for words.

As they crossed the street Mary suddenly touched his arm.

"Look!" she whispered.

A girl was leaning up against the wall, her face buried in her hands, sobbing bitterly. They both watched her for a moment. It was Amy Hardinge.

"I will go and speak to her," Mary whispered.

Brooks drew her away.

"Not one word, even of advice," he said. "Let us keep to our principles. The end will be surer."

They turned the corner of the street. Above the shouting of an angry woman and the crazy song of a drunken man the girl's sobs still lingered in their ears.

CHAPTER VIII
MR. BULLSOM IS STAGGERED

Mr. Bullsom looked up from his letters With an air of satisfaction.

"Company to dinner, Mrs. Bullsom!" he declared. "Some more of your silly old directors, I suppose," said Selina, discontentedly. "What a nuisance they are."

Mr. Bullsom frowned.

"My silly old directors, as you call 'em," he answered, "may not be exactly up to your idea of refinement, but I wouldn't call 'em names if I were you. They've made me one of the richest men in Medchester."

"A lot we get out of it," Louise grunted, discontentedly.

"You get as much as you deserve," Mr. Bullsom retorted. "Besides, you're so plaguing impatient. You don't hear your mother talk like that."

Selina whispered something under her breath which Mr. Bullsom, if he heard, chose to ignore.

"I've explained to you all before," he continued, "that up to the end of last year we've been holding the entire property—over a million pounds' worth, between five of us. Our time's come now. Now, look here—I'll listen to what you've got to say—all of you. Supposing I've made up my mind to launch out. How do you want to do it? You first, mother."

Mrs. Bullsom looked worried.

"My dear Peter," she said, "I think we're very comfortable as we are. A larger household means more care, and a man-servant about the place is a thing I could never abide. If you felt like taking sittings at Mr. Thompson's as well as our own chapel, so that we could go there when we felt we needed a change, I think I should like it sometimes. But it seems a waste of good money with Sundays only coming once in seven days."

Mr. Bullsom shook with good-humoured laughter.

"Mother, mother," he said, "we shall never smarten you up, shall we, girls? Now, what do you say, Selina?"

"I should like a country house quite ten on fifteen miles away from here, lots of horses and carriages, and a house in town for the season," Selina declared, boldly.

"And you, Louise?"

"I should like what Selina has said."

Mr. Bullsom looked a little grave.

"The house in London," he said, "you shall have, whether I buy it or only hire it for a few months at a time. If we haven't friends up there, there are always the theatres and music-halls, and lots going on. But a country house is a bit different. I thought of building a place up at Nicholson's Corner, where the trains stop. The land belongs to me, and there's room for the biggest house in Medchester."

Selina tossed her head.

"Of course," she said, "if we have to spend all our lives in this hateful suburb it doesn't much matter whether you stay here on build another house, no one will come to see us. We shall never get to know anybody."

"And supposing you go out into the country," Mr. Bullsom argued. "How do you know that you will make friends there?"

"People must call," Selina answered, "if you subscribe to the hounds, and you must get made a magistrate."

"We have lived here for a good many years," Mr. Bullsom said, "and there are very superior people living almost at our doors whom even you girls don't know to bow to."

Selina tossed her head.

"Superior, you call them, do you? A silly stuck-up lot, I think. They form themselves into little sets, and if you don't belong, they treat you as though you had small-pox."

"The men are all pleasant enough," Mr. Bullsom remarked. "I meet them in the trains and in business, and they're always glad enough to pass the time o' day."

"Oh, the men are all right," Selina answered. "It's easy enough to know them. Mr. Wensome trod on my dress the other day, and apologized as though he'd torn it off my back, and the next day he gave me his seat in the car. I always acknowledge him, and he's glad enough to come and talk, but if his wife's with him, she looks straight ahead as though every one else in the car were mummies."

Mr. Bullsom cut the end of a cigar thoughtfully, and motioned Louise to get him a light.

"You see, your mother and I are getting on in life," he said, "and it's a great thing to ask us to settle down in a place where there's no slipping off down to the club in the evening, and no chance of a friend dropping in for a chat. We've got to an age when we need some one to talk to. I ain't going to say that a big house in the country isn't a nice thing to have, and the gardens and that would be first-class. But it's a big move, and it ain't to be decided about all in a hurry."

"Why, father, there's the shooting," Selina exclaimed. "You're fond of that, and men will go anywhere for really good shooting, and make their wives go, too. If you could get a place with plenty of it, and a fox-covert or two on the estate, I'm perfectly certain we should be all right."

Mr. Bullsom looked still a little doubtful.

"That's all very well," he said, "but I don't want to bribe people into my house with shooting and good cooking, and nursing their blooming foxes. That ain't my idea of making friends."

"It's only breaking the ice-just at first," Selina argued. "Afterwards I'm sure you'd find them friendly enough."

"I tell you what I shall do," Mr. Bullsom said, deliberately; "I shall consult the friend I've got coming to dinner to-night."

Selina smiled contemptuously.

"Pshaw!" she exclaimed. "What do any of them know about such things?"

"You don't know who it is," Mr. Bullsom replied, mysteriously.

The girls turned towards him almost simultaneously.

"Is it Mr. Brooks?"

Mr. Bullsom nodded. Selina flushed with pleasure and tried to look unconscious.

"Only the day before yesterday," Mr. Bullsom said, "as chairman of the committee, I had the pleasure of forwarding to Brooks a formal invitation to become the parliamentary candidate for the borough. He writes to me by return to say that he will be here this afternoon, as he wishes to see me personally."

"I must say he hasn't lost much time," Louise remarked, smiling across at Selina.

Mr. Bullsom grunted.

"I don't see how he could do much less," he said. "After all, though every one admits that he's a clever young chap and uncommonly conscientious, he's not well known generally, and he hasn't the position in the town or anywhere which people generally look for in a parliamentary candidate. I may tell you, girls, and you, mother, that he was selected solely on my unqualified support and my casting vote."

"I hope," Mrs. Bullsom said, "that he will be properly grateful."

"I'm sure it's very good of you, pa," Selina declared, affably. She liked the idea of Brooks owing so much to her father.

"There's no young man," Mr. Bullsom said, "whom I like so much or think so much of as Mr. Brooks. If I'd a son like that I'd be a proud man. And as we're here all alone, just the family, as it were, I'll go on to say this," Mr. Bullsom continued, his right thumb finding its way to the armhole of his waistcoat. "I'm going to drop a hint at the first opportunity I get, quite casually, that whichever of you girls gets married first gets a cheque from me for one hundred thousand pounds."

Even Selina was staggered. Mrs. Bullsom was positively frightened.

"Mr. Bullsom!" she said. "Peter, you ain't got as much as that? Don't tell me!"

"I am worth to-day," Mr. Bullsom said, solemnly, "at least five hundred thousand pounds."

"Peter," Mrs. Bullsom gasped, "has it been come by honest?"

Mr. Bullsom smiled in a superior way.

"I made it," he answered, "by locking up forty thousand, more than half of what I was worth, for five years. But I knew what I was about, and so did the others. Mason made nearly as much as I did."

Selina looked at her father with a new respect. He rose and brushed the ashes of his cigar from his waistcoat.

"Now I'm off," he declared. "Brooks and I will be back about seven, and I shall try and get him to sleep here. Fix yourselves up quiet and ladylike, you girls. Good-bye, mother."

* * * * *

"We have about an hour before dinner," Mr. Bullsom remarked, sinking into his most comfortable chair and lighting a cigar. "Just time for a comfortable chat. You'll smoke, Brooks, won't you?"

Brooks excused himself, and remained standing upon the hearthrug, his elbow upon the mantelpiece. He hated this explanation he had to make. However, it was no good in beating about the bush.

"I am going to surprise you very much, Mr. Bullsom," he began.

Mr. Bullsom took the cigar from his mouth and looked up with wide-open eyes. He had been preparing graciously to wave away a torrent of thanks.

"I am going to surprise you very much," Brooks repeated. "I cannot accept this magnificent offer of yours. I cannot express my gratitude sufficiently to you, or to the committee. Nothing would have made me happier than to have been able to accept it. But I am absolutely powerless."

"You don't funk it?" Mr. Bullsom asked.

"Not I. The fact is, there are circumstances connected with myself which make it inadvisable for me to seek any public position at present."

Mr. Bullsom's first sensations of astonishment were augmented into stupefaction. He was scarcely capable of speech. He found himself wondering idly how heinous a crime a man must commit to be branded ineligible.

"To explain this to you," Brooks continued, "I am bound to tell you something which is only known to two people in the country. The Marquis of Arranmore is my father."

Mr. Bullsom dropped his cigar from between his fingers, and it lay for a moment smouldering upon the carpet. His face was a picture of blank and hopeless astonishment.

"God bless my soul!" he exclaimed, faintly. "You mean that you—you, Kingston Brooks, the lawyer, are Lord Arranmore's son?"

Brooks nodded.

"Yes! It's not a pleasant story. My father deserted my mother when I was a child, and she died in his absence. A few months ago, Lord Arranmore, in a leisurely sort of way, thought well to find me out, and after treating me as an acquaintance for some time—a sort of probationary period, I suppose—he told me the truth. That is the reason of my resigning from the firm of Morrison and Brooks almost as soon as the partnership deed was signed. I went to see Mr. Ascough and told him about your offer, and he, of course, explained the position to me."

"But,"—Mr. Bullsom paused as though striving to straighten out the matter in his own mind, "but if you are Lord Arranmore's son there is no secret about it, is there? Why do you still call yourself Mr. Brooks?"

Mr. Bullsom, whose powers of observation were not remarkably acute, looking steadily into his visitor's face, saw there some signs of a certain change which others had noticed and commented upon during the last few months—a hardening of expression and a slight contraction of the mouth. For Brooks had spent many sleepless nights pondering upon this new problem which had come into his life.

"I do not feel inclined," he said, quietly, "for many reasons, to accept the olive-branch which it has pleased my father to hold out to me after all these years. I have still some faint recollections of the close of my mother's life—hastened, I am sure, by anxiety and sorrow on his account. I remember my own bringing up, the loneliness of it. I remember many things which Lord Arranmore would like me now to forget. Then, too, my father and I are as far apart as the poles. He has not the least sympathy with my pursuits or the things which I find worth doing in life. There are other reasons which I need not trouble you with. It is sufficient that for the present I prefer to remain Mr. Brooks, and to lead my own life."

"But—you won't be offended, but I want to understand. The thing seems such a muddle to me. You've given up your practice—how do you mean to live?"

"There is an income which comes to me from the Manor of Kingston," Brooks answered, "settled on the eldest sons of the Arranmore peerage, with which my father has nothing to do. This alone is comparative wealth, and there are accumulations also."

"It don't seem natural," Mr. Bullsom said. "If you'll excuse my saying so, it don't sound like common-sense. You can live on what terms you please with your father, but you ought to let people know who you are. Great Scott," he added, with a little chuckle, "what will Julia and the girls say?

"You will understand, Mr. Bullsom," Brooks said, hastily, "that I trust you to preserve my confidence in this matter. I have told you because I wanted you to understand why I could not accept this invitation to contest the borough, also because you were one of my best friends when I was here. But you are the only person to whom I have told my secret."

Mr. Bullsom sighed. It would have been such a delightful disclosure.

"As you wish, of course," he said. "But my it don't seem possible! Lord Arranmore's son—the Marquis of Arranmore! Gee whiz!"

"Some day, of course," Brooks said, "it must come out. But I don't want it to be yet awhile. If that clock is right hadn't I better be going up-stairs?"

Mr. Bullsom nodded.

"If you'll come with me," he said, "I'll show you your room."

CHAPTER IX
GHOSTS

Brooks, relieved that his explanation with Mr. Bullsom was over, was sufficiently entertaining at dinner-time. He sat between Selina and Louise, and made himself agreeable to both. Mr. Bullsom for half the time was curiously abstracted, and for the remainder almost boisterous. Every now and then he found himself staring at Brooks as though at some natural curiosity. His behaviour was so singular that Selina commented upon it.

"One would think, papa, that you and Mr. Brooks had been quarrelling," she remarked, tartly. "You seem quite odd to-night."

Mr. Bullsom raised his glass. He had lately improved his cellar.

"Drink your health, Brooks," he said, looking towards him. "We had an interesting chat, but we didn't get quarrelling, did we?"

"Nor are we ever likely to," Brooks answered, smiling. "You know, Miss Bullsom, your father was my first client of any importance, and I shan't forget how glad I was to get his cheque."

"I'm very pleased that he was useful to you," Selina answered, impressively. "Will you tell me something that we want to know very much?"

"Certainly!"

"Are you really not coming back to Medchester to live?"

Brooks shook his head.

"No. I am settling down in London. I have found some work there I like."

"Then are you the Mr. Brooks who has started what the Daily Courier calls a 'Whiteby's Charity Scheme' in the East End?"

"Quite true, Miss Bullsom. And your cousin is helping me."

Selina raised her eyebrows.

"Dear me," she said, "I had no idea that Many had time to spare for that sort of thing, had you, father?

"Many can look after herself, and uncommonly well too," Mr. Bullsom answered.

"She comes mostly in the evening," Brooks explained, "but she is one of my most useful helpers."

"It must be so interesting to do good," Louise said, artlessly. "After dinner, Mr. Brooks, will you tell us all about it?"

"It seems so odd that you should care so much for that sort of thing," Selina remarked. "As a rule it is the frumpy and uninteresting people who go in for visiting the poor and doing good, isn't it? You seem so young, and so—oh, I don't think I'd better go on."

"Please do," Brooks begged.

"Well, you won't think I was trying to flatter, will you, but I was going to say, and too clever for that sort of thing."

Brooks smiled.

"Perhaps," he said, "the reason that social reform is so urgently needed in so many ways is for that very reason, Miss Bullsom—that the wrong sort of person has been going in for it. Looking after the poor has meant for most people handing out bits of charity on the toasting-fork of religion. And that sort of thing doesn't tend to bridge over the gulf, does it?"

"Toasting-fork!" Selina giggled. "How funny you are, Mr. Brooks."

"Am I?" he answered, good-humouredly. "Now let me hear what you have been doing since I saw you in town."

Selina was immediately grave—not to say scornful.

"Doing! What do you suppose there is to do here?" she exclaimed, reproachfully. "We've been sitting still waiting for something to happen. But—have you said anything to Mr. Brooks yet, papa?"

Mr. Bullsom shook his head.

"Haven't had time," he answered. "Brooks had so much to say to me. You knew all about our land company, Brooks, of course? You did a bit of conveyancing for us."

"Of course I did," Brooks answered, "and I told you from the first that you were going to make a lot of money by it."

Mr. Bullsom glanced around the room. The two maid-servants were at the sideboard.

"Guess how much."

Brooks shook his head.

"I never knew your exact share," he said.

"It's half a million," Mr. Bullsom said, pulling down his waistcoat, and squaring himself to the table. "Not bad, eh, for a country spec?"

"It's wonderful," Brooks admitted. "I congratulate you heartily."

"Thanks," Mr. Bullsom answered.

"We want papa to buy a house in the country, and go to town for the season," Selina said. "So long as we can afford it I am dying to get out of Medchester. It is absolutely the most commercial town I have ever been in.

"Your father should stand for Parliament himself," Brooks suggested.

It is really possible that Mr. Bullsom, being a man governed entirely by one idea at a time, had never seriously contemplated the possibility of himself stepping outside the small arena of local politics. It is certain at any rate that Brooks' words came to him as an inspiration. He stared for a moment into his glass—then at Brooks. Finally he banged the table with the flat of his hand.

"It's an idea!" he exclaimed. "Why not?"

"Why not, indeed?" Brooks answered. "You'd be a popular candidate for the borough."

"I'm chairman of the committee," Mr. Bullsom declared; "I'll propose myself. I've taken the chair at political dinners and meetings for the last twenty years. I know the runs, and the people of Medchester know me. Why not, indeed? Mr. Brooks, sir, you're a genius."

"You 'ave given him something to think about," Mrs. Bullsom murmured, amiably. "I'd be willing enough but for the late hours. They never did agree with Peter—did they? He's always been such a one for his rest."

Mr. Bullsom's thumbs made their accustomed pilgrimage.

"In the service of one's country," he said, "one should be prepared to make sacrifices. The champagne, Amy. Besides, one can always sleep in the morning."

Selina and Louise exchanged glances, and Selina, as the elder, gave the project her languid approval.

"It would be nice for us in a way," she remarked. "Of course you would have a house in London then, papa, and being an M.P. you would get cards for us to a lot of 'at homes' and things. Only I wish you were a Conservative."

"A Liberal is much more fashionable than he was," Brooks assured her, cheerfully.

"Fashionable! I know the son of a Marquis, a Lord himself, who's a Liberal, and a good one," Mr. Bullsom remarked, with a wink to Brooks.

"Well, my dears," Mrs. Bullsom said, making an effort to rise, and failing at the first attempt, "shall we leave the gentlemen to talk about it over their wine?"

"Oh, you sit down again, mother," Selina directed.

"That sort of thing's quite old-fashioned, isn't it, Mr. Brooks? We're going to stay with you. You can smoke. Ann, bring the cigars."

Mrs. Bullsom, who was looking forward to a nap in a quiet corner of the drawing-room, obeyed with resignation written large on her good-natured, somewhat flushed face. But Mr. Bullsom, who wanted to revert to the subject which still fascinated him, grunted.

"Hang these new ideas," he said. "It's you they're after, Mr. Brooks. As a rule, they're off before I can get near my cigar-box."

Selina affected a little consciousness, which she felt became her.

"Such foolishness, papa. You don't believe it, do you, Mr. Brooks?"

"Am I not to, then?" he asked, looking down upon her with a smile. Whereupon Selina's consciousness became confusion.

"How stupid you are," she murmured. "You can believe just what you like. What are you looking at over in the corner of the room?"

"Ghosts," he answered.

Yet very much as those images flitted at that moment through his brain, so events were really shaping themselves in that bare clean-swept room into which his eyes had for a moment strayed away. Mary Scott was there, her long apron damp with soap-suds and her cheeks red with exertion, for she had just come from bathing twelve youngsters, who, not being used to the ordeal, had given trouble. There were other of his helpers too, a dozen of them up to their eyes in work, and a long string of applicants patiently waiting their turn. The right sort too—the sort from underneath—pale-faced, hollow-eyed, weary, yet for a moment stirred from their lethargy of suffering at the prospect of some passing relief. There was a young woman, hollow-cheeked, thin herself as a lath, eager for work or chance of work for her husband—that morning out of hospital, still too delicate to face the night air and the hot room. He knew shorthand, could keep books, typewrite, a little slip about his character, but that was all over and done with. A bank clerk with L90 a year, obliged to wear a silk hat, who marries a penniless girl on his summer holiday. They must live, both of them, and the gold passed through his fingers day by day, an endless shower. The magistrates had declined to sentence him, but the shame—and he was never strong. Brooks saw the card made out for that little cottage at

Hastings, and enclosed with the railway ticket Owston was picking up fast there—and smiled faintly. He saw the girl on her breathless way home with the good news, saw her wet face heaven turned for the first time for many a month. There were men and women in the world with hearts then. They were not all puppets of wood and stone, even as those bank directors. Then, too, she would believe again that there might be a God.

Ghosts! They were plentiful enough. There was the skin-dresser—his fingers still yellow with the dye of the pith. Things were bad in Bermondsey. The master had gone bankrupt, the American had filched away his trade. No one could find him work. He was sober enough except at holiday time and an odd Saturday—a good currier—there might be a chance for him in the country, but how was he to get there? And in any case now, how could he? His wife had broken down, lay at home with no disease that a hospital would take her in for, sinking for want of good food, worn out with hard work, toiling early and late to get food for the children until her man should get a job. There was the workhouse, but it meant separation, perhaps for ever, and they were man and wife, as much needed the one by the other, perhaps more, as their prototype in the world of plenty. Again Brooks smiled. He must have seen Flitch, a capital chap Flitch, making up that parcel in the grocery department and making an appointment for three days' time. And Menton, too, the young doctor, as keen on the work as Brooks himself, but paid for his evenings under protest, overhears the address—why, it was only a yard or two. He would run back with the man and have a look at his wife. He had some physic—he felt sure it was just what she wanted. So out into the street together, and no wonder the yellow-stained fingers that grasped the string of the parcel shook, and the man felt an odd lump in his throat, and a wave of thankfulness as he passed a flaring public-house when half-an-hour ago he had almost plunged madly in to find pluck for the river—devil's pluck. The woman. Nothing the matter with her but what rest and good food would cure. Another case for that little cottage. Lucky there were others being made ready.

"What sort of ghosts, Mr. Brooks?" Selina asked, a little more sharply.

He started, and withdrew his eyes at last.

"Ah, Miss Bullsom," he answered, "just the ghosts we all carry with us, you know, the ghosts of our thoughts, living and dead, good and evil."

"How funny you are, Mr. Brooks," she exclaimed.

CHAPTER X
A NEW DON QUIXOTE

Brooks reached London the next evening to find himself famous. The evening papers, one of which he had purchased en route, were one and all discussing his new charitable schemes. He found himself held up at once to ridicule and contempt—praised and blamed almost in the same breath. The Daily Gazette, in an article entitled "The New Utopia," dubbed him the "Don Quixote of philanthropy" the St. James's made other remarks scarcely so flattering. He drove at once to Stepney, and found his headquarters besieged by a crowd which his little staff of helpers was wholly unable to cope with, and half-a-dozen reporters waiting to snatch a word with him. Mary watched his entrance with a little sigh of relief.

"I'm so glad you have come," she exclaimed. "It is hard to send these people away, but do you know, they have come from all parts of London? Neither Mr. Flitch nor I can make them understand that we can only deal with cases in the immediate neighbourhood. You must try."

Brooks stood up at once.

"I am very sorry," he said, "if there has been any misunderstanding, but I want you all to remember this. It is impossible for us to deal with any cases to-night unless you are residents of the immediate neighbourhood. The list of streets is on the front door. Please do not present yourselves before any of the desks unless you lodge or live in one of them."

There was a murmur of disappointment, and in the background a few growls.

"I hope before very long," Brooks continued, "that we shall have a great many more branches open, and be able to offer help to all of you. But at present we cannot make any exceptions. Will every one except our neighbours please help us by leaving the room."

For the most part he was obeyed, and then one of the reporters touched him on the shoulder.

"Good-evening, Mr. Brooks. I am representing the Evening Courier. We should be glad to know what your ideas are as to the future of this new departure of yours, and any other information you might cane to give us. There are some others here, I see, on the same errand. Any exclusive information you cared to place at my disposal would be much valued, and we should take especial pains to put your case fairly before the public."

Brooks smiled.

"Really," he said, "it seems as though I were on my defence."

The reporter took out his pencil.

"Well, you know," he said, "some of the established charitable institutions are rather conservative, and they look upon you as an interloper, and your methods as a little too broad."

"Well," Brooks said, "if it is to be war between us and the other charitable institutions you name, I am ready for it, but I cannot talk to you now. As you see, I have an evening's work before me."

"When can you spare me half-an-hour, sir?"

"At midnight—my rooms, in, Jermyn Street."

The reporter closed his book.

"I don't wish to waste your time, sir," he answered. "If you are not going to say anything to the others before then I will go away."

Brooks nodded. The reporters whispered together.

"May we stay and watch for a few minutes?" one of them asked.

Brooks agreed, and went on with his work. Once more the human flotsam and jetsam, worthy and unworthy, laid bare the sore places in their lives, sometimes with the smooth tongue of deceit, sometimes with the unconscious eloquence of suffering long pent up. One by one they found their way into Brooks' ledgers as cases to be reckoned out and solved. And meanwhile nearly all of them found some immediate relief, passing out into the night with footsteps a little less shuffling, and hearts a little lighter. The night's work was a long one. It was eleven o'clock before Brooks left his seat with a little gesture of relief and lit a cigarette.

"I must go and get something to eat," he said. "Will you come Miss Scott?"

She shook her head.

"I have to make out a list of things we want for my department," she said. "Last night they were nearly all women here. Don't bother about me. Mr. Flitch will put me in an omnibus at London Bridge. You must see those reporters. You've read the evening papers, haven't you?"

Brooks nodded.

"Yes. I knew we should have opposition. This isn't even the beginning of it. It won't hurt us."

Nevertheless Brooks was anxious to be properly understood, and he talked for a long time with the reporter, whom he found awaiting him in Jermyn Street—a pleasant young fellow just back from the war, with the easy manner and rattling conversation of his order.

"You ought to call in and have a chat with the chief, Mr. Brooks," he said. "He'd be delighted to hear your views personally, I'm sure, and I believe you'd convert him. He's a bit old-fashioned, you know, that is for a sub—believes in the orthodox societies, and makes a great point of not encouraging idleness."

"I'd be glad to some time," Brooks answered. "But I can tell you this. If we can get the money, and I haven't asked for a penny yet, nothing in the shape of popular opinion is going to stop us. Idleness and drunkenness, deceit and filthy-mindedness, and all those vices which I admit are like a pestilence amongst these people, are sins which we are responsible for, not them, and, of course, we must suffer to some extent from them. But we've got to grapple with them. We shall be taken advantage of, and grossly deceived continually. I know of one or two cases already. We expect it—count upon it. But in the end we shall come out on the top. If we are consistent the thing will right itself."

"You are a young man to be so interested in philanthropic work, Mr. Brooks Every one seems to consider philanthropy the pursuit of the old," Brooks answered. "I don't know why, I am sure."

"And may I ask if that is a sample of your daily correspondence?" he asked, pointing to the table.

Brooks looked at the enormous pile of letters and shook his head.

"I have never had more than twenty letters at a time in my life," he answered. "There seems to be almost as many thousands there. It is, I suppose, a result of the Press booming our modest little show. I can scarcely feel as grateful as I should like to. Have another pipe, will you—or a cigar? I think unless there's anything else you'd like to ask I'd better begin on these."

"Nothing more, thanks," the pressman answered; "but if I might I'd like to stay while you open a few. There might be something interesting. If you'll forgive my remarking it, there seem to be a good many registered letters. I understood that you had not appealed to the public for subscriptions."

"Neither have I," Brooks answered, stretching out his hand. "If there is money in these it is entirely unsolicited."

He plunged into a correspondence as various as it was voluminous. There were letters of abuse, of sympathy, of friendship, of remonstrance, of reproof. There were offers of help, money, advice, suggestions, and advertisements. There were small sums of money, and a few larger ones. He was amused to find that a great many people addressed him as an infidel—the little mission preacher had certainly been busy, and everywhere it seemed to be understood that his enterprise was an anti-Christian one. And finally there was a long packet, marked as having been delivered by hand, and inside—without a word of any sort, on a single clue as to its sender—a bank-note for one thousand pounds.

Brooks passed it over to his companion, who saw the amount with a little start.

"A thousand pounds—not even registered—in a plain envelope. And you have no idea from whom it came?"

"None whatever," Brooks answered.

The pressman folded it up silently, and passed it back. He looked at the huge pile of correspondence and at Brooks—his dark thoughtful face suddenly lit up with a rare gleam of excitement. In his own mind he was making a thumb-nail sketch of these things. There was material for one of those broad, suggestive articles which his editor loved. He wished Brooks good-night.

"I'm much obliged for all you've told me," he said. "If you don't mind, I'd like to drop in now and again down at Stepney. I believe that this is going to be rather a big thing for you."

Brooks smiled.

"So do I," he answered. "Come whenever you like."

Brooks sank into an easy-chair, conscious at last of a more than ordinary exhaustion. He looked at the pile of newspapers at his feet, the sea of correspondence on the table—his thoughts travelled back to the bare, dusty room in Stepney, with its patient, white-faced crowd of men and women and children. Perhaps, after all, then he had found his life's work here. If so he need surely regret no longer his lost political opportunities. Yet in his heart he knew that it had been from the House of Commons he had meant to force home his schemes. To work outside had always seemed to him to be labouring under a disadvantage, to be missing the true and best opportunity of impressing upon the law-makers of the country their true responsibilities. But of that there was no longer any hope. Of the House of Lords he thought only with a cold shiver. No, political life was denied to him. He must do his best for the furtherance of his work outside.

He fell asleep to awake in the cold grey of the morning, stiff and cramped, and cold to the bone. Stamping up and down the room in a vigorous attempt to restore his lost circulation, he noticed as he passed the corner of the table a still unopened letter addressed to him in a familiar handwriting. He took it over to the window, and, glancing at the faintly-sketched coronet on time back, turned it over and broke the seal.

"ST. JAMES'S HOUSE, LONDON.

"Thursday.

"MY DEAR BROOKS,

"I have read with an amusement which I am sure you will not fail to share, the shower of condemnation, approval, and remonstrance which by your doings in Stepney you appear to have brought down upon your head. The religious element especially, you seem to have set by the ears. I sat within hearing of our premier bishop last night at dinner, and his speculations with regard to you and your ultimate aims were so amusing that I passed without noticing it my favourite entree.

"You will have observed that it is your anonymity which is the weapon of which your antagonists make most use. Why not dissipate it and confound them? A Mr. Brooks of unknown antecedents might well be supposed capable of starting a philanthropic work for his own good; the same suspicion could never fall on Lord Kingston Ross, a future marquis. You will notice that I make no appeal to you from any personal motive. I should suggest that we preserve our present relations without alteration. But if you care to accept my suggestion I would propose that you nominate me trustee of your society, and I will give, as a contribution to its funds, the sum of five thousand pounds."

Brooks looked down the long street, quiet and strangely unfamiliar in the dawning light, and for a moment he hesitated. The letter he held in his hand crushed up into a shapeless ball. It would make things very easy. And then—a rush of memories. He swung round and sat down at his desk, drawing paper and ink towards him.

"DEAR LORD ARRANMORE," he wrote, "I am much obliged to you for the suggestion contained in your letter, but I regret that its acceptance would involve the carrying out on my part of certain obligations which I am not at present prepared to undertake. We will, therefore, if you please, allow matters to remain on this footing.

"Yours sincerely,

"KINGSTON BROOKS."

Bareheaded he stole out into the street, and breathed freely only when he heard it drop into the pillar-box. For only he himself knew what other things went with the rejection of that offer.

He crept up-stairs to lie down for a while, and 'on the way he laughed softly to himself.

"What a fool she would think me!" he muttered. "What a fool I am!"

PART III

CHAPTER I
AN ARISTOCRATIC RECRUIT

An early spring came with a rush of warm west wind, sunshine, and the perfume of blossoming flowers. The chestnuts where out at the Park fully a week before their time, and already through the great waxy buds the colour of the coming rhododendrons was to be seen in sheltered corners of the Park. London put out its window boxes, and remembered that it had, after all, for two short months a place amongst the beautiful cities of the world. 'Bus conductors begun to whistle, and hansom cab drivers to wear a bunch of primroses in their coats. Kingston Brooks, who had just left his doctor, turned into the Park and mingled idly with the throng of people.

For the first time for many months he suffered his thoughts to travel over a wider range than usual. The doctor's words had been sharp and to the point. He must have instant change—change, if not of scene, at least of occupation. Scarcely to be wondered at, Brooks thought to himself, with a faint smile, when he thought of the last twelve months, full to the brim of strenuous labour, of ceaseless striving within a herculean task. Well, he was in smoother waters now. He might withdraw his hand for a while, if necessary. He had gone his way, and held his own so far against all manner of onslaught. Just then he heard himself called by name, and, looking up, found himself face to face with Sybil Caroom.

"Mr. Brooks! Is it really you, then, at last?"

He set his teeth hard, but he could not keep the unusual colour from his cheeks.

"It is really I, Lady Sybil. How do you do?"

Sybil was charming in a lilac-coloured dress and hat as fresh and dainty as her own complexion. She looked straight into his eyes, and told him that he ought to be ashamed of himself.

"Oh, it's not the least use your looking as though you were going to edge away every moment," she declared, laughing. "I am going to keep you for quite a long time, and make you tell me about everything."

"In which case, Lady Sybil," her escort remarked, good-humouredly, "you will perhaps find a better use for me at some future time."

"How sweet of you," she answered, blandly. "Do you know Mr. Brooks? Mr. Kingston Brooks, Lord Bertram. Mr. Brooks is a very old friend, and I have so many questions I want to ask him."

Lord Bertram, a slim, aristocratic young man, raised his hat, and glanced with some interest at the other man.

"The Mr. Kingston Brooks of the East End? Lavvy's friend?" he asked, politely.

Brooks smiled.

"I am afraid," he said, "that I am the person who is being exposed—isn't that the word? I warn you, Lady Sybil, that I am a questionable character."

"I will take the risk," she answered, gaily.

"I think you may safely do so," Lord Bertram answered, raising his hat. "Good-morning, Lady Sybil—morning, Mr. Brooks!"

She led him towards the chairs.

"I am going to take the risk of your being in an extravagant frame of mind," she said, "and make you pay for two chairs—up here, on the back now. Now, first of all, do you know that you look shockingly ill?"

"I have just come from-n my doctor," Brooks answered. "He agrees with you."

"I am glad that you have had the sense to go to him," she said. "Tell me, are you just run down, on is there anything more serious the matter?

"Nothing serious at all," he answered. "I have had a great deal to do, and no holiday during the past year, so I suppose I am a little tired."

"You look like a ghost," she said. "You have been overworking yourself ridiculously. Now, will you be so good as to tell me why you have never been to see us?"

"I have been nowhere," he answered. "My work has claimed my undivided attention."

"Nonsense," she answered. "You have been living for a year within a shilling cab ride of us, and you have not once even called. I really wonder that I am sitting here with you, as though prepared to forgive you. Do you know that I have written you three times asking you to come to tea?"

He turned a very white face upon her.

"Won't you understand," he said, "that I have been engrossed in a work which would admit of no distractions?"

"You could find time to go down to Medchester, and make speeches for your friend Mr. Bullsom," she answered.

"That was different. I was deeply indebted to Mr. Bullsom, and anxious to see him returned. That, too, was work. It is only pleasures which I have denied myself."

"That," she remarked, "is the nicest—in fact, the only nice thing you have said. You have changed since Enton."

"I have been through a good deal," he said, wearily.

She shuddered a little.

"Don't look like that," she exclaimed. "Forgive me, but you made me think—do you remember that night at Enton, when Lord Arranmore spoke of his work amongst the poor, how the hopelessness of it began to haunt him and weigh upon him till he reached the verge of madness. You had something of that look just now."

He smiled faintly.

"Believe me, it was fancy," he answered, earnestly. "Remember, I am a little out of sorts to-day. I am not discouraged; I have no cause to be discouraged. A good many of the outside public misunderstand my work, and Mr. Lavilette thinks I make money out of it. Then, of course, all the organized charities are against me. But in spite of all I am able to go on and increase day by day."

"It is wonderful," she declared. "I read everything in the papers about you—and I get the monthly reports, for of course I am a subscriber—so is mother. But—that brings your shameful neglect of us back into my mind. I wrote to you begging to be allowed to inspect one of your branches, and all I got back was a polite reply from your secretary to the effect that the general public—even subscribers—were never allowed in any of the branches as sightseers, and that all I could see was the stores and general arrangements, for which he enclosed a view-card."

"Well," Brooks said, "you don't think that poor people who come to you for help should be exposed to the casual inspection of visitors who want to see how it is done, do you? I have always been very particular about that. We should not allow the Prince of Wales in the room whilst we were dealing with applicants."

"Well, you might have written yourself, or come and seen us," Sybil declared, a little irrelevantly. "Why couldn't I be an occasional helper?"

"There is not the slightest reason why you should not," he answered. "We have seventeen hundred on the books, but we could always do with more, especially now we are opening so many more branches. But, you know, we should expect you to come sometimes, and how would Lady Caroom like that?" She laughed.

"You know how much mother and I interfere with one another," she answered. "Besides, I have several friends who are on your list, and who are sent for now and then—Edie Gresham and Mary Forbrooke." "It is rough work," he said; "but, of course, if you like, my secretary shall put your name down, and you will get a card then telling you what week to come. It will be every afternoon for a week, you know. Then you are qualified, and we might send for you at any time if we were short."

"I should come," she said.

A coach passed by, with its brilliant load of women in bright gowns and picture hats, and two or three immaculate men. They both looked up, and followed it with their eyes.

"Lord Arranmore," Sybil exclaimed, "and that is the Duchess of Eversleigh with him on the box. It doesn't seem—the same man, does it?"

Brooks smiled a little bitterly.

"The same man," he repeated. "No!"

They were silent for a few moments. Then Sybil turned towards him with a little impetuous movement.

"Come," she said, "let us talk about yourself now. What are you going to do?"

"To do?" he repeated, vaguely. "Why—"

"About your health, of course. You admitted a few minutes ago that you had been to see your doctor."

"Why—I suppose I must ease up a little."

"Of course you must. When will you come and dine quietly with us in Berkeley Square, and go to the theatre?"

He shook his head.

"It is kind of you," he said, "but—"

"When will you come and have tea with me, then?"

He set his teeth. He had done his best.

"Whenever you choose to ask me," he answered, with a sort of dogged resignation.

She looked at him half curiously, half tenderly.

"You are so much changed," she murmured, "since those days at Enton. You were a boy then, although you were a thoughtful one—now you are a man, and when you speak like that, an old man. Come, I want the other Mr. Brooks."

He sat quite still. Perhaps at that moment of detachment he realized more keenly than ever the withering nature of this battle through which he had passed. Indeed, he felt older. Those days at Enton lay very far back, yet the girl by his side made him feel as though they had been but yesterday. He glanced at her covertly. Gracious, fresh, and as beautiful as the spring itself. What demon of mischief had possessed her that she should, with all her army of admirers, her gay life, her host of pleasures, still single him out in this way and bring back to his memory days which he had told himself he had wholly forgotten? She was not of the world of his adoption, she belonged to the things which he had forsworn.

"The other Mr. Brooks," he murmured, "is dead. He has been burned in the furnace of this last wonderful year. That is why I think—I fear it is no use your looking for him—and you would not wish to have a stranger to tea with you."

"That," she said, "is ingenious, but not convincing. So you will please come to-morrow at four o'clock. I shall stay in for you.

"At four o'clock," he repeated, helplessly.

Lady Caroom waved to them from the path.

"Sybil, come here at once," she exclaimed, "and bring Mr. Brooks with you. Dear me, what troublesome people you have been to find. I am very glad indeed to see you again."

She looked Brooks in the face as she held his hand, and With a little start he realized that she knew.

"You most quixotic of young men," she exclaimed, "come home with us at once, and explain how you dared to avoid us all this time. What a ghost you look. I hope it is your conscience. Don't pretend you can't sit with your back to the horse, but get in there, sir, and—James, the little seat—and make yourself as comfortable as you can. Home, James! Upon my word, Mr. Brooks, you look like one of those poor people whom you have been working for in the slums. If starvation was catching, I should think that you had caught it. You must try my muffins."

Sybil caught his eye, and laughed.

"Mother hasn't altered much, has she?" she asked.

CHAPTER II
MR. LAVILETTE INTERFERES

"What is this Kingston Brooks' affair that Lavilette has hold of now?" yawned a man over his evening papers. "That fellow will get into trouble if he doesn't mind."

"Some new sort of charity down in the East End," one of the little group of club members replied. "Fellow has a lot of branches, and tries to make 'em a sort of family affair. He gets a pile of subscriptions, and declines to publish a balance-sheet. Lavilette seems to think there's something wrong somewhere."

"Lavilette's such a suspicious beggar," another man remarked. "The thing seems all right. I know people who are interested in it, who say it's the most comprehensive and common-sense charity scheme of the day."

"Why doesn't he pitch into Lavilette, then? Lavilette's awfully insulting. Brooks the other day inserted an acknowledgment in the papers of the receipt of one thousand pounds anonymous. You saw what Lavilette said about it?"

"No. What?"

"Oh, he had a little sarcastic paragraph—declined to believe that Brooks had ever received a thousand pounds anonymously—challenged him to give the number of the note, and said plainly that he considered it a fraud. There's been no reply from Brooks."

"How do you know?"

"This week's Verity. Here it is!"

"We have received no reply from Mr. Kingston Brooks up to going to press with respect to our remark concerning the thousand pounds alleged to have been received by him from an anonymous giver. We may add that we scarcely expected it. Yet there is another long list of acknowledgments of sums received by Mr. Brooks this morning. We are either the most credulous nation in the world, or there are a good many people who don't know what to do with their money. We should like to direct their attention to half-a-dozen excellent and most deserving charities which we can personally recommend, and whose accounts will always stand the most vigorous examination."

"H'm! That's pretty strong," the first speaker remarked. "I should think that that ought to stay the flow of subscriptions."

Lord Arranmore, who was standing on the hearthrug smoking a cigarette, joined languidly in the conversation.

You think that Brooks ought to take some notice of Lavilette's impudence, then?"

"Well, I'm afraid his not doing so looks rather fishy," the first speaker remarked. "That thousand pounds note must have been a sort of a myth."

"I think not," Lord Arranmore remarked, quietly. "I ought to know, for I sent it myself,"

Every man straightened himself in his easy-chair. There was a little thrill of interest.

"You're joking, Arranmore."

"Not I! I've sent him three amounts—anonymously."

"Well, I'd no idea that sort of thing was in your line," one of the men exclaimed.

"More it is," Arranmore answered. "Personally, I don't believe in charity—in any modern application of it at any rate. But this man Brooks is a decent sort."

"You know who Brooks is, then?"

"Certainly. He was my agent for a short time in Medchester."

Mr. Hennibul, who was one of the men sitting round, doubled his copy of Verity up and beat the air with it.

"I knew I'd heard the name," he exclaimed. "Why, I've met him down at Enton. Nice-looking young fellow."

Arranmore nodded.

"Yes. That was Brooks."

Mr. Hennibul's face beamed.

"Great Scott, what a haul!" he exclaimed. "Why, you've got old Lavilette on toast—you've got him for suing damages too. If this is why Brooks has been hanging back—just to let him go far enough—by Jove, he's a smart chap."

"I don't fancy Brooks has any idea of the sort," Lord Arranmore answered. "All the same I think that Lavilette must be stopped and made to climb down."

Curiously enough he met Brooks the same afternoon in Lady Caroom's drawing-room.

"This is fortunate," he remarked. "I wished for a few minutes' conversation with you."

"I am at your service," Brooks answered, quietly.

The room was fairly full, so they moved a little on one side. Lord Arranmore for a moment or two studied his son's face in silence.

"You show signs of the struggle," he remarked.

"I have been overworked," Brooks answered. "A week or two's holiday is all I require—and that I am having. As for the rest," he answered, looking Lord Arranmore in the face, "I am not discouraged. I am not even depressed."

"I congratulate you—upon your zeal."

"You are very good."

"I was going to speak to you," Lord Arranmore continued, "concerning the paragraph in this week's Verity, and these other attacks which you seem to have provoked."

Brooks smiled.

"You too!" he exclaimed.

"I also!" Lord Arranmore admitted, coolly. "You scarcely see how it concerns me, of course, but in a remote sense it does."

"I am afraid that I am a little dense," Brooks remarked.

"I will not embarrass you with any explanation," Lord Arranmore remarked. "But all the same I am going to surprise you. Do you know that I am very much interested in your experiment?"

Brooks raised his eyebrows.

"Indeed!"

"Yes, I am very much interested," Lord Arranmore repeated. "I should like you to understand that my views as to charity and charitable matters remain absolutely unaltered. But at the same time I am anxious that you should test your schemes properly and unhampered by any pressure from outside. You are all the sooner likely to grow out of conceit with them. Therefore let me offer you a word of advice. Publish your accounts, and sue Lavvy for a thousand pounds."

Brooks was silent for a moment.

"My own idea," he said, slowly, "was to take no notice of these attacks. The offices where the financial part of our concern is managed are open to our subscribers at any time, and the books are there for their inspection. It is only at the branches where we do not admit visitors."

"You must remember," Lord Arranmore said, "that these attacks have been growing steadily during the last few months. It is, of course, no concern of mine, but if they are left unanswered surely your funds must suffer."

"There have been no signs of it up to the present," Brooks answered. "We have large sums of money come in every day."

"This worst attack," Lord Arranmore remarked, "only appeared in this week's Verity. It is bound to have some effect."

Brooks shrugged his shoulders.

"I do not fear it," he answered, calmly. "As a matter of fact, however, I am going to form a council to take the management of the financial organization. It is getting too large a thing for me with all my other work. Is there anything else you wished to say to me?"

The eyes of the two men met for a moment both unflinchingly. Perhaps they were each searching for something they could not find.

"There is nothing else. Don't let me detain you."

Brooks, who was the leaving guest, stepped quietly away, and Lord Arranmore calmly outstayed all the other callers.

"Your manners," Lady Caroom told him, as the last of her guests departed, "are simply hoydenish. Who told you that you might sit out all my visitors in this bare-faced way?"

"You, dear lady, or rather your manner," he answered, imperturbably. "It seemed to me that you were saying all the time, 'Do not desert me! Do not desert me!' And so I sat tight."

"An imagination like yours," she declared, "is positively unhealthy. Arranmore, what an idiot you are.

"Well?"

"Oh, you know all about it—and one hears! Are you tired of your life?"

"Very, very tired of it!" he answered. "Isn't everybody?"

"Of course not. Neither are you really. It is only a mood. Some day you will succeed in what you seem trying so hard to do, and then you will be sorry—and perhaps some others!"

"If one could believe that," he murmured.

"Two months ago," she continued, "every one was saying that you had made up your mind to end your days in the hunting-field. All Melton was talking about your reckless riding, and your hairbreadth escapes."

"Both shockingly exaggerated," he said, under his breath.

Perhaps; but apart from the papers I have seen people who were out and who have told me that you rode with absolute recklessness, simply and purely for a fall, and that you deserved to break your neck a dozen times over. Then there was your week in Paris with Prince Comfrere, and now your supper-parties are the talk of London."

"They are justly famed," he answered, gravely, "for you know I brought home the chef from Voillard's. I am sorry that I cannot ask you to one."

"Don't be ridiculous, Arranmore. Why do you do these things? Does it amuse you, give you any satisfaction?"

"Upon my word I don't know," he answered.

"Then why do you do it?"

"Because," he said slowly, "there is a shadow which dogs me. I am always trying to escape—and it is always hard on my heels. You are a woman, Catherine, and you don't know the suffering of the most intolerable form of ennui—loneliness."

"And do you?" she asked, looking at him with softening eyes.

"Always. It rode with me in the turnkey frill—and sometimes perhaps it lifted my spurs—why not? And at these suppers you speak of, well, they are all very gay—it is I only who have bidden them, who reap no profit. For whosoever may sit there the chair at my side is always empty."

"You speak sadly," she said, "and yet—"

"Yet what?"

"To hear you talk, Arranmore, with any real feeling about anything is always a relief," she said. "Sometimes you speak and act as though every emotion which had ever filled your life were dead, as though you were indeed but the shadow of your former self. Even to know that you feel pain is better than to believe you void of any feeling whatever."

"Then you may rest content," he told her quietly, "for I can assure you that pain and I are old friends and close companions."

"You have so much, too, which should make you happy—which should keep you employed and amused," she said, softly.

"'Employed and amused.'" His eyes flashed upon her with a gleam of something very much like anger. "It pleases you to mock me!"

"Indeed no!" she protested. "You must not say such things to me."

"Then remember," he said, bitterly, "that sympathy from you comes always very near to mockery. It is you and you alone who can unlock the door for me. You show me the key—but you will not use it."

A belated caller straggled in, and Arranmore took his leave. Lady Caroom for the rest of the afternoon was a little absent. She gave her visitors cold tea, and seriously imperiled her reputation as a charming and sympathetic hostess.

CHAPTER III
THE SINGULAR BEHAVIOUR OF MARY SCOTT

The looking-glass was, perhaps, a little merciless in that clear north light, but Mary's sigh as she looked away from it was certainly unwarranted. For, as a matter of fact, she had improved wonderfully since her coming to London. A certain angularity of figure had vanished—the fashionable clothes which Mr. Bullsom had insisted upon ordering for her did ample justice to her graceful curves and lithe buoyant figure. The pallor of her cheeks, too, which she had eyed just now with so much dissatisfaction, was far removed from the pallor of ill-health; her mouth, which had lost its discontented droop, was full of pleasant suggestions of humour. She was distinctly a very charming and attractive young woman—and yet she turned away with a sigh. She was twenty-seven years old, and she had been unconsciously comparing herself with a girl of eighteen.

She drew down one of the blinds and set the tea-tray where she could sit in the shadow. She was conscious of having dressed with unusual care—she had pinned a great bunch of fragrant violets in her bosom. She acknowledged to herself frankly that she was anxious to appear at her best. For there had come to her, in the midst of her busy life—a life of strenuous endeavour mingled with many small self-denials—a certain sense of loneliness—of insufficiency—a new thing to her and hard to cope with in this great city where friends were few. And last night, whilst she had been thinking of it, came this note from Brooks asking if he might come to tea. She had been ashamed of herself ever since. It was maddening that she should sit waiting for his coming like a blushing schoolgirl—the colour ready enough to stream into her face at the sound of his footstep.

He came at last—a surprise in more ways than one. For he had abandoned the blue serge and low hat of his daily life, and was attired in frock coat and silk hat—his tie and collar of a new fashion, even his bearing altered—at least so it seemed to her jealous observation. He was certainly looking better. There was colour in his pale cheeks, and his eyes were bright once more with the joy of life. Her dark eyes took merciless note of these things, and then found seeing at all a little difficult.

"My dear Mary," he exclaimed, cheerfully—he had fallen into the way of calling her Mary lately "this is delightful of you to be in. Do you know that I am really holiday-making?"

"Well," she answered, smiling, "I imagined that you were not on your way eastwards."

"Where can I sit? May I move these?" He swept aside a little pile of newspapers and books, and took possession of the seat which she had purposely appropriated. "The other chairs are so far off, and you seem to have chosen a dark corner. Eastwards, no. I have been at the office all the morning, and we have bought the property in Poplar Grove and the house in Bermondsey. Now I have finished for the day. Doctor's orders."

"If any one has earned a holiday," she said, quietly, "you have. There is some cake on the table there."

"Thanks. Well, it was hard work at first. How we stuck at it down at Stepney, didn't we? Six in the morning till twelve at night. And then how we rushed ahead. It seems to me that we have been doing nothing but open branches lately."

"I wonder," she said, "that you have stood it so well. Why don't you go away altogether for a time? You have such splendid helpers now.

"Oh, I'm enjoying myself," he answered, lightly, "and I don't care to be out of touch with it all."

"You enjoy contrasts," she remarked. "I saw your name in the paper this morning as one of Lady Caroom's guests last night."

He nodded.

"Yes, Lady Caroom has been awfully good to me, and I seem to have got to know a lot of pleasant people in an incredulously short time."

"You are a curious mixture," she said, looking at him thoughtfully.

"Of what?" he asked, passing his cup for some more tea.

"Of wonderful self-devotion," she answered, "and a genuine and natural love of enjoyment. After all, you are only a boy."

"I fancy," he remarked, smiling, "that my years exceed yours."

"As a matter of fact they don't," she answered, "but I was not thinking of years, I was thinking of disposition. You have set going the greatest charitable scheme of the generation, and yet you are so young, so very young."

He laughed a little uneasily. In some vague way he felt that he had displeased her.

"I never pretended," he said, "that I did not enjoy life, that I was not fond of its pleasures. It was only while my work was insecure that I made a recluse of myself. You, too," he said, "it is time that you slackened a little. Come, take an evening off and we will dine somewhere and go to the theatre." How delightful it sounded. She felt a warm rush of pleasure at the thought. They would want her badly at Stepney, but "This evening?" she asked.

"Yes. No, hang it, it can't be this evening. I'm dining with the Carooms—nor to-morrow evening. Say Thursday evening, will you?"

Something seemed suddenly to chill her momentary gush of happiness.

"Well," she said, "I think not just yet. We have several fresh girls, you know—it is a bad time to be away. Perhaps you will ask me later on."

He laughed softly.

"What a funny girl you are, Mary. You'd really rather stew in that hot room, I believe, than go anywhere to enjoy yourself. Such women as you ought to be canonized. You are saints even in this life. What can be done for you in the next?"

Mary bit her lip hard, and she bent low over the tea-cups. In another moment she felt that her self-control must go. Fortunately he drifted away from the subject.

"Very soon," he said, "we must all have a serious talk about the future. The management is getting too big for me. I think there should be a council elected—something of the sort must be done, and soon."

"That," she remarked, "is what Mr. Lavilette says, isn't it?"

He looked at her with twinkling eyes.

"Oh, you needn't think I'm being scared into it," he answered. "All the same, Lavvy's right enough. No one man has the right to accept large subscriptions and not let the public into his confidence."

"Lavilette doesn't believe in our anonymous subscriptions, does he?" she asked.

"No! He's rather impudent about that, isn't he? I suppose I ought really to set him right. I should have done so before, but he went about it in such an offensive manner. Well, to go on with what I was saying. You will come on the council, Mary?"

"I? Oh, surely not!"

"You will! And, what is more, I am going to split all the branches up into divisions, and appoint superintendents and manageresses, at a reasonable salary. And you," he concluded, "are going to be one of the latter."

She shook her head firmly.

"No! I must remain my own mistress."

"Why not? I want to allot to you the work where you can do most good. You know more about it than any one. There is no one half so suitable. I want you to throw up your other work come into this altogether, be my right hand, and let me feel that I have one person on the council whom I can rely upon."

She was silent for a moment. She leaned back in her chair, but even in the semi-obscurity the extreme pallor of her face troubled him.

"You must remember, too," he said, "that the work will not be so hard as now. Lately you have given us too much of your time. Indeed, I am not sure that it is not you who need a holiday more than I."

She raised her eyes.

"This is—what you came to say to me?"

"Yes. I was anxious to get your promise."

There was another short silence. Then she spoke in dull even tones.

"I must think it over. You want my whole time, and you want to pay me for it."

"Yes. It is only reasonable, and we can afford it. I should draw a salary myself if I had not a little of my own."

She raised her eyes once more to his mercilessly, and drew a quick little breath. Yes, it was there written in his face—the blank utter indifference of good-fellowship. It was all that he had come to ask her, it was all that he would ever ask her. Suddenly she felt her heart throbbing in quick short beats-her cheeks burned. They were alone—even her little maid had gone out. Why was he so miserably indifferent? She stumbled to her feet, and suddenly stooping down laid her burning cheeks against his.

"Kingston," she said, "you are so cruel—and I am so lonely. Can't you see that I am miserable? Kiss me!"

Brooks sat petrified, utterly amazed at this self-yielding on the part of the last woman in this world whom he would ever have thought capable of anything of the sort.

"Kiss me—at once."

He touched her lips timorously. Then she sprang away from him, her cheeks aflame, her eyes on fire, her hair strangely ruffled. She pointed to the door.

"Please go—quickly."

He picked up his hat.

"But, Mary! I—"

"Please!"

She stamped her foot.

"But—"

"I will write. You shall hear from me to-morrow. But if you have any pity for me at all you will go now—this moment."

He rose and went. She heard him turn the handle of the door, heard his footsteps upon the stone stairs outside.

She counted them idly. One, two, three, four now he was on the next landing. She heard them again, less distinctly, always less distinctly. Then silence. She ran to the window. There he was upon the pavement, now he was crossing the road on his way to the underground station. She tore at her handkerchief, waved it wildly for a moment—and then stopped. He was gone—and she. The hot colour came rushing painfully into her cheeks. She threw herself face downwards upon the sofa.

CHAPTER IV
LORD ARRANMORE IN A NEW ROLE

"The epoch-making nights of one's life," Mr. Hennibul remarked, "are few. Let us sit down and consider what has happened."

"A seat," Lady Caroom sighed. "What luxury! But where?"

"My knowledge of the geography of this house," Mr. Hennibul answered, "has more than once been of the utmost service to me, but I have never appreciated it more than at this moment. Accept my arm, Lady Caroom."

They made a slow circuit of the room, passed through an ante-chamber and came out in a sort of winter-garden looking over the Park. Lady Caroom exclaimed with delight.

"You dear man," she exclaimed. "Of course I knew of this place—isn't it charming?—but I had no idea that we could reach it from the reception-rooms. Let us move our chairs over there. We can sit and watch the hansoms turn into Piccadilly."

"It shall be as you say," he answered. "I wonder if all London is as excited to-night as the crowd we have just left."

"To me," she murmured, "London seems always imperturbable, stonily indifferent to good or evil. I believe that on the eve of a revolution we should dine and go to the theatre, choose our houses at which to spend the evening, and avoid sweet champagne with the same care. You and I may know that to-night England has thrown overboard a national policy. Yet I doubt whether either of us will sleep the less soundly."

"Not only that," he said, "but the Government have to-day shown themselves possessed of a penetration and appreciation of mind for which I for one scarcely gave them credit. They have made me a peer."

She looked at him with an amused smile.

"They make judges and peers for two reasons" she remarked.

"That, Lady Caroom, is unkind," he said. "I can assure you that throughout my career I have never made a nuisance of myself to any one. In the House I have been a model member, and I have always obeyed my whip in fear and trembling. At the Bar I have been mildness itself. The /St. James's Gazette/ speaks of my urbanity, and the courtesy with which I have always conducted the most arduous cross-examination. You should read the /St. James's Gazette/, Lady Caroom. I do not know the biographical editor, but it is easy to predict a future for him. He has common-sense and insight. The paragraph about myself touched me. I have cut it out, and I mean to keep it always with me."

"The Press," she said, "have all those things cut and dried. No doubt if you made friends with that young man he would let you read your obituary notice. I have a friend who has corrected the proofs of his already."

Hennibul smiled.

"My cousin Avenal, the police magistrate," he said, "actually read his in the Times. He was bathing at Jersey and was carried away by currents, and picked up by a Sark fishing-smack. They took him to Sark, and he was so charmed with his surroundings and the hospitality of the people that he quite forgot to let anybody know where he was. When he read his obituary notice he almost decided to remain dead. He declared that it was quite impossible to live up to it."

"Our charity now-a-days," she remarked, "always begins with the dead."

"Let me try and awaken yours towards the living!" he said.

She laughed.

"Are you smitten with the Brooks' fever?" she asked.

"Mine is a fever," he answered, "but it has nothing to do with Brooks. I would try to awaken your charity on behalf of a perfectly worthy object, myself—/vide/ the /St. James's Gazette/."

"And what do you need from me more than you have?" she asked. "Haven't you the sole possession of my society, the right to bore me or make me happy, perhaps presently the right to feed me?"

"For a few minutes," he answered.

"Don't be so sure. It may be an hour."

"I want it," he said, "for longer."

Something in his tone suddenly broke through the easy lightness of their conversation. She stole a swift side-glance at him, and understood.

"Come," she said, "you and I are setting every one here a bad example. This is not an occasion for /tete-a-tetes/. We should be doing our duty and talking a little to every one. Let us go back and make up for lost time."

She rose to her feet, but found him standing in the way. For once the long humorous mouth was set fast, his eyes were no longer full of the shadow of laughter, his tone had a new note in it, the note which a woman never fails to understand.

"Dear Lady Caroom," he said, "I was not altogether jesting."

She looked him in the eyes.

"Dear friend," she answered, "I know that you were not, and so I think that we had better go back."

He detained her very gently.

"It is the dearest hope I have in life," he said, softly. "Do not let me run the risk of being misunderstood. Will you be my wife?"

She shook her head. There were tears in her eyes, but her gesture was significant enough.

"It is impossible," she said. "I have loved another man all my life."

He offered her his arm at once.

"Then I believe," he said, in a low tone, "in the old saying—that a glimpse of paradise is sufficient to blind the strongest man...."

They passed into the reception-room, and came face to face with Brooks. She held out her hand.

"Come, you have no right here," she declared. "You are not even a Member of Parliament." He laughed.

"What about you?"

"Oh, I am an inspiration!"

"I don't believe," he said, "that you realize in the least what is going to happen."

"I do!" she answered. "I am going to make you relieve Lord Hennibul, and take me to have an ice."

They moved off together. Hennibul stood looking after them for a moment. Then he sighed and turned slowly away.

"If it's Arranmore," he said to himself, "why on earth doesn't he marry her?"

Lady Caroom was more silent than usual. She complained of a headache, and Brooks persuaded her to take champagne instead of the ice.

"What is the matter with you to-night?" she asked, looking at him thoughtfully. "You look like a boy—with a dash of the bridegroom."

He laughed joyously.

"You should read the evening papers—you would understand a little the practical effect of our new Tariff Bill. Mills in Yorkshire and Lancashire are being opened that have been shut down for years; in Medchester, Northampton, and the boot-centres the unemployed are being swept into the factories. Manufacturers who have been struggling to keep their places open at all are planning extensions already. The wages bill throughout the country will be the largest next week that has been paid for years. Travellers are off to the Colonies with cases of samples—every manufacturing centre is suddenly alive once more. The terrible struggle for existence is lightened. Next week," Brooks continued, with an almost boyish twinkle in his eyes, "I shall go down to Medchester and walk through the streets where it used to make our hearts ache to see the unemployed waiting about like dumb suffering cattle. It will be a holiday—a glorious holiday."

"And yet behind it all," she remarked, watching him closely, "there is something on your mind. What is it?"

He looked at her quickly.

"What an observation."

"Won't you tell me?"

He shook his head.

"It is only one of the smallest cupboards," he said. "The ghost will very soon be stifled."

She sighed.

"Did you see Lord Arranmore this evening?"

"Yes. He was talking to the duke just now. What of him?"

"I have been watching him. Did you ever see a man look so ill?",

"He is bored," Brooks answered, coldly. "This sort of thing does not amuse him."

She shook her head.

"He is always the same. He has always that weary look. He is living with absolute recklessness. It cannot possibly last long."

"He knows the price," Brooks answered. "He lives as he chooses."

"I wonder," she murmured. "Sometimes I wonder whether we do not misjudge him—you and I, Kingston. For you know we have been his judges. You must not shake your head. It is true. You have judged him to be unworthy of a son, and I—I have judged him to be unworthy of a wife.

You don't think—that we could possibly have made a mistake—that underneath there is a little heart left—eaten up with pride and loneliness?"

"I have never seen," Brooks answered, "the slightest trace of it."

"Nor I," she answered. "Yet I knew him when he was young. He was so different, and annihilation is very hard, isn't it? Supposing he were to die, and we were to find out afterwards?"

"You," he said, slowly, "must be the judge of your own actions. For my part I see in him only the man who abandoned my mother, who spent the money of other people in dissipation and worse than dissipation. Who came to England and accepted my existence after a leisurely interval as a matter of course. I have never seen in any one of his actions, or heard in his tone one single indication of anything save selfishness so incarnate as to have become the only moving impulse of his life. If ever I could believe that he cared for me, would find in me anything save a convenience, I would try to forget the past. If he would even express his sorrow for it, show himself capable of any emotion whatsoever in connection with anything or any person save himself, I would be only too thankful to escape from my ridiculous position."

Then they were silent for a moment, each occupied with their own thoughts, and Lord Arranmore, pale and spare, taller than most men there, notwithstanding a recently-acquired stoop, came wearily over to them.

"Dear me," he remarked, "what gloomy faces—and I expected to see Brooks at least radiant. Am I intruding?"

"Don't be absurd, Arranmore," she said kindly. "Why don't you bring up that chair and sit down? You look tired."

He laughed—a little hardly.

"I have been tired so long," he said, "that it has become a habit. Brooks, will you think me guilty of an impertinence, I wonder? I have intruded upon your concerns."

Brooks looked up with his eyes full of questioning. "That fellow Lavilette," Arranmore continued, seemed worried about your anonymous subscription. I was in an evil temper yesterday afternoon, and Verity amused me. So I wrote and confounded the fellow by explaining that it was I who sent the money—the thousand pounds you had."

"You?" Lady Caroom exclaimed, breathlessly.

"You sent me that thousand pounds?" Brooks cried.

They exchanged rapid glances: A spot of colour burned in Lady Caroom's cheeks. She felt her heart quicken, an unspoken prayer upon her lips.

Brooks, too, was agitated.

"Upon my word," Lord Arranmore remarked, coldly, "I really don't know why my whim should so much astound you. I took care to explain that I sent it without the slightest sympathy in the cause—merely out of compliment to an acquaintance. It was just a whim, nothing more, I can assure you. I think that I won it at Sandown or something."

"It was not because you were interested in this work, then?" Lady Caroom asked, fearfully.

"Not in the slightest," he answered. "That is to say, sympathetically interested. I am curious. I will admit that. No more."

The colour faded from Lady Caroom's cheeks. She shivered a little and rose to her feet. Brooks' face had hardened.

"We are very much obliged to you for the money," he said. "As for Lavilette, I had not thought it worth while to reply to him."

Lord Arranmore shrugged his shoulders.

"Nor should I in your place," he answered. "My position is a little different, of course. I am positively looking forward to my next week's Verity. You are leaving now, I see. Good-night!"

"I have kept Mr. Brooks away from his friends," she said, looking at him. "Will you see me to my carriage?"

He offered her his arm with courtly grace. They passed down the crowded staircase together.

"You are looking ill, Philip," she said, softly. "You are not taking care of yourself."

"Care of myself," he laughed. "Why, for whom? Life is not exactly a playground, is it?"

"You are not making the best of it!"

"The best! Do you want to mock me?"

"It is you," she whispered, "who stand before a looking-glass, and mock yourself. Philip, be a man. Your life is one long repression. Break through just once! Won't you?"

He sighed. "Would you have me a hypocrite, Catherine?"

She shook her head. Suddenly she looked up at him.

"Philip, will you promise me this? If ever your impulse should come—if you should feel the desire to speak, to act once more as a man from your heart—you will not stifle it. Promise me that." He looked at her with a faint, tired smile. "Yes, I promise," he answered.

CHAPTER V
LADY SYBIL LENDS A HAND

Brooks glanced at the card which was brought in to him, at first carelessly enough, afterwards with mingled surprise and pleasure.

"Here is some one," he said to Mary Scott, "whom I should like you to meet. Show the young lady in," he directed.

Some instinct seemed to tell her the truth.

"Who is it?" she asked quickly. "I am very busy this morning."

"It is Lady Sybil Caroom," he answered. "Please don't go. I should like you to meet her."

Mary looked longingly at the door of communication which led into the further suite of offices, but it was too late to think of escape. Sybil had already entered, bringing into the room a delicious odor of violets, herself almost bewilderingly beautiful. She was dressed with extreme simplicity, but with a delicate fastidiousness which Mary at any rate was quick to appreciate. Her lips were slightly parted in a natural and perfectly dazzling smile. She came across to Brooks with outstretched hand and laughter in her eyes.

"Confess that you are horrified," she exclaimed. "I don't care a bit. I've waited for you to take me quite long enough. If you won't come now I shall go by myself."

"Go where?" he exclaimed.

"Why, to one of the branches—I don't care which. I can help for the rest of the day." He laughed.

"Well, let me introduce you to Miss Scott," he said, turning round. "Mary, this is Lady Sybil Caroom. Miss Scott," he continued, turning to the younger girl, "has been my right hand since we first started. If ever you do stand behind our counter it will have to be under her auspices."

Sybil turned courteously but with some indifference towards the girl, who was standing by Brooks' chair. In her plain black dress and white linen collar Mary perhaps looked more than her years, especially by the side of Sybil. As the eyes of the two met, Sybil saw that she was regarded with more than ordinary attention. She saw, too, that Mary was neither so plain nor so insignificant as she had at first imagined.

"I am sure you are very much to be congratulated, Miss Scott," she said. "Mr. Brooks' scheme is a splendid success, isn't it? You must be proud of your share in it."

"My share," Mary said, in quiet, even tones, "has been very small indeed. Mr. Brooks is alone responsible for it. The idea was his, and the organization was his. We others have been no more than machines."

"Very useful machines, Mary," Brooks said, with a kind glance towards her. "Come, we mustn't any of us belittle our share in the work."

Mary took up some papers from the desk.

"I think," she said, "that if you have no more messages for Mr. Flitch I had better start. We are very busy in Stepney just now."

"Please don't hurry," Brooks said. "We must try and manage something for Lady Sybil."

Mary looked up doubtfully.

"Unless you ask Lady Sybil to look on," she said, "I don't quite see how it is possible for her to come."

"Lady Sybil knows the conditions," Brooks answered. "She wants to have a try as a helper."

Mary raised her eyebrows slightly.

"The chief work in the morning is washing children," she remarked. "They come to us in a perfectly filthy condition, and we wash about twenty each, altogether."

Sybil laughed.

"Well, I'm not at all afraid of that," she declared. "I could do my share. I rather like kiddies."

"The other departments," Mary went on, "all need some instruction. Would you think it worth while for one day? If so, I should be pleased to do what I can for you."

Sybil hesitated. She glanced towards Brooks.

"I don't want to give a lot of unnecessary trouble, of course," she said. "Especially if you are busy. But it might be for more than one day. You have a staff of supernumerary helpers, haven't you, whom you send for when you are busy? I thought that I might be one of those."

"In that case," Mary answered, "I shall be very glad, of course, to put you in the way of it. I am going to my own branch this morning at Stepney. Will you come with me?"

"If you are sure I shan't be a nuisance," Sybil answered, gratefully. "Good-bye, Mr. Brooks. I'm awfully obliged to you, and will talk it all over at the Henages' to-night."

The two girls drove off in Sybil's brougham. Mary, in her quiet little hat and plain jacket, seemed to her companion, notwithstanding her air of refinement, to be a denizen of some other world. And between the two there was from the first a certain amount of restraint.

"Do you give up your whole time to this sort of work?" Sybil asked, presently.

"I do now," Mary answered. "I had other employment in the morning, but I gave that up last week. I am a salaried official of the Society from last Monday."

Sybil stole a swift side-glance at her.

"Do you know, I think that it must be a very satisfactory sort of life," she said.

Mary's lips flickered into the faintest of smiles. "Really!"

"Oh, I mean it," Sybil continued. "Of course, I like going about and enjoying myself, but it is hideously tiring. And then after a year or two of it you begin to realize a sort of sameness. Things lose their flavour. Then you have odd times of serious thought, and you know that you have just been going round and round in a circle, that you have done nothing at all except made some show at enjoying yourself. Now that isn't very satisfactory, is it?"

"No," Mary answered, "I don't suppose it is."

"Now you," Sybil continued, "you may be dull sometimes, but I don't suppose you are, and whenever you leave off and think—well, you must always feel that your time, instead of having been wasted, has been well and wholesomely spent. I wish I could have that feeling sometimes."

Despite herself, Mary felt that she would have to like this girl. She was so pretty, so natural, and so deeply in earnest.

"There is no reason why you shouldn't, is there?" she said, more kindly than she had as yet spoken. "I can assure you that I very often have the blues, and I don't consider mine by any means the happiest sort of life. But, of course, one feels differently a little if one has tried to do something—and you can if you like, you know."

Sybil's face was perfectly brilliant with smiles.

"You think that I can?" she exclaimed. "How nice of you. I don't mind how hard it is at first. I may be a little awkward, but I don't think I'm stupid."

"You think this sort of work is the sort you would like best?"

"Why, yes. It seems so practical, you know," Sybil declared. "You must be doing good, even if some of the people don't deserve it. I don't know about the washing, but I don't mind it a bit. Do you think it will be a busy morning?"

"I am sure it will," Mary answered. "A number of the people are getting to work again now, since the Tariff Revision Bill passed, and they keep coming to us for clothes and boots and things. I shall give you the skirts and blouses to look after as soon as the washing is over."

"Delightful," Sybil exclaimed. "I am sure I can manage that."

"And on no account must you give any money to any one," Mary said. "That is most important."

"I will remember," Sybil promised.

Two hours later she broke in upon her mother and half-a-dozen callers, her hat obviously put on without a looking-glass, her face flushed, and her hair disordered, and smelling strongly of disinfectant.

"Some tea, mother, please," she exclaimed, nodding to her visitors. "I have had one bun for luncheon, and I am starving. Can you imagine what I have been doing?"

No one could. Every one tried.

"Skating!"

"Ping-pong!"

Getting theatre-tickets at the theatre! She waved them aside with scorn.

"I have washed fourteen children," she declared, impressively, "fitted at least a dozen women with blouses and skirts, and three with boots. Besides a lot of odd things."

Lord Arranmore set down his cup with a little shrug of the shoulders.

"You have joined Brooks' Society?" he remarked.

"Yes! I have been down at the Stepney branch all the morning. And do you know, we're disinfected before we leave."

"A most necessary precaution, I should think," Lady Caroom exclaimed, reaching for her vinaigrette, "but do go and change your things as quickly as you can."

"I must eat, mother, or starve," Sybil declared. "I have never been so hungry."

A somewhat ponderous lady, who was the wife of a bishop, felt bound to express her disapprobation.

"Do you really think, dear," she said, "that you are wise in encouraging a charity which is not in any way under the control of the Church?"

"Oh, isn't it?" Sybil remarked. "I'm sure I didn't know. But then the Church hasn't anything quite like this, has it? Mr. Brooks is so clever and original in all his ideas."

The disapprobation of the bishop's wife became even more marked.

"The very fact," she said, "that the Church has not thought it wise to institute a charitable scheme upon such—er—sweeping lines, is a proof, to my mind, that the whole thing is a mistake. As a matter of fact, I happen to know that the bishop strongly disapproves of Mr. Brooks' methods."

"That's rather a pity, isn't it?" Sybil asked, sweetly. "The Society has done so much good, and in so short a time. Every one admits that."

"I think that the opinion is very far from universal," the elder lady remarked, firmly. "There appears to be no discrimination shown whatever in the distribution of relief. The deserving and the undeserving are all classed together. I could not possibly approve of any charity conducted upon such lines, nor, I think, could any good churchwoman."

"Mr. Brooks thinks," Sybil remarked, with her mouth full of cake, "that it is the undeserving who are in the greatest need of help."

"One could believe anything," the bishop's wife said stiffly, "of a man who adopted such principles as that. And although I do not as a rule approve of Mr. Lavilette or his paper, I am seriously inclined to agree with him in some of his strictures upon Mr. Brooks."

Sybil laughed softly.

"I hadn't read them," she remarked. "Mother doesn't allow the man's paper in the house. Do you really mean that you have it at the palace, Mrs. Endicott?"

The bishop's wife stiffened.

"Mr. Lavilette has at times done great service to the community by his exposure of frauds of all sorts, especially charitable frauds," she said. "It is possible that he may shortly add to the number."

Lord Arranmore shook his head slowly.

"Mr. Lavilette," he said, "has also had to pay damages in one or two rather expensive libel cases. And, between you and me, Mrs. Endicott, if our young friend Brooks chose to move in the matter, I am afraid Mr. Lavilette might have to sign the largest cheque he has ever signed in his life for law costs."

The bishop's wife rose with an icy smile.

"I seem to have found my way into Mr. Brooks' headquarters," she remarked. "Lady Caroom, I shall hope to see you at the palace shortly."

"Poor me," Sybil exclaimed, as their visitor departed. "She only asked you, mummy, so as to exclude me. And poor Mr. Brooks! I wish he'd been here. What fun we should have had."

"Oh, these Etrusians," Lord Arranmore murmured. "I thought that a bishop was very near heaven indeed, all sanctity and charity, and that a bishop's wife was the concentrated essence of these things—plus the wings."

Sybil laughed softly.

"Sanctity and charity," she repeated, "and Mrs. Endicott. Oh!"

CHAPTER VI
THE RESERVATION OF MARY SCOTT

The two girls were travelling westwards on the outside of an omnibus, in itself to Sybil a most fascinating mode of progression, and talking a good deal spasmodically.

"It's really too bad of you, Miss Scott," Sybil declared. "Now to-day, if you will come, luncheon shall be served in my own room. We shall be quite cosy and quiet, and I promise you that you shall not see a soul except my mother—whom I want you to know."

Mary shook her head.

"Don't think me unkind," she said. "I really must not begin visiting. I have only just time for a hurried lunch, and then I must look in at the office and get down to Bermondsey."

"You might just as well have that hurried lunch with me," Sybil declared. "I'll send you anywhere you like afterwards in the carriage."

"It is very kind of you," Mary answered, "but my visiting days are over. I am not a social person at all, you know. My role is usefulness, and nothing else."

"You are too young to talk like that," Sybil said. "I am ten years older than you are," Mary reminded her. "You are twenty-eight," Sybil answered. "I think it is beautiful of you to be so devoted to this work, but I am quite sure a little change now and then is wholesome."

"In another ten years I may think of it," Mary said. "Just now I have so much upon my hands that I dare not risk even the slightest distraction."

"In another ten years," Sybil said, "you will find it more difficult to enlarge your life than now. I can't believe that absorption in any one thing is natural at your age."

Mary looked steadfastly down at the horses.

"We must all decide what is best for ourselves," she said. "I have not your disposition, remember."

"Nothing in the world," Sybil said, "would convince me that it is well for any girl of your age to crowd everything out of her life except work, however fine and useful the work may be. Now you have admitted that except for Mr. Brooks and the people you have met in connection with his work you have no friends in London. I want you to count me a friend, Miss Scott. You have been very kind to me, and made everything delightfully easy. Why can't you let me try and repay it a little?"

"I have only done my duty," Mary answered, quietly. "I am supposed to show new helpers what to do, and you have picked it up very quickly. And as for the rest—don't think me unkind, but I have no room for friendships in my life just now."

"I am sorry," Sybil answered, softly, for though Mary's tone had been cold enough, she had nevertheless for a single moment lifted the curtain, and Sybil understood in some vague manner that there were things behind into which she had no right to inquire.

The two girls parted at Trafalgar Square, and Sybil, still in love with the fresh air, turned blithely westward on foot. In the Haymarket she came face to face with Brooks.

He greeted her with a delightful smile.

"You alone, and walking," he exclaimed. "What fortune. May I come?"

"Of course," she answered. "You know where I have come from, I suppose?"

He glanced at her plain clothes and realized that the odour of disinfectants was stronger even than the perfume of the handful of violets which she had just bought from a woman in the street.

"Stepney!" he exclaimed.

"Quite right. I had a card last evening, and was there at nine o'clock this morning. I suppose I look a perfect wreck. I was dancing at Hamilton House at three o'clock."

He looked towards her marvelling. Her cheeks were prettily flushed, and she walked with the delightful springiness of perfect health.

"I have never seen you look better," he answered.

"And you," she remarked, glancing in amusement at his blue serge clothes, which, to tell the truth, badly needed brushing. "What are you doing in the West End at this time in the morning?

"I have been to Drury Lane," he answered, "with some surveyors from the County Council. There is a whole court there I mean to get condemned. Then I looked in at our new place there, but there was such a howling lot of children that I was glad to get away. How they hate being washed!"

"Don't they!" she exclaimed, laughing. "I had the dearest, naughtiest little girl this morning, and, do you know, when I got her clean, her own brothers and sisters didn't know her again. I'm so glad I've seen you, Mr. Brooks. I want to ask you something." "Well?"

"About Miss Scott. She's been so good to me, and I like her awfully. We've just come up on the omnibus together."

"She has been my right hand from the very first," Brooks said, slowly. "I really don't see how I could have done without her. She is such a capital organizer, too."

"I know all that," Sybil declared. "She's wonderful. I don't want, of course, to be inquisitive," she went on, after a moment's hesitation, "but she interests me so much, and it was only this morning that I felt that I understood her a little bit."

Brooks nodded.

"She is a very reserved young woman," he said.

"Yes, but isn't there some reason for it?" Sybil continued, eagerly. "I have asked her lots of times to come and see me. She admits that she has no friends in London, and I wanted to have her come very much. You see, I thought she would be sure to like mother, and if she doesn't care for society, we might go to the theatre or the opera, a it would be a little change for her, wouldn't it?"

"I think it is very kind of you indeed," Brooks said.

"Well, she has always refused, but I have been very persistent. I just thought that she was perhaps a little shy, or found it difficult to break through her retirement—people get like that, you know, when they live alone. So this morning I really went for her, and I happened to be looking, and I saw something in her face which puzzled me. It stopped my asking her any more. There is something underneath her quiet manner and self-devotion. She has had trouble of some sort."

"How do you know?" he asked.

"A girl can always tell," Sybil answered. "Her self-control is wonderful, but she just let it slip—for a moment. She has some trouble, I am sure. I thought perhaps you might know. Isn't there anything we could do? I am so sorry for her."

Brooks was very grave, and his face was curiously pale.

"Are you quite sure?" he asked.

"Certain!"

They walked on in silence for a few moments.

"You have asked me a very difficult question," he said at last. "She has had a very unhappy sort of life. Her father and mother died in Canada—her father shot himself, and her mother died of the shock. She went to live with an uncle at Medchester, who was good to her, but his household could scarcely have been very congenial. I met her there—she was interested in charitable works then, and she came to London to try and attain some sort of independence. At first she had a position on a lady's magazine which took up her mornings, but we have just induced her to accept a small salary and give us all her time." "That seems like a comprehensive sketch of her life," Sybil remarked, thoughtfully, "but are you sure—that you have not missed anything out?"

"So far as I know," he answered, gravely, "there is nothing new to tell."

They walked the rest of the way to Berkeley Square in absolute silence.

"You will come in to lunch?" she said.

He looked down at his clothes.

"I think not," he answered.

"We are almost certain to be alone," she said. "You haven't seen mother for a long time."

He suffered himself to be persuaded, and almost immediately regretted it. For there were a dozen people or more round the luncheon-table, and he caught a glimpse of more than one frock coat. Further, from the dead silence which followed their entrance, it seemed more than probable that he himself had formed the subject of conversation.

Lady Caroom greeted him as kindly as ever, and found a place for him by her side. Brooks, whose self-possession seldom failed him, smiled to himself as he recognized the bishop, who was his /vis-a-vis/. Hennibul, however, from a little lower down nodded to him pleasantly, and Lord Arranmore spoke a few words of dry greeting.

"Your friend Bullsom," he remarked, "has soon distinguished himself. He made quite a decent speech the other night on the Tariff Bill."

"He has common-sense and assurance," Brooks answered. "He ought to be a very useful man."

Lord Hennibul leaned forward and addressed Arranmore with blank surprise on his face.

"You don't mean to say that you read the debates in the House of Commons, Arranmore?" he exclaimed.

Lord Arranmore shrugged his shoulders.

"Since the degeneration of English humour," he remarked, "one must go somewhere for one's humour."

"I should try the House of Lords, then," a smart young under-secretary remarked under his breath, with a glance at the bishop. "There is more hidden humour in the unshaken gravity of the Episcopal Bench than in both Houses of Parliament put together."

"They take themselves so seriously," Sybil murmured.

"To our friend there," the younger man continued, "the whole world's a congregation—and, by Jove, here comes the text."

For the bishop had deliberately cleared his throat, and leaning forward addressed Brooks across the table.

"I believe," he said, "that I have the pleasure of speaking to Mr. Brooks—Mr. Kingston Brooks?"

"That is my name," Brooks answered civilly, wondering what avalanche was to be hurled upon him.

"Would you consider a question, almost a personal question, from a stranger an impertinence—when the stranger is twice your age?" the bishop asked.

"By no means," Brooks answered. "On the contrary, I should be delighted to answer it if I can."

"These aspersions which Mr.—er—Lavilette has been making so freely in his paper against your new departure—I mean against the financial management of it—do you propose to answer them?"

"Well," Brooks said, "I have not altogether made up my mind. Perhaps your lordship would permit me—since you have mentioned the matter—to ask for your advice."

The bishop inclined his head. This was by no means the truculent sort of young man he had expected.

"You are very welcome to it, Mr. Brooks," he answered. "I should advise you most earnestly to at once justify yourself,—not to Mr. Lavilette, but to the readers of his paper whom he may have influenced by his statements. One charitable institution, however different its foundation, or its method of working, or its ultimate aims, leans largely upon another. Mr. Lavilette's attack, if unanswered, may affect the public mind with regard to many other organizations which are grievously in need of support."

"If that is your opinion," Brooks said, after a moment's hesitation, "I will take the steps you suggest, and set myself right at once."

"If you can do that thoroughly and clearly," the bishop said, "you will render a service to the whole community."

"There should not be much difficulty," Brooks remarked, helping himself to omelette. "I never appealed for subscriptions, but directly they began to come in I engaged a clerk and a well-known firm of auditors, through whose banking-account all the money has passed. They have been only too anxious to take the matter up."

"I am more than pleased at your decision, Mr. Brooks," the bishop said, genially. "I rejoice at it. You will pardon my remarking that you seem very young to have inaugurated and to carry the whole responsibility of a work of such magnitude."

"The work," Brooks answered, "has largely grown of itself. But I have an excellent staff of helpers."

"The sole responsibility though rests with you.

"I am arranging to evade it," Brooks answered. "I am going to adopt commercial methods and inaugurate a Board of Directors."

The bishop hesitated.

"Again, Mr. Brooks," he said, "I must address a suggestion to you which might seem to require an apology. You have adopted methods and expressed views with regard to your scheme which are in themselves scarcely reconcilable with the point of view with which we churchmen are bound to regard the same question. But if you thought it worth while before finally arranging your Board to discuss the whole subject with me, it would give me the greatest pleasure to have you visit me at the palace at any time convenient to yourself."

"I shall consider it a great privilege," Brooks answered, promptly, "and I shall not hesitate to avail myself of it."

The little party broke up soon afterwards, but Lady Caroom touched Brooks upon his shoulder.

"Come into my room for a few minutes," she said. "I want to talk with you."

CHAPTER VII
FATHER AND SON

"Do you know," Lady Caroom said, motioning Brooks to a seat by her side, "that I feel very middle-class and elderly and interfering. For I am going to talk to you about Sybil."

Brooks was a little paler than usual. This was one of those rare occasions when he found his emotions very hard to subdue. And it had come so suddenly.

"After we left Enton," Lady Caroom said, thoughtfully, "I noticed a distinct change in her. The first evidences of it were in her treatment of Sydney Molyneux. I am quite sure that she purposely precipitated matters, and when he proposed refused him definitely."

"I do not think," Brooks found voice to say, "that she would ever have married Sydney Molyneux."

"Perhaps not," Lady Caroom admitted, "but at any rate before our visit to Enton she was quite content to have him around—she was by no means eager to make up her mind definitely. After we left she seemed to deliberately plan to dispose of him finally. Since then—I am talking in confidence, Kingston-she has refused t e Duke of Atherstone."

Brooks was silent. His self-control was being severely tested. His heart was beating like a sledgehammer—he was very anxious to avoid Lady Caroom's eyes.

"Atherstone," she said, slowly, "is quite the most eligible bachelor in England, and he is, as you know, a very nice, unaffected boy. There is only one possible inference for me, as Sybil's mother, to draw, and that is that she cares, or is beginning to think that she cares, for some one else."

"Some one else? Do you know whom?" Brooks asked.

"If you do not know," Lady Caroom answered, "I do not."

Brooks threw aside all attempt at disguise. He looked across at Lady Caroom, and his eyes were very bright.

"I have never believed," he said, "that Sybil would be likely to care for me. I can scarcely believe it now."

Lady Caroom hesitated.

"In any case," she said, "could you ask her to marry you? You must see that as things are it would be impossible!"

"Impossible!" he muttered. "Impossible!"

"Of course," she answered, briskly. "You must be a man of the world enough to know that. You could not ask a girl in Sybil's position to share a borrowed name, nor would the other conditions permit of your marrying her. That is why I want to talk to you."

"Well?"

"Is there any immediate chance of your reconciliation with the Marquis of Arranmore?"

"None," Brooks answered.

"Well, then," Lady Caroom said, "there is no immediate chance of your being in a position to marry Sybil. Don't look at me as though I were saying unkind things. I am not. I am only talking common-sense. What is your income?"

"About two thousand pounds, but some of that half, perhaps more—goes to the Society."

"Exactly. It would be impossible for you to marry Sybil on the whole of it, or twice the whole of it."

"You want me then," Brooks said, "to be reconciled to my father. Yet you—you yourself will not trust him."

"I have not expressed any wish of the sort," Lady Caroom said, kindly. "I only wished to point out that as things are you were not in a position to ask Sybil to marry you, and therefore I want you to keep away from her. I mean this kindly for both of you. Of course if Sybil is absolutely in earnest, if the matter has gone too far, we must talk it all over again and see what is to be done. But I want you to give her a chance. Keep away for a time. Your father may live for twenty-five years. If your relations with him all that time continue as they are now, marriage with a girl brought up like Sybil would be an impossibility."

Brooks was silent for several moments. Then he looked up suddenly.

"Has Lady Sybil said anything to you—which led you to speak to me?"

Lady Caroom shook her head.

"No. She is very young, you know. Frankly, I do not believe that she knows her own mind. You have not spoken to her, of course?" "No!"

"And you will not?"

"I suppose," Brooks said, "that I must not think of it."

"You must give up thinking about her, of course," Lady Caroom said, "until—" Until what?

"Until you can ask her—if ever you do ask her—to marry you in your proper name."

Brooks set his teeth and walked up and down the little room.

"That," he said, "may be never."

"Exactly," Lady Caroom agreed. "That is why I am suggesting that you do not see her so often."

He stopped opposite her.

"Does he—does Lord Arranmore know anything of this?"

She shook her head.

"Not from me. He may have heard whispers. To tell you the truth, I myself have been asked questions during the last few days. You have been seen about a good deal with Sybil, and you are rather a mystery to people. That is why I felt compelled to speak." He nodded. "I see!"

"You must not blame me," she went on, softly. "You know, Kingston, that I like you, that I would give you Sybil willingly under ordinary circumstances. I don't want to speak to her if I can help it. And, Kingston, there is one thing more I must say to you. It is on my mind. It keeps me awake at night. I think that it will make an old woman of me very soon. If—if we should be wrong?"

"There is no possibility of that," he answered, sadly. "Lord Arranmore is candour itself, even in his selfishness."

"His face haunts me," she murmured. "There is something so terribly impersonal, so terribly sad about it. He looks on at everything, he joins in nothing. They say that he gambles, but he never knows whether he is winning or losing. He gives entertainments that are historical, and remains as cold as ice to guests whom a prince would be glad to welcome. His horse won that great race the other day, and he gave up his place on the stand, just before the start, to a little girl, and never even troubled to watch the race, though his winnings were enormous. He bought the Frivolity Theatre, produced this new farce, and has never been seen inside the place. What does it mean, Kingston? There must be suffering behind all this—terrible suffering."

"It is a law of retribution," Brooks said, coldly. "He has made other people suffer all his life. Now perhaps his turn has come. He spends fortunes trying to amuse himself and cannot. Are we to pity him for that?"

"I have heard of people," she said, looking at him intently, "who are too proud to show the better part of themselves, who rather than court pity or even sympathy will wear a mask always, will hide the good that is in them and parade the bad."

"You love him still?" he said, wonderingly.

"Kingston, I do. If I were a brave woman I would risk everything. Sometimes when I see him, like a Banquo at a feast, with his eyes full of weariness and the mummy's smile upon his lips, I feel that I can keep away no longer. Kingston, let us go to him, you and I. Let us see if we can't tear off the mask."

He shook his head.

"He would laugh at us!"

"Will you try?"

He hesitated.

"No! But, Lady Caroom, you have no such debt of bitterness against him as I have. I cannot advise you—I would not dare. But if there is a spark of soul left in the man, such love as yours must fan it into warmth. If you have the courage—risk it."

Brooks left without seeing Sybil again, and turned northward. In Pall Mall he heard his name called from the steps of one of the great clubs. He looked up and found Lord Arranmore leisurely descending.

"A word with you, Brooks," he said, coolly, "on a matter of business. Will you step inside?"

Brooks hesitated. It was beginning to rain, and neither of them had umbrellas.

"As you will," he answered. "I have an appointment in half-an-hour."

"I shall not detain you ten minutes," Lord Arranmore answered. "There is a comfortable strangers' room here where we can chat. Will you have anything?"

"Nothing to drink, thanks," Brooks answered. "A cigarette, if you are going to smoke."

Lord Arranmore pushed his cigarette-case across the small round table which stood between their easy-chairs. The room was empty.

"You will find these tolerable. I promised to be brief, did I not? I wished to speak for a moment upon a subject which it seems to me might require a readjustment of our financial relations."

Brooks looked up puzzled but made no remark.

"I refer to the possibility of your desiring to marry. Be so good as not to interrupt me. I have seen you once or twice with Sybil Caroom, and there has been a whisper—but after all that is of no consequence. The name of the young lady would be no concern of mine. But in case you should be contemplating anything of the sort, I thought it as well that you should know what the usual family arrangements are."

"I am sorry," Brooks said, "but I really don't understand what you mean by family arrangements."

"No!" Lord Arranmore remarked, softly. "Perhaps if you would allow me to explain—it is your own time which is limited, you know. The eldest son of our family comes in, as you have been told, on his twenty-first birthday, to two thousand pounds a year, which income you are now in possession of. On his marriage that is increased to ten thousand a year, with the possession of either Enton or Mangohfred. in the present case you could take your choice, as I am perfectly indifferent which I retain. That is all I wished to say. I thought it best for you to understand the situation. Mr. Ascough will, at any time, put it into legal shape for you."

"You speak of this—arrangement," Brooks said, slowly, "as though it were a corroboration of the settlement upon the eldest son. This scarcely seems possible. There can be no such provision legally."

"I scarcely see," Lord Arranmore said, wearily, "what that has to do with it, The ten thousand pounds a year is, of course, not a legal charge upon the estates. But from time immemorial it has been the amount which has been the admitted portion of the eldest son upon marriage. It is no gift from me. It is the income due to Lord Kingston of Ross. If you wish for any future explanation I must really refer you to Mr. Ascough. The discussion of business details is by no means a favourite occupation of mine."

Brooks rose to his feet. His eyes were fixed steadily, almost longingly upon Lord Arranmore's. His manner was not wholly free from nervousness.

"I am very much obliged to you, Lord Arranmore," he said. "I quite understand that you are making me the offer of a princely settlement out of the Arranmore estates to which I have no manner of claim. It is not possible for me to accept it."

There was a moment's silence. A great clock in the corner ticked noisily. A faint unusual colour stole into Lord Arranmore's cheeks.

"Accept it! I accord you no favour, I offer you no gift. The allowance is, I repeat, one which every Lord Kingston has drawn upon his marriage. Perhaps I have spoken before it was necessary. You may have had no thoughts of anything of the sort?"

Brooks did not answer.

"I have noticed," Lord Arranmore continued in measured tones, "an intimacy between you and Lady Sybil Caroom, which suggested the idea to me. I look upon Lady Sybil as one of the most charming young gentlewomen of our time, and admirably suited in all respects to the position of the future Marchioness of Arranmore. I presume that as head of the family I am within my rights in so far expressing my opinion?"

"Marriage," Brooks said, huskily, "is not possible for me at present."

"Why not?"

"I cannot accept this money from you. The terms on which we are do not allow of it."

There was an ominous glitter in Lord Arranmore's eyes. He, too, rose to his feet, and remained facing Brooks, his hand upon the back of his chair.

"Are you serious? Do you mean that?"

"I do!" Brooks answered. Lord Arranmore pointed to the door.

"Then be off," he said, a note of passion at last quivering in his tone. "Leave this room at once, and let me see as little of you in the future as possible. If Sybil cares for you, God help her! You are a damned obstinate young prig, sir. Be off!"

Brooks walked out of the club and into the street, his ears tingling and his cheeks aflame. The world seemed topsy-turvy. It was long indeed before he forgot those words, which seemed to come to him winged with a wonderful and curious force.

CHAPTER VIII
THE ADVICE OF MR. BULLSOM

At no time in his life was Brooks conscious of so profound a feeling of dissatisfaction with regard to himself, his work, and his judgment, as during the next few weeks. His friendship with Mary Scott, which had been a more pleasant thing than he had ever realized, seemed to him to be practically at an end, he had received a stinging rebuke from the one man in the world whose right to administer it he would have vigorously denied, and he was forced to admit to himself that his last few weeks had been spent in a fool's paradise, into which he ought never to have ventured. He had the feeling of having been pulled up sharply in the midst of a very delightful interlude—and the whole thing seemed to him to come as a warning against any deviation whatsoever from the life which he had marked out for himself. So, after a day of indecision and nerveless hesitation, he turned back once more to his work. Here, at any rate, he could find absorption.

He formed his Board—without figure-heads, wholly of workers. There was scarcely a name which any one had ever heard of before. He had his interview with the bishop, who was shocked at his views, and publicly pronounced his enterprise harmful and pauperizing, and Verity, with the names of the Board as a new weapon, came for him more vehemently than ever. Brooks, at last goaded into action, sent the paper to his solicitors and went down to Medchester to attend a dinner given to Mr. Bullsom.

It was at Medchester that he recovered his spirits. He knew the place so well that it was easy for him to gauge and appreciate the altered state of affairs there. The centre of the town was swept clean at last of those throngs of weary-faced men and youths looking for a job, the factories were running full time-there seemed to his fancy to be even an added briskness in the faces and the footsteps of the hurrying crowds of people. Later on at the public dinner which he had come down to attend, he was amply assured as to the sudden wave of prosperity which was passing over the whole country. Mr. Bullsom, with an immense expanse of white shirt, a white waistcoat and a scarlet camellia in his button-hole, beamed and oozed amiability upon every one. Brooks he grasped by both hands with a full return to his old cordiality, indulgence in which he had rather avoided since he had been aware of the social gulf between them.

"Brooks," he said, "I owe this to you. It was your suggestion. And I don't think it's turned out so badly, eh? What do you think?"

"I think that you have found your proper sphere," Brooks answered, smiling. "I can't think why you ever needed me to suggest it to you."

"My boy, I can't either," Mr. Bullsom declared. "This is one of the proudest nights of my life. Do you know what we've done up there at Westminster, eh? We've given this old country a new lease of life. How they were all laughing at us up their sleeve, eh! Germans, and Frenchmen, and Yankees. It's a horse of another colour now. John Bull has found out how to protect himself. And, Brooks, my boy, it's been mentioned to-night, and I'm a proud man when I think of it. There were others who did the showy part of the work, of course, the speechmaking and the bill-framing and all that, but I was the first man to set the Protection snowball rolling. It wasn't much I had to say, but I said it. A glass of wine with you, Sir Henry? With pleasure, sir!

"I wonder how long it will last," Brooks' neighbour remarked, cynically. "The manufacturers are like a lot of children with a new toy. What about the Colonies? What are they going to say about it?"

"We have no Colonies," Brooks answered, smiling. "You are only half an Imperialist. Don't you know that they have been incorporated in the British Empire?

"Hope they'll like it," his neighbour remarked, sardonically. "Plenty of glory and a good price to pay for it. What licks me is that every one seems to imagine that this Tariff Bill is going to give the working-classes a leg-up. To my mind it's the capitalist who's going to score by it."

"The capitalist manufacturer," Brooks answered. "But after all you can't under our present conditions dissociate capital and labour. The benefit of one will be the benefit of the other. No food stuffs are taxed, you know."

His neighbour grunted.

"Pity Cobden's ghost can't come and listen to the rot those fellows are talking," he remarked. "We shall see in a dozen years how the thing works."

The dinner ended with a firework of speeches, and an ovation to their popular townsman and member, which left Mr. Bullsom very red in the face and a little watery about the eyes. Brooks and he drove off together afterwards, and Mr. Bullsom occupied the first five minutes or so of the journey with a vigorous mopping of his cheeks and forehead.

"A great night, Brooks," he exclaimed, faintly. "A night to remember. Don't mind admitting that I'm more than a bit exhausted though. Phew!"

Brooks laughed, and leaning forward looked out of the windows of the carriage.

"Are we going in the right direction?" he asked. "This isn't the way to 'Homelands.'"

Mr. Bullsom smiled.

"Little surprise for you, Brooks!" he remarked. "We found the sort of place the girls were hankering after, to let furnished, and we've took it for a year. We moved in a fortnight ago."

"Do I know the house?" Brooks asked. "It's Woton Hall," Mr. Bullsom remarked, impressively. "Nice old place. Dare say you remember it."

"Remember it! Of course I do," Brooks answered. "How do the young ladies like it?"

Mr. Bullsom laid hold of the strap of the carriage. The road was rough, the horses were fresh, and Mr. Bullsom's head had felt steadier.

"Well," Mr. Bullsom said, "you'd think to hear em we'd stepped straight into heaven. We're close to the barracks, you know, and I'm blest if half the officers haven't called already. They drop in to luncheon, or dinner, or whatever's going on, in the most friendly way, just as they used to, you know, when Sir Henry lived there, him as took wine with me, you remember. Lord, you should hear Selina on the military. Can't say I take to 'em much myself. I'll bet there'll be one or two of them hanging about the place to-night. Phew!"

Mr. Bullsom mopped his forehead again. The carriage had turned in at the drive, and he glanced towards Brooks a little uneasily.

"Do I look-as though I'd been going it a bit?" he asked. "Since Selina's got these band-box young men hanging around she's so mighty particular."

Brooks leaned forward and rescued Mr. Bullsom's tie from underneath his ear.

"You're all right," he said, reassuringly. "You mustn't let the girls bully you, you know."

Mr. Bullsom sat bolt upright.

"You are quite right, Brooks," he declared. "I will not. But we took on the servants here as well, and they're a bit strange to me. After all, though, I'm the boss. I'll let 'em know it, too."

A footman threw open the door and took Brooks' dressing-case. A butler, hurrying up from the background, ushered them into the drawing-room. Mr. Bullsom pulled down his waistcoat and marched in; whistling softly a popular tune. Selina and Louise, in elaborate evening gowns, were playing bridge with two young men.

Selina rose and held out her hand to Brooks a little languidly.

"So glad to see you, Mr. Brooks," she declared. "Let me introduce Mr. Suppeton, Captain Meyton!"

The two young men were good enough to acknowledge the introduction, and Brooks shook hands with Louise. Selina was surveying her father with uplifted eyebrows.

"Why, father, where on earth have you been?" she exclaimed. "I never saw anybody such a sight. Your shirt is like a rag, and your collar too."

"Never you mind me, Selina," Mr. Bullsom answered, firmly. "As to where I've been, you know quite well. Political dinners may be bad for your linen, and there may be more healths drunk than is altogether wise, but a Member of Parliament has to take things as he finds 'em. Don't let us interrupt your game. Brooks and I are going to have a game at billiards."

One of the young men laid down his cards.

"Can't we join you?" he suggested. "We might have a game of pool, if it isn't too late."

"You are soon tired of bridge," Selina remarked, reproachfully. "Very well, we will all go into the billiard-room."

The men played a four-handed game. Between the shots Selina talked to Brooks.

"Were you surprised?" she asked. "Had you heard?"

"Not a word. I was astonished," he answered.

"You hadn't seen it in the papers either? Most of them mentioned it—in the county notes."

"I so seldom read the newspapers," he said. "You like it, of course?"

Selina was bereft of words.

"How we ever existed in that hateful suburb," she whispered under her breath. "And the people round here too are so sociable. Papa being a member makes a difference, of course. Then the barracks—isn't it delightful having them so close? There is always something going on. A cricket match to-morrow, I believe. Louise and I are going to play. Mrs. Malevey—she's the Colonel's wife, you know persuaded us into it."

"And your mother?" Brooks asked a minute or two later.

Selina tossed her head.

"Mother is so foolish," she declared. "She misses the sound of the trains, and she actually calls the place dead alive, because she can't sit at the windows and see the tradesmen's carts and her neighbours go by. Isn't it ridiculous?"

Brooks hesitated.

"I suppose so," he answered. "Your mother can have her friends out here, though. It really is only a short drive to Medchester."

"She won't have them oftener than I can help," Selina declared, doggedly. "Old Mrs. Mason called the other day when Captain Meyton and Mrs. Malevey were here. It was most awkward. But I don't know why I tell you all these things," she declared, abruptly. "Somehow I always feel that you are quite an old friend."

Selina's languishing glance was intercepted by one of her admirers from the barracks, as she had intended it to be. Brooks went off to play his shot and returned smiling.

"I am only too happy that you should feel so," he declared. "Your father was very kind to me."

"Isn't it almost a pity that you didn't stay in Medchester, Mr. Brooks?" Selina remarked, with a faint note of patronage in her tone. "Papa is so much more influential now, you know, and he was always so fond of you."

"It is rather a pity," Brooks remarked, with twinkling eyes. "One can't foresee these things, you know."

Selina felt it time to bestow her attention elsewhere, and the game soon came to an end. The girls glanced at the clock and reluctantly withdrew.

"Remember, Miss Bullsom, that we are relying upon you to-morrow," the younger of the two officers remarked, as he opened the door. "Two o'clock sharp—but you lunch with Mrs. Malevey first, don't you?"

"We shan't forget," Selina assured him, graciously. "Good-night."

The two young men left soon afterwards. Mr. Bullsom mixed himself a whisky-and-soda, and stood for a few minutes on the hearthrug before retiring.

"You're not up to the mark, Brooks, my boy," he said, kindly.

Brooks shrugged his shoulders. "I am about as usual," he answered.

Mr. Bullsom set down his glass.

"Look here, Brooks," he said, "you've given me many a useful piece of advice, even when you used to charge me six and eightpence for it. I'm going to turn the tables. One doesn't need to look at you twice to see that things aren't going altogether as they should do with you. See here! Are you sure that you're not cutting off your nose to spite your face, eh?"

"Perhaps I am," Brooks answered. "But it is too late to draw back now."

"It is never too late," Mr. Bullsom declared, vigorously. "I've no fancy for weathercocks, but I haven't a ha'porth of respect for a man who ain't smart enough to own up when he's made a mistake, and who isn't willing to start again on a fresh page. You take my advice, Brooks. Be reconciled with your father, and let 'em all know who you are. I've seen a bit of Lord Arranmore, and I'll stake my last shilling that he's not a bad 'un at heart. You make it up with him, Brooks. Come, that's a straight tip, and it's a good one."

Brooks threw away his cigarette and held out his hand.

"It is very good advice, Mr. Bullsom," he said, "under any ordinary circumstances. I wish I could take it. Good-night."

Mr. Bullsom grasped his hand.

"You're not offended, my boy?" he asked, anxiously.

"Not I," Brooks answered, heartily. "I'm not such an idiot."

"I don't want to take any liberties," Bullsom said, "and I'm afraid I forget sometimes who you are, but that's your fault, seeing that you will call yourself only Mr. Kingston Brooks when you're by rights a lord. But if you were the Prince of Wales I'd still say that my advice was good. Forgive your father anything you've got against him, and start afresh."

"Well, I'll think about it," Brooks promised.

CHAPTER IX
A QUESTION AND AN ANSWER

Brooks returned to London to find the annual exodus already commenced. Lady Caroom and Sybil had left for Homburg. Lord Arranmore was yachting in the Channel. Brooks settled down to work, and found it a little wearisome.

He saw nothing of Mary Scott, whose duties now brought her seldom to the head office. He began to think that she was avoiding him, and there came upon him about this time a sense of loneliness to which he was sometimes subject. He fought it with hard work—early and late, till the colour left his cheeks and black lines bordered his eyes. They pressed him to take a holiday, but he steadily declined. Mr. Bullsom wrote begging him to spend a week-end at least at Woton Hall. He refused this and all other invitations.

One day he took up a newspaper which was chiefly concerned with the doings of fashionable people, and Lady Caroom's name at once caught his eye. He read that her beautiful daughter Lady Sybil was quite the belle of Homburg, that the Duke of Atherstone was in constant attendance, that an interesting announcement might at any moment be made. He threw aside the paper and looked thoughtfully out into the stuffy little street, where even at night the air seemed stifling and unwholesome. After all, was he making the best of his life? He had started a great work. Hundreds and thousands of his fellow creatures would be the better for it. So far all was well enough. But personally—was this entire self-abnegation necessary?—was he fulfilling his duty to himself? was he not rather sacrificing his future to a prejudice—an idea? In any case he knew that it was too late to retract. He had renounced his proper position in life, it was too late for him now to claim it. And there had gone with it—Sybil. After all, why should he arrogate to himself judgment? The sins of his father were not his concern. It was chiefly he who suffered by his present attitude, yet he had chosen it deliberately. He could not draw back. He had cut himself off from her world—he saw now the folly of his ever for a moment having been drawn into it. It must be a chapter closed.

The weeks passed on, and his loneliness grew. One day the opening of still another branch brought him for a moment into contact with Mary Scott. She too was looking pale, but her manner was bright, even animated. She seemed to feel none of the dejection which had stolen away from him the whole flavour of life. Her light easy laugh and cheerful conversation were like a tonic to him. He remembered those days at Medchester After all, she was the first woman whom he had ever looked upon as a comrade, whom he had ever taken out of her sex and considered singly.

She spoke of his ill-looks kindly and with some apprehension.

"I am all right," he assured her, "but a little dull. Take pity on me and come out to dinner one night this week."

They dined in the annex of a fashionable restaurant practically out of doors—a cool green lawn for a carpet and a fountain playing close at hand. Mary wore a white dinner-gown, gossamer-like and airy. Her rich brown hair was tastefully arranged, her voice had never seemed to him so soft and pleasant. All around was the hum of cheerful conversation. A little world of people seemed to be there whose philosophy of life after all was surely the only true one, where hearts were light with the joy of the moment. The dinner was carefully served, the wine, which in his solitude he had neglected, stole through his veins with a pleasant warmth. Brooks felt his nerves relax, the light came back to his eyes and the colour to his cheeks. Their conversation grew brighter—almost gay. They both carefully avoided all mention of their work—it was a holiday. The burden of his too carefully thought out life seemed to pass away. Brooks felt that his youth was coming to him a little late, but with delicious freshness.

He smoked a cigarette and sipped his coffee, glancing every now and then at his companion with approving eyes. For Mary, whose dress was so seldom a matter of moment to her, chanced to look her best that night. The delicate pallor of her cheeks under the rich tone of her hair seemed quite apart from any suggestion of ill-health, her eyes were wonderfully full and soft, a quaint pearl ornament hung by a little gold chain from her slender, graceful neck. A sort of dreamy content came over Brooks. After all, why should he throw himself in despair against the gates of that other world, outside which he himself had elected to dwell? It was only madness for him to think of Sybil. While Lord Arranmore lived he must remain Kingston Brooks—and for Kingston Brooks it seemed that even friendship with her was forbidden. He could live down those memories. They were far better crushed. He thought of that moment in Mary's sitting-room, that one moment of her self-betrayal, and his heart beat with an unaccustomed force. Why not rob her of the bitterness of that memory? He looked at the white hand resting for a moment on the table so close to his, and a sudden impulse came over him to snatch it up, to feel his loneliness fade away for ever before the new light in her face.

"Let us go and sit on the other side of the lawn," he said, leaning over towards her. "We can hear the music better."

They found a quiet seat where the music from the main restaurant reached them, curiously mingled with the jingling of cab bells from Piccadilly. Brooks leaned over and took her hand. "Mary," he said, "will you marry me?"

She looked at him as though expecting to find in his face some vague sign of madness, some clue to words which seemed to her wholly incomprehensible. But he had all the appearance of being in earnest. His eyes were serious, his fingers had tightened over hers. She drew a little away, and every vestige of colour had vanished from her cheeks.

"Marry you?" she exclaimed.

He bent over her, and he laughed softly in the darkness. A mad impulse was upon him to kiss her, but he resisted it.

"Why not? Does it sound so dreadful?"

She drew her fingers away slowly but with determination.

"I had hoped," she said, "that you would have spared me this."

"Spared you!" he repeated. "I do not understand. Spared you!"

She looked at him with flashing eyes.

"Oh, I suppose I ought to thank you," she said, bitterly. "Only I do not. I cannot. You were kinder when you joined with me and helped me to ignore—that hateful moment. That was much kinder."

"Upon my honour, Mary," Brooks declared, earnestly, "I do not understand you. I have not the least idea what you mean."

She looked at him incredulously.

"You have asked me to marry you," she said. "Why?"

"Because I care for you."

"Care for me? Does that mean that you—love me?"

"Yes."

She noted very well that moment's hesitation.

"That is not true," she declared. "Oh, I know. You ask me out of pity—because you cannot forget. I suppose you think it kindness. I don't! It is hateful!"

A light broke in upon him. He tried once more to take her hand, but she withheld it.

"I only half understand you, Mary," he said, earnestly, "but I can assure you that you are mistaken. As to asking you out of pity—that is ridiculous. I want you to be my wife. We care for the same things—we can help one another—and I seem to have been very lonely lately."

"And you think," Mary said, with a curious side-glance at him, "that I should cure your loneliness. Thank you. I am very happy as I am. Please forget everything you have said, and let us go."

Brooks was a little bewildered—and manlike a little more in earnest.

"For some reason or other," he said, "you seem disinclined to take me seriously. I cannot understand you, Mary. At any rate you must answer me differently. I want you to be my wife. I am fond of you—you know that—and I will do my best to make you happy."

"Thank you," Mary said, hardly. "I am sorry, but I must decline your offer—absolutely. Now, let us go, shall we?"

She would have risen, but he laid his hand firmly upon her shoulder.

"Not till I have some sort of explanation," he said. "Is it that you do not care for me, Mary?"

She turned round upon him with colour enough in her cheeks and a strange angry light burning in her eyes.

"You might have spared me that also," she exclaimed. "You are determined to humiliate me, to make me remember that hateful afternoon in my rooms—oh, I can say it if I like—when I kissed you. I knew then that sooner or later you would make up your mind that it was your duty to ask me to marry you. Only you might have done it by letter. It would have been kinder. Never mind. You have purged your conscience, and you have got your answer. Now let us go."

Brooks looked at her for a moment amazed beside himself with wonder and self-reproach.

"Mary," he said, quietly, "I give you my word that nothing which I have said this evening has the least connection with that afternoon. I give you my word that not for a moment have I thought of it in connection with what I have said to you to-night."

She looked at him steadfastly, and her eyes were full of things which he could not understand.

"When did you make up your mind—to ask me this?"

He pointed to the little table where they had been sitting.

Only a few minutes ago. I confess it was an impulse. I think that I realized as we sat there how dear you had grown to me, Mary—how dull life was without you."

"You say these things to me," she exclaimed, "when all the time you love another woman."

He started a little. She smiled bitterly as she saw the shadow on his face.

"What do you mean?"

"I mean," she said, deliberately, "that you love Sybil Caroom. Is it not true?"

His head drooped a little. He had never asked himself even so much as this. He was face to face now with all the concentrated emotions which lately had so much disturbed his life. The problem which he had so sedulously avoided was forced upon him ruthlessly, with almost barbaric simplicity.

"I do not know," he answered, vaguely. "I have never asked myself. I do not wish to ask myself. Why do you speak of her? She is not of our world, the world to which I want to belong. I want to forget her."

"You are a little mad to-night, my friend," Mary said. "To-morrow you will feel differently. If Sybil Caroom cares for you, what does it matter which world she belongs to? She is not the sort of girl to be bound by old-fashioned prejudices. But I do not understand you at all to-night. You are not yourself. I think that you are—a little cruel." "Cruel?" he repeated.

Her face darkened.

"Oh, it is only natural," she said, with a note of suppressed passion in her how tone. "It is just the accursed egotism of your sex. What right have you to make us suffer so—to ask me to marry you—and sit by my side and wonder whether you care for another woman? Can't you see how humiliating it all is? It is an insult to ask a woman to marry you to cure your loneliness, to make you a home to settle your indecision. It is an insult to ask a woman to marry you for any reason except that you care for her more than any other woman in the world, and can tell her so trustfully, eagerly. Please to put me in a cab at once, and never speak of these things again."

She was half-way across the lawn before he could stop her, her head thrown back, carrying herself proudly and well, moving as it seemed to him with a sort of effortless dignity wholly in keeping with the vigour of her words. He obeyed her literally. There was nothing else for him to do. His slight effort to join her in the cab she firmly repulsed, holding out her hand and speaking a few cheerful words of thanks for her evening's entertainment. And when the cab rolled away Brooks felt lonelier than ever.

CHAPTER X
LADY SYBIL SAYS "YES"

The carriage plunged into the shadow of the pine-woods, and commenced the long uphill ascent to Saalburg. Lady Caroom put down her parasol and turned towards Sybil, whose eyes were steadfastly fixed upon the narrow white belt of road ahead.

"Now, Sybil," she said, "for our talk."

"Your talk," Sybil corrected her, with a smile.

I'm to be listener."

"Oh, it may not be so one-sided after all," Lady Caroom declared. "And we had better make haste, or that impetuous young man of yours will come pounding after us on his motor before we know where we are. What are you going to do about him, Sybil?"

"I don't know."

"Well, you'll have to make up your mind. He's getting on my nerves. You must decide one way or another."

Sybil sighed.

"He's quite the nicest young man I know—of his class," she remarked.

"Exactly," Lady Caroom assented. "And though I think you will admit that I am one of the least conventional of mothers, I must really say I don't think that it is exactly a comfortable thing to do to marry a man who is altogether outside one's own circle."

"Mr. Brooks," Sybil said, "is quite as well bred as Atherstone."

"He is his equal in breeding and in birth," Lady Caroom declared. "You know all about him. I admit," she continued, "that it sounds like a page out of a novel. But it isn't. The only pity is—from one point of view—that it makes so little difference."

"You think," Sybil asked, "that he will really keep his word—that he will not be reconciled with Lord Arranmore?"

"I am sure of it, my dear," Lady Caroom answered. "Unless a miracle happens, he will continue to be Mr. Kingston Brooks for the next ten or fifteen years, for Lord Arranmore's lifetime, and you know that they are a long-lived race. So you see the situation remains practically unaltered by what I have told you. Mr. Kingston Brooks is a great favourite of mine. I am very fond of him indeed. But I very much doubt—even if he should ask you—whether you would find your position as his wife particularly comfortable. You and I, Sybil, have no secrets from one another. I wish you would tell me exactly how you feel about him."

Sybil smiled—a little ruefully.

"If I knew—exactly," she answered, "I should know exactly what to do. But I don't. You know how uninteresting our set of young men are as a rule. Well, directly I met Mr. Brooks at Enton I felt that he was different. He interested me very much. Then I have always wanted to do something useful, to get something different into my life, and he found me exactly the sort of work I wanted. But he has never talked to me as though he cared particularly though I think that he does a little."

"It is easy to see," Lady Caroom remarked, "that you are not head over ears in love."

"Mother," Sybil answered, "do you believe that girls often do fall head over ears in love? If Mr. Brooks and I met continually, and if he and his father were reconciled, well, I think it would be quite easy for me very soon to care for him a great deal. If even now he had followed me here, was with us often, and showed that he was really very fond of me, I think that I should soon be inclined to return it—perhaps even—I don't know—to risk marrying him, and giving up our ordinary life. But as it is I like to think of him, I should like him to be here; but I am not, as you say, head over ears in love with him."

"And now about Atherstone?" Lady Caroom said.

"Well, Atherstone has improved a great deal," Sybil answered, thoughtfully. "There are a great many things about him which I like very much. He is always well dressed and fresh and nice. He enjoys himself without being dissipated, and he is perfectly natural. He is rather boyish perhaps, but then he is young. He is not afraid to laugh, and I like the way he enters into everything. And I think I like his persistence."

"As his wife," Lady Caroom said, "you would have immense opportunities for doing good. He has a great deal of property in London, besides three huge estates in Somerset."

"That is a great consideration," Sybil said, earnestly. "I shall always be thankful that I met Mr. Brooks. He made me think in a practical way about things which have always troubled me a little. I should hate to seem thoughtless or ungrateful to him. Will you tell me something, mother?" Of course."

"Do you think that he cares—at all?"

I think he does—a little!

"Enough to be reconciled with his father for my sake?"

"No! Not enough for that," Lady Caroom answered.

Sybil drew a little breath.

"I think," she said, "that that decides me."

The long ascent was over at last. They pulled up before the inn, in front of which the proprietor was already executing a series of low bows. Before they could descend there was a familiar sound from behind, and a young man, in a grey flannel suit and Panama hat, jumped from his motor and came to the carriage door.

"Don't be awfully cross!" he exclaimed, laughing. "You know you half promised to come with me this afternoon, so I couldn't help having a spin out to see whether I could catch you up. Won't you allow me, Lady Caroom? The step is a little high."

"It isn't any use being cross with you," Sybil remarked. "It never seems to make any impression."

"I am terribly thick-skimmed," he answered, "when I don't want to understand. Will you ladies have some tea, or come and see how the restoration is getting on?"

"We were proposing to go and see what the German Emperor's idea of a Roman camp was," Sybil answered.

"Oh, you can't shake me off now, can you, Lady Caroom?" he declared, appealing to her. "We'll consider it an accident that you found me here, if you like, but it is in reality a great piece of good fortune for you."

"And why, may I ask?" Sybil inquired, with uplifted eyebrows.

"Oh, I'm an authority on this place—come here nearly every day to give the director, as he calls himself, some hints. Come along, Lady Caroom. I'll show you the baths and the old part of the outer wall."

Lady Caroom very soon had enough of it. She sat down upon a tree and brought out her sketchbook.

"Give me a quarter of an hour, please," she begged, "not longer. I want to be home for tea."

They strolled off, Atherstone turning a little nervously to Sybil.

"I say, we've seen the best part of the ruins," he remarked. "The renovation's hideous. Let's go in the wood—and I'll show you a squirrel's nest."

Sybil hesitated. Her thoughts for a moment were in confusion. Then she sighed once and turned towards the wood.

"I have never seen a squirrel's nest," she said. "Is it far?"

Lady Caroom put her sketch away as she heard their approaching footsteps, and looked up. Atherstone's happiness was too ridiculously apparent. He came straight over to her.

"You'll give her to me, won't you?" he exclaimed. "'Pon my word, she shall be the happiest woman in England if I can make her so. I'm perfectly certain I'm the happiest man."

Lady Caroom pressed her daughter's hand, and they all turned to descend the hill.

"Of course I'm charmed," Lady Caroom said. "Sybil makes me feel so elderly. But I don't know what I shall do for a chaperon now."

Atherstone laughed.

"I'm your son-in-law," he said. "I can take you out."

Sybil shook her head.

"No, you won't," she declared. "The only woman I have ever been really jealous of is mother. She has a way of absorbing all the attention from every one when she is around. I'm not going to have her begin with you."

"I feel," Atherstone said, "like the man who married a twin—said he never tried to tell the difference, you know, when a pal asked him how he picked out his own wife."

"If you think," Sybil said, severely, "that you have made any arrangements of that sort I take it all back. You are going to marry me, if you behave yourself."

He sighed.

"Three months is a beastly long time," he said.

Lady Caroom drove back alone. The motor whizzed by her half-way down the hill—Sybil holding her hat with both hands, her hair blowing about, and her cheeks pink with pleasure. She waved her hand gaily as she went by, and then clutched her hat again. Lady Caroom watched them till they were out of sight, then she found herself looking steadfastly across the valley to the dark belt of pine-clad hills beyond. She could see nothing very clearly, and there was a little choking in her throat. They were both there, father and son. Once she fancied that at last he was holding out his arms towards her—she sat up in the carriage with a little cry which was half a sob. When she drove through the hotel gates it was he who stood upon the steps to welcome her.

CHAPTER XI
BROOKS HEARS THE NEWS

Unchanged! Her first eager glance into his face told her that. Waxen white, his lips smiled their courteous greeting upon her, his tone was measured and cold as ever. She set her teeth as she rose from her seat, and gathered her skirts in her hand.

"You, too, a pilgrim?" she exclaimed. "I thought you preferred salt water."

"We had a pleasant fortnight's yachting," he answered. "Then I went with Hennibul to Wiesbaden, and I came on here to see you."

"Have you met Sybil and Atherstone?" she asked him.

"Yes," he answered, gravely.

"Come into my room," she said, "and I will give you some tea. These young people are sure to have it on the terrace. I will join you when I have got rid of some of this dust."

He was alone for ten minutes. At the end of that time she came out through the folding-doors with the old smile upon her lips and the old lithesomeness in her movements. He rose and watched her until she had settled down in her low chair.

"So Sybil is going to marry Atherstone!"

"Yes. He really deserves it, doesn't he? He is a very nice boy."

Arranmore shrugged his shoulders.

"What an everlasting fool Brooks is," he said, in a low tone.

"He keeps his word," she answered. "It is a family trait with you, Arranmore. You are all stubborn, all self-willed, self-centred, selfish!"

"Thank you!"

"You can't deny it."

I won't try. I suppose it is true. Besides, I want to keep you in a good humour."

"Do tell me why!"

"If Sybil is going to be married you can't live alone."

"I won't admit that, but what about it? Do you know of a nice respectable companion?"

"Myself."

She shook her head.

"You may be nice," she answered, "but you certainly aren't respectable."

"I am what you make me," he answered, in a low tone. "Catherine! A moment ago you accused me of stubbornness. What about yourself?"

"I?"

"Yes, you. You have been the one woman of my life. You are free, you know that there is no other man who could make you happy as I could, yet you will not come to me—for the sake of an idea. If I am heartless and callous, an infidel, an egotist, whatever you choose, at least I love you. You need never fear me. You would always be safe."

She shook her head.

"Arranmore," she said, "this is so painful to me. Do let us cease to discuss it. I have tried so hard to make you understand how I feel. I cannot alter. It is impossible!"

"You tempt me," he cried, "to play the hypocrite."

"No, I do not, Arranmore," she answered, gently, "for there is no acting in this world which would deceive me."

"You do not doubt that I should make you a good husband?"

"I believe you would," she answered, "but I dare not try it."

"And this is the woman," he murmured, sadly, "who calls me stubborn."

Tea was brought in. Afterwards they walked in the gardens together. The band was playing, and they were surrounded on all sides by acquaintances. A great personage stopped and talked to them for a while. Lady Caroom admitted the news of Sybil's engagement. After that every one stopped to express pleasure. It was not until the young people appeared themselves, and at once monopolized all attention, that Arranmore was able to draw his companion away into comparative solitude.

"Do you by any chance correspond with Brooks?" he asked her.

She shook her head.

"No!" she answered. "I was thinking of that. I should like him to know from one of us. Can't you write him, Arranmore?"

"I could," he answered, "but it would perhaps come better from you. Have you ever had any conversation with him about Sybil?"

"Once," she answered, "yes!

"Then you can write—it will be better for you to write. I should like to ask you a question if I may."

"Yes."

"Have you any idea whether the news will be in any way a blow to him?"

"I think perhaps it may," she admitted.

Arranmore was silent. She watched him half eagerly, hoping for some look, some expression of sympathy. She was disappointed. His face did not relax. It seemed almost to grow harder.

"He has only himself to blame," he said, slowly. "But for this ridiculous masquerading his chance was as good as Atherstone's. Quixoticism such as his is an expensive luxury."

She shivered a little.

"That sounds hard-hearted," she said. "He is doing what he thinks right."

Then Lord Arranmore told her what he had told Brooks himself.

"My son is quite a model young man," he said, "but he is a prig. He thinks too much about what is right and wrong, about what is due to himself, and he values his own judgment too highly. However, I have no right to complain, for it is he who suffers, not I. May I dine at your table to-night? I came over alone."

"Certainly."

They were interrupted a few minutes later by Sybil and Atherstone, and a small host of their friends. But in consequence of Lord Arranmore's visit to Homburg, Brooks a few days later received two letters. The first was from Lord Arranmore.

"RITTER's HOTEL.

"DEAR MR. BROOKS,

"The news which I believe Lady Caroom is sending you to-day may perhaps convince you of the folly of this masquerading. I make you, therefore, the following offer. I will leave England for at least five years on condition that you henceforth take up your proper position in society, and consent to such arrangements as Mr. Ascough and I may make. In any case I was proposing to myself a somewhat extensive scheme of travel, and the opportunity seems to me a good one for you to dispense with an incognito which may lead you some day into even worse complications. I trust that for the sake of other people with whom you may be brought into contact you will accept the arrangement which I propose.

"I remain,

"Yours faithfully,

"ARRANMORE."

The other letter was from Lady Caroom.

"RITTER'S HOTEL.

"MY DEAR 'MR. BROOKS,'

"I want to be the first to tell you of Sybil's engagement to the Duke of Atherstone, which took place this afternoon. He has been a very persistent suitor, and he is a great favourite, I think, deservedly, with every one. He will, I am sure, make her very happy.

"I understand that you are still in London. You must find this weather very oppressive. Take my advice and don't overwork yourself. No cause in the world, however good, is worth the sacrifice of one's health.

"I hope that my news will not distress you. You realized, of course, that your decision to remain known, or rather unknown, as Kingston Brooks, made it at some time or other inevitable, and I hope to see a good deal of you when we return to town, and that you will always believe that I am your most sincere friend,

"CATHERINE CAROOM."

Brooks laid the two letters down with a curious mixture of sensations. He knew that a very short time ago he might have considered himself brokenhearted, and he knew that as a matter of fact he was nothing of the sort. He answered Lady Caroom's letter first.

"27, JERMYN STREET, W.

"DEAR LADY CAROOM,

"It was very kind of you to write to me, and to send me the news of Sybil's engagement so promptly. I wish her most heartily every happiness. After all, it is the most suitable thing which could have happened.

"You are right in your surmise. After our conversation I realized quite plainly that under my present identity I could not possibly think of Lady Sybil except as a very charming and a very valued friend. I was, therefore, quite prepared for the news which you have sent me.

"I am going for a few days' golf and sea-bathing into Devonshire, so don't waste too much sympathy upon me. My best regards to Lady Sybil. Just now I imagine that she is overwhelmed with good wishes, but if she will add mine to the number, I can assure you and her that I offer them most heartily.

"Yours most sincerely,

"KINGSTON BRGOKS."

"P.S.—Have you heard that your friend the Bishop is going to bring a Bill before the House of Lords which is to exterminate me altogether?"

Lady Caroom sighed for a moment as she read the letter, but immediately afterwards her face cleared.

"After all, I think it is best," she murmured, "and Atherstone is such a dear."

CHAPTER XII
THE PRINCE OF SINNERS SPEAKS OUT

The bishop sat down amidst a little murmur of applause. He glanced up and saw that his wife had heard his speech, and he noted with satisfaction the long line of reporters, for whose sake he had spoken with such deliberation and with occasional pauses. He felt that his indictment of this new charitable departure had been scathing and logical. He was not altogether displeased to see Brooks himself in the Strangers' Gallery. That young man would be better able to understand now the mighty power of the Church which he had so wantonly disregarded.

But it was not the bishop's speech which had filled Brooks with dismay, which had made his heart grow suddenly cold within him. For this he had been prepared—but not for the adversary who was now upon his feet prepared to address the House. At least, he said to himself, bitterly, he might have been spared this. It was Lord Arranmore, who, amidst some murmurs of surprise, had risen to address the House—pale, composed, supercilious as ever. And Brooks felt that what he could listen to unmoved from the Bishop of Beeston would be hard indeed to bear from this man.

The intervention of Lord Arranmore so early in the debate was wholly unexpected. Every one was interested, and those who knew him best prepared themselves for a little mild sensation. The bishop smiled to himself with the satisfaction of a man who has secured a welcome but unexpected ally. Lord Arranmore's views as to charity and its dispensation were fairly well known.

So every one listened—at first with curiosity, afterwards with something like amazement. The bishop abandoned his expression of gentle tolerance for one of manifest uneasiness. It seemed scarcely credible that he heard aright. For the Marquis of Arranmore's forefinger was stretched out towards him—a gesture at once relentless and scornful, and the words to which he was forced to listen were not pleasant ones to hear.

"It is such sentiments as these," the Marquis of Arranmore was saying—and his words came like drops of ice, slow and distinct—"such sentiments as these voiced by such men as the Lord Bishop of Beeston in such high places as this where we are now assembled, which have created and nourished our criminal classes, which have filled our prisons and our workhouses, and in time future if his lordship's theology is correct will people Hell. And as for the logic of it, was ever the intelligence of so learned and august a body of listeners so insulted before? Is charity, then, for the deserving and the deserving only? Are we to put a premium upon hypocrisy, to pass by on the other side from those who have fallen, and who by themselves have no power to rise? This is precisely his lordship's proposition. The one great charitable institution of our times, founded upon a logical basis, carried out with a devotion and a self-sacrifice beyond all praise, he finds pernicious and pauperizing, because, forsooth, the drunkard and criminals are welcome to avail themselves of it, because it seeks to help those who save for such help must remain brutes themselves and a brutalizing influence to others."

There was a moment's deep silence. To those who were watching the speaker closely, and amongst them Brooks, was evident some sign of internal agitation. Yet when he spoke again his manner was, if possible, more self-restrained than ever. He continued in a low clear tone, without any further gesture and emotion.

"My lords, I heard a remark not intended for my ears, upon my rising, indicative of surprise that I should have anything to say upon such a subject as this. Lest my convictions and opinions should seem to you to be those of an outsider, let me tell you this. You are listening to one who for twelve years lived the life of this unhappy people, dwelt amongst them as a police-court missionary—one who was driven even into some measure of insanity by the horrors he saw and tasted, and who recovered only by an ignominious flight into a far-off country. His lordship the Bishop of Beeston has shown you very clearly how little he knows of the horrors which seethe beneath the brilliant life of this wonderful city. He has brought it upon himself and you—that one who does know shall tell you something of the truth of these things."

There was an intense and breathless silence. This was an assembly amongst whom excitement was a very rare visitant. But there were many there now who sat still and spellbound with eyes riveted upon the speaker. To those who were personally acquainted with him a certain change in his appearance was manifest. A spot of colour flared in his pale cheeks. There was a light in his eyes which no one had ever seen there before. After years of self-repression, of a cynicism partly artificial, partly inevitable, the natural man had broken out once more, stung into life by time smooth platitudes of the great churchman against whom his attack was directed. He was reckless of time fact that Lady Caroom, Brooks, and many of his acquaintances were in the Strangers' Gallery. For the motion before the House was one to obtain legal and ecclesiastical control over all independent charities appealing to the general public for support, under cover of which the Church, in the person of the Bishop of Beeston, had made a solemn and deliberate attack upon Brooks' Society, Brooks himself, its aims and management.

As the words fell, deliberately, yet without hesitation, from his lips, vivid, scathing, forceful, there was not one there but knew that this man spoke of the things which he had felt. The facts he marshalled before them were appalling, but not a soul doubted them. It was truth which he hurled at them, truth before which the Bishop sat back in his seat and felt his cheeks grow paler and his eyes more full of trouble. A great deal of it they had heard before, but never like this—never had it been driven home into their conscience so that doubt or evasion was impossible. And this man, who was he? They rubbed their eyes and wondered. Ninth Marquis of Arranmore, owner of great estates, dilettante, sportsman, cynic, latter-day sinner—or an apostle touched with fire from Heaven to open men's eyes, gifted for a few brief minutes with the tongue of a saintly Demosthenes. Those who knew him gaped like children and wondered. And all the time his words stung them like drops of burning rain.

"This," he concluded at last, "is the Hell which burns for ever under this great city, and it is such men as his lordship the Bishop of Beeston who can come here and speak of their agony in well-rounded periods and congratulate you and himself upon the increasing number of communicants in the East End—who stands in the market-place of the world with stones for starving people. But I, who have been down amongst those fires, I, who know, can tell you this: Not all the churches of Christ, not all the religious societies ever founded, not all the combined labours of all the missionaries who ever breathed, will quench or even abate those flames until they go to their labours in the name of humanity alone, and free themselves utterly from all the cursed restrictions and stipulations of their pet creed. Starving men will mock at the mention of a God of Justice, men who are in torture body and soul are scarcely likely to respond to the teachings of a God of Love. Save the bodies of this generation, and the souls of the next may be within your reach."

They thought then that he had finished. He paused for an unusually long time. When he spoke again he seemed to have wholly regained his usual composure. The note of passion had passed from his tone. His cheeks were once more of waxen pallor. The deliberately-chosen words fell with a chill sarcasm from his lips.

"His lordship the Bishop of Beeston," he said, "has also thought fit, on the authority, I presume, of Mr. Lavilette and his friends, to make slighting reference to the accounts of the Society in question. As one of the largest subscribers to that Society, may I be allowed to set at rest his anxieties? Before many days the accounts from its very earliest days, which have all the time been in the hands of an eminent firm of accountants, will be placed before the general public. In the meantime let me tell you this. I am willing to sign every page of them. I pledge my word to their absolute correctness. The author of this movement has from the first, according to my certain knowledge, devoted a considerable part of his own income to the work. If others who are in the enjoyment of a princely stipend for their religious labours"—he looked hard at the bishop—"were to imitate this course of action, I imagine that there are a good many charitable institutions which would not now be begging for donations to keep them alive."

He sat down without peroration, and almost immediately afterwards left the House. The first reading of the bishop's Bill was lost by a large majority.

Arranmore sat by himself in his study, and his face was white and drawn. A cigarette which he had lit on entering the room had burnt out between his fingers. This sudden upheaval of the past, coming upon him with a certain spasmodic unexpectedness, had shaken his nerves. He had not believed himself capable of anything of the sort. The unusual excitement was upon him still. All sorts of memories and fancies long ago buried, thronged in upon him. So he sat there and suffered, striving in vain to crush them, whilst faces mocked him from the shadows, and familiar voices rang strangely in his ears. He scarcely heard the softly-opened door. The light footsteps and the rustling of skirts had their place amongst the throng of torturing memories. But his eyes—surely his eyes could not mock him. He started to his feet.

"Catherine!"

She did not speak at once, but all sorts of things were in her eyes. He ground his teeth together, and made one effort to remain his old self.

"You have come to offer—your sympathy. How delightful of you. The bishop got on my nerves, you know, and I really am not answerable for what I said. Catherine!"

She threw her arms around his neck.

"You dear!" she exclaimed. "I am not afraid of you any more. Kiss me, Philip, and don't talk nonsense, because I shan't listen to you."

Brooks drove up in hot haste. The butler stopped him respectfully.

"His lordship is particularly engaged, sir."

"He will see me," Brooks answered. "Please announce me—Lord Kingston of Ross!"

"I beg your pardon, sir," the man stammered.

"Lord Kingston of Ross," Brooks repeated, casting off for ever the old name as though it were a disused glove. "Announce me at once."

It was the Arranmore trick of imperiousness, and the man recognized it. He threw open the study door with trembling fingers, but he was careful to knock first.

"Lord Kingston of Ross."

He walked to his father with outstretched hand.

"You were right, sir," he said, simply. "I was a prig!"

They stood for a moment, their hands locked. It was a silent greeting, but their faces were eloquent. Brooks looked from his father to Lady Caroom and smiled.

"I could not wait," he said. "I was forced to come to you at once. But I think that I will go now and pay another call."

He stood outside on the kerb while they fetched him a hansom. The fresh night wind blew in his face, cool and sweet. From Piccadilly came the faint hum of tram, and the ceaseless monotonous beat of hurrying footsteps. The hansom pulled up before him with a jerk. He sprang lightly in.

"No. 110, Crescent Flats, Kensington."